Conveyancing (

Second editic

Related titles from Law Society Publishing:

Coal Mining and Brine Subsidence Claim Searches: Directory and Guidance
The Law Society and the Coal Authority

Commonhold
Gary Cowen, James Driscoll and Laurence Target

Conveyancing Forms and Procedures
Annette Goss, Lorraine Richardson and Michael Taylor

Conveyancing Handbook
General Editor: Frances Silverman, Consultant Editors: Annette Goss,
Russell Hewitson, Peter Reekie, Anne Rodell and Michael Taylor

Leasehold Enfranchisement and the Right to Manage
Christopher Sykes

Licensing for Conveyancers
Tim Hayden and Jane Hanney

Understanding Property Insurance
Gerald Sherriff

Understanding Stamp Duty Land Tax
Reg Nock

Titles from Law Society Publishing can be ordered from all good bookshops or direct
(telephone 0870 850 1422, email **lawsociety@prolog.uk.com** or visit our online shop at
www.lawsociety.org.uk/bookshop).

Conveyancing Checklists

Second edition

Frances Silverman and Russell Hewitson

The Law Society

ISBN–13: 978–1–85328–749–7

Crown copyright material is reproduced here with the permission of the Controller of HMSO.

First edition 2007

This edition published in 2010 by the Law Society
113 Chancery Lane, London WC2A 1PL

Typeset by Columns Design Ltd, Reading
Printed by CPI Antony Rowe, Chippenham, Wiltshire

FSC

Mixed Sources

Product group from well-managed
forests and other controlled sources

Cert no. SGS-COC-2953
www.fsc.org
© 1996 Forest Stewardship Council

The paper used for the text pages of this book is FSC certified. FSC (the Forest Stewardship Council) is an international network to promote responsible management of the world's forests.

Contents

Preface to the second edition

This new edition has been comprehensively revised to take account of the many changes which have taken place in the practice of conveyancing since the first edition was published in 2006. As previously, we emphasise that the checklists and letters included are necessarily subjective and we welcome readers suggestions for additions an improvements.

The checklists have been adapted from those in the 16th Edition of the Law Society's Conveyancing Handbook and it should be stressed that this book is not intended as a substitute for the fuller guidance provided in that work.

The Appendix material is up to date as at the date of publication but readers may wish to check the relevant websites from time to time to ensure that they are aware of any changes to the content of these documents .

Just as this new edition was due to go to print the Land Registry announced that it will be withdrawing the facility for lenders and their intermediaries to send Electronic Notification of Discharges (ENDs) for registered charges at midnight on 3 January 2010.

The material included in this edition is current as at November 2009.

Frances Silverman
Russell Hewitson
November 2009

PART A
Checklists

1

General matters

1.1 FLOWCHART OF TYPICAL CONVEYANCING TRANSACTION

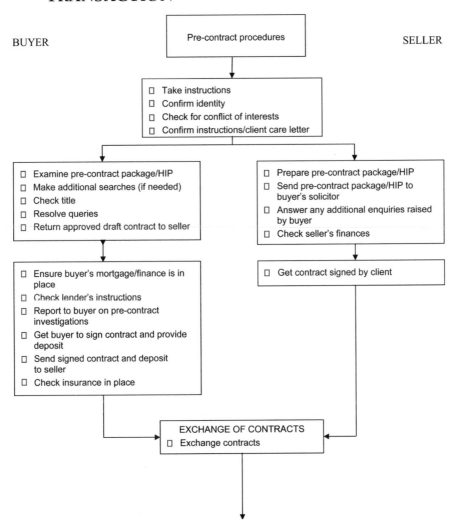

BUYER

SELLER

Pre-contract procedures

- ☐ Take instructions
- ☐ Confirm identity
- ☐ Check for conflict of interests
- ☐ Confirm instructions/client care letter

- ☐ Examine pre-contract package/HIP
- ☐ Make additional searches (if needed)
- ☐ Check title
- ☐ Resolve queries
- ☐ Return approved draft contract to seller

- ☐ Prepare pre-contract package/HIP
- ☐ Send pre-contract package/HIP to buyer's solicitor
- ☐ Answer any additional enquiries raised by buyer
- ☐ Check seller's finances

- ☐ Ensure buyer's mortgage/finance is in place
- ☐ Check lender's instructions
- ☐ Report to buyer on pre-contract investigations
- ☐ Get buyer to sign contract and provide deposit
- ☐ Send signed contract and deposit to seller
- ☐ Check insurance in place

- ☐ Get contract signed by client

EXCHANGE OF CONTRACTS
- ☐ Exchange contracts

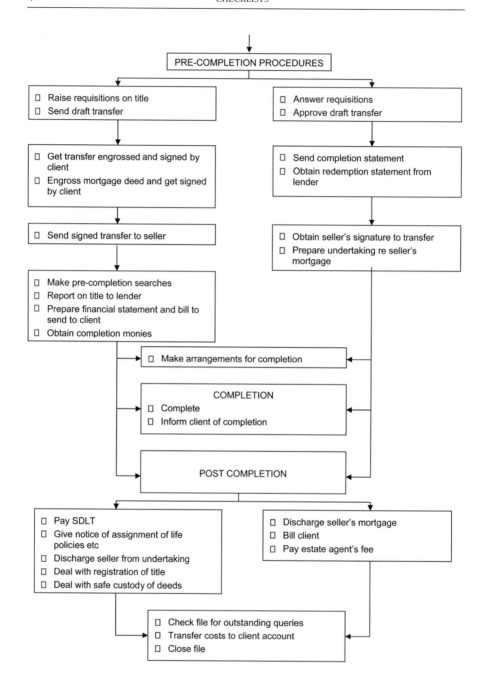

1.2   CHECKLIST FOR FILE COVER: SELLER

- ☐ Instructions confirmed
- ☐ Home Information Pack supplied
- ☐ Contact buyer's conveyancer
- ☐ Contact estate agent
- ☐ Contact seller's lender
- ☐ Draft contract approved
- ☐ Exchange of contracts
- ☐ Deposit
- ☐ Requisitions
- ☐ Transfer
- ☐ Completion arrangements
- ☐ Undertakings
- ☐ Completion
- ☐ Discharge seller's mortgage
- ☐ Discharge from undertaking
- ☐ Bill and statement to client
- ☐ Costs paid.

1.3   CHECKLIST FOR FILE COVER: BUYER

- ☐ Instructions confirmed
- ☐ Home Information Pack supplied
- ☐ Contact seller's conveyancer
- ☐ Contact estate agent
- ☐ Contact lender
- ☐ Searches
- ☐ Draft contract approved
- ☐ Buyer's mortgage arrangements
- ☐ Deposit
- ☐ Insurance
- ☐ Exchange of contracts
- ☐ Requisitions
- ☐ Transfer
- ☐ Pre-completion searches
- ☐ Completion arrangements
- ☐ Bill and statement to client
- ☐ Undertakings
- ☐ Completion
- ☐ SDLT
- ☐ Registration of title
- ☐ Discharge seller's conveyancer from undertaking
- ☐ Documents to lender
- ☐ Notices to lender re life policy, to tenants, etc.
- ☐ Costs paid.

2

Taking instructions

2.1 TAKING INSTRUCTIONS FROM THE SELLER

Item	Reason for Question
☐ Date instructions taken	Record keeping
☐ Full names, addresses of seller(s) and buyer(s) and home and business telephone numbers	Needed in contract and for contact with client
☐ Name and address of person at estate agents	For contact
☐ Find out where title deeds are and obtain client's authority to obtain them if in the hands of a third party	To deduce title
☐ Ask clients for title number (if known)	To obtain official copy entries of the title
☐ Name of other parties' solicitors or representatives	For contact
☐ Do we act for the other party also?	Conflict of interest, breach of Rule 3
☐ Full address of property to be sold	Needed in contract
☐ Situation of property – position of footpaths/railways/rivers, etc.	Need for plan or special searches
☐ Tenure: freehold/leasehold	Needed in contract
☐ Price	Needed in contract, Stamp Duty Land Tax (SDLT) considerations
☐ Has any preliminary deposit been paid? If so, how much? Receipt obtained?	Take account in calculating deposit on exchange
☐ Which fixtures are to be removed?	Needed in contract
☐ Which fittings are to remain? Additional price for fittings?	Needed in contract and may affect SDLT
☐ Anticipated completion date	To advise client on likely duration of transaction and to assess urgency of matter. To discuss redemption of present mortgage, i.e. interest charges up to end of month
☐ Present/proposed use of property	Planning aspects/restrictive covenants
☐ Does the transaction attract VAT?	May be needed in contract and client may need advice
☐ Who is resident in the property?	Occupiers' rights, overriding interests

☐	Is the transaction dependent on the purchase?	Synchronisation
☐	Any other terms agreed between the parties?	Needed in contract
☐	Any correspondence between the parties?	Existence of a contract, or other terms agreed
☐	Vacant possession/details of tenancies	Needed in contract
☐	Advice as to costs	Required by Rule 2
☐	Interest on deposit	Deposit interest considerations
☐	Do a financial calculation, including costs	To ensure the client can afford the transaction
☐	Time taken in interview	Time costing/recording
☐	Did we act on purchase?	Look at old file prior to interview to gain relevant information
☐	Are there any outstanding mortgages? How much and to whom?	Calculation of financial statement and will normally need to be redeemed on completion
☐	Ask for seller's mortgage account number or reference	Needed in order to obtain deeds from lender and to obtain a preliminary redemption statement
☐	Advise seller not to cancel mortgage repayments or insurance until completion	So that redemption figure obtained on completion is not higher than presently anticipated
☐	How much deposit required?	Advise client on dangers of reduced deposit, use of deposit in related purchase
☐	What is to happen to the proceeds of sale?	Accounting to the client, investment advice
☐	Does the sale attract capital gains tax?	Advise the client
☐	Discuss making a local search and enquiries and any other relevant searches	
☐	Check identity of client	A precaution against mortgage fraud and money laundering.

2.2 TAKING INSTRUCTIONS FROM THE BUYER

Item		Reason for Question
☐	Date instructions taken	Record keeping
☐	Full names and addresses of seller(s) and buyer(s) and home and business telephone numbers	Needed in contract and for contact with client
☐	Name and address of person at estate agents	For contact
☐	Name of other parties' solicitors or representatives	For contact and Land Registry requirements

☐	Do we act for the other party also?	Conflict of interest, breach of Rule 3
☐	Full address of property to be bought	Needed in contract
☐	Situation of property – position of footpaths/railways/rivers, etc.	Need for plan or special searches
☐	Tenure: freehold/leasehold	Needed in contract
☐	Price	Needed in contract, SDLT considerations
☐	Has any preliminary deposit been paid? If so, how much? Receipt obtained?	Take account in calculating deposit on exchange
☐	Which fixtures are to be removed?	Needed in contract
☐	Which fittings are to remain? Additional price for fittings? Apportionment of purchase price?	Needed in contract and may affect SDLT
☐	Anticipated completion date	To advise client on likely duration of transaction and to assess urgency of matter. Effect of date on first payment under mortgage
☐	Present/proposed use of property	Planning aspects/restrictive covenants
☐	Does the transaction attract VAT?	May be needed in contract and client may need advice
☐	Who is resident in the property?	Occupiers' rights, overriding interests
☐	Is the transaction dependent on the sale of another property?	Synchronisation
☐	Any other terms agreed between the parties?	Needed in contract
☐	Any correspondence between the parties?	Existence of a contract, or other terms agreed
☐	Vacant possession/details of tenancies	Needed in contract
☐	Advice as to costs	Required by Rule 2
☐	Interest on deposit	Deposit interest considerations
☐	Do a financial calculation, including costs	To ensure the client can afford the transaction
☐	Time taken in interview	Time costing/recording
☐	How will the deposit be funded?	Is bridging finance needed? Need to give notice if funds invested? Client's authority if undertaking to be given
☐	How is the balance of the price to be funded? Has the client obtained a mortgage certificate or offer? Does client have outstanding mortgage on any other property?	Advice on sources of finance and/or tax relief on interest. Lenders may insist that all outstanding mortgages are repaid as a condition of the new loan
☐	Survey arrangements	Advise the client
☐	Insurance: Property? Life? Contents? Other? e.g. employee liability	Advise the client

☐ How is property to be held by co-owners?	Advise the client
☐ Custody of deeds	Instructions needed if property not mortgaged
☐ Client's present property?	Need to give notice to determine tenancy? Penalty on mortgage redemption
☐ Check client's identity	A precaution against mortgage fraud and money laundering and required by the CML Lenders' Handbook
☐ Stamp Duty Land Tax	Advise client of responsibility to complete Land Tax Return

2.3 SITUATIONS WHERE INSTRUCTIONS MUST BE DECLINED

Instructions may be accepted provided that there is no breach of Rules 1 or 2 Solicitors' Code of Conduct 2007 (Rule 1 – core duties; Rule 2 – client relations). Instructions must be declined *inter alia* in the following circumstances:

☐ Where to act would involve the solicitor in a breach of the law, e.g. a fraudulent conveyance

☐ Where the solicitor would be involved in a breach of the rules of conduct, e.g. dealing with more than one prospective buyer without disclosing this to all prospective buyers

☐ Where a conflict of interest exists or is likely to exist

☐ Where the solicitor lacks the expertise to carry out the client's instructions competently

☐ Where the solicitor does not have sufficient time to devote to the client's affairs

☐ Where the instructions are tainted by duress or undue influence, e.g. an elderly client is 'persuaded' by her relatives to sell the family home

☐ Where the solicitor, one of his partners, employees or close relatives holds some office or appointment the holding of which might lead the client or the general public to infer that the solicitor had some influence over the outcome of the matter, e.g. a solicitor who is a member of the local planning committee should not accept instructions to act in a planning appeal against the authority of which he is a member

☐ Where another solicitor has already been instructed in the matter and that other solicitor's retainer has not been terminated

☐ Where the client's freedom of choice to instruct the solicitor of his choosing has been impaired in some way, e.g. the client has received a discount from a builder on the condition that a certain solicitor is instructed

☐ Subject to the exceptions outlined above the solicitor cannot decline to act on the basis of the colour, race, national or ethnic origins of the client nor on the basis of the client's sex or sexual orientation, marital status, disability, religion, belief or age.

2.4   CONFIRMATION OF INSTRUCTIONS

Instructions should be confirmed to the client in writing. The letter should include:

- ☐ Information relating to the name and status of the person who will be carrying out the work for the client and the name of the partner who has overall responsibility for the matter
- ☐ Details of whom the client should contact in the event of a complaint about the solicitor's services
- ☐ An explanation of how the client will be kept informed of progress
- ☐ Information as to costs and disbursements including liability for third party costs
- ☐ A repetition of the advice regarding any agreement under Rule 9 of the Solicitors' Code of Conduct 2007 (referrals of business) (where relevant)
- ☐ Information regarding the payment of Stamp Duty Land Tax (SDLT)
- ☐ Advice regarding the evidence of identification needed under money laundering legislation and information about the acceptable means of payment
- ☐ A résumé of the information received and advice given at the interview in order to ensure that no misunderstanding exists between solicitor and client
- ☐ Confirmation of any action agreed to be taken by the solicitor
- ☐ A reminder to the client of anything which he promised to do, e.g. obtain service charge receipts
- ☐ A request for a payment on account in relation to disbursements.

2.5   SPECIFIC INFORMATION FOR BUYER CLIENT ON SDLT

The client care letter sent to the buyer following the interview should also make the following points regarding the completion of the SDLT return form:

- ☐ That it is the client's duty to submit the form within the time limit of 30 days, although the solicitor may send the form on behalf of the client
- ☐ That there are penalties for a failure to submit the form on time (£100 for up to three months' delay, thereafter £200 together with tax-related penalty if there is a failure to file for 12 months)
- ☐ If the solicitor does complete the form on behalf of the client, the form will be completed based on information provided by the client and that the client is responsible for the accuracy of the information and for any penalty which may be incurred if the form is returned for correction
- ☐ That failure to submit the form on time may result in delays in registering the purchase of the property
- ☐ The client is liable for the payment of any tax due and where there are co-buyers the liability is joint and several
- ☐ That if the solicitor is named on the form as 'tax agent', the solicitor will not accept any responsibility for the form, he will merely be the person with whom HM Revenue & Customs will communicate and to whom the land transaction return certificate will be sent

☐ That HM Revenue & Customs may enquire into the transaction and the client may be liable to pay additional tax after any enquiry

☐ That should an enquiry take place, any costs incurred by the solicitor will be additional to those paid for the conveyancing transaction

☐ That the client should keep any documents relating to the transaction for a minimum period of six years

☐ That any documents in the solicitor's possession will be available for a minimum period of six years and what will happen to them after that period has expired.

2.6 ACTION FOLLOWING INSTRUCTIONS (BOTH PARTIES)

☐ Confirm instructions to client
☐ Make full attendance note of instructions
☐ Establish contact with the other party's representatives
☐ Establish contact with the estate agent
☐ Establish contact with the client's lender
☐ If the identity of the other party's solicitor is not known, his or her status should be checked with the Law Society (check licensed conveyancer's status with the Council for Licensed Conveyancers).

2.7 ACTION FOLLOWING INSTRUCTIONS FOR THE SELLER

☐ Obtain title deeds
☐ Obtain official copy entries of the title (registered land)
☐ Ask estate agent for copy of the particulars
☐ Requisition local search and enquiries and other searches (if so instructed by the client)
☐ Investigate title before drafting contract
☐ Prepare abstract or epitome of title (unregistered land)
☐ Make Land Charges Department search against seller
☐ Check seller's replies to pre-contract enquiries
☐ Prepare home information pack (if not already done)

2.8 ACTION FOLLOWING INSTRUCTIONS FOR THE BUYER

☐ Make search applications appropriate to the property and its location (if not to be supplied by seller)
☐ Deal with buyer's mortgage and survey arrangements if required
☐ Check the identity of the buyer(s)
☐ Check the identity of the seller's representative if not known
☐ Obtain estate agent's particulars
☐ Consider draft contract when received from seller.

2.9 CONTENTS OF THE HOME INFORMATION PACK (HIP)

☐ The Home Information Pack (No.2) Regulations 2007 (SI 2007/1667) prescribe the contents of the home information pack (HIP). Only documents and information that are defined as 'Required' or 'Authorised' by the Regulations can be included in a HIP.

☐ Required documents must be included

☐ Authorised documents are recommended as they may affect a buyer's decision whether or not to buy the property.

2.9.1 Required documents

Regulation 8(a)–(n) of the Home Information Pack (No.2) Regulations 2007 lists the documents which must be included in the HIP (references below to Schedules are to Schedules to these Regulations):

☐ A HIP index that complies with Schedule 1, listing and explaining the contents of the pack

☐ A property information questionnaire (complying with Schedule 11 if the property is not a new home; or complying with Schedule 12 where the property is a new home)

☐ An energy performance certificate and recommendation report or a predicted energy assessment (for property which is not physically complete)

☐ A sustainability certificate, or nil-rated certificate (for property finished before or at the first point of marketing and which is marketed as a new home), or an interim sustainability certificate (for property not finished before or at the first point of marketing and which is marketed as a new home)

☐ A sale statement in the form set out in Schedule 2. This includes information as to the nature of the interest being sold: freehold, leasehold or commonhold

☐ An official copy of the title register and an official copy of the title plan (for property with a registered title)

☐ A certificate of an official search of the index map and such other documents on which the seller can reasonably be expected to rely in order to deduce title (for property with an unregistered title)

☐ The replies to enquiries of local authority

☐ The replies to a search of the local land charges register

☐ The replies to drainage and water enquiries

☐ Any leases or licences to which the property is subject or will be subject following completion of the sale (e.g. the sale of the freehold of two linked properties, house and granny-flat, one with vacant possession and other tenanted) where the property is sold in the circumstances set out in the Housing Act 2004, s.171(2)

☐ Results of searches and enquiries which provide the information listed in Schedules 8, 9 and 10. This is the same information as required by the official local land charges search, CON 29 Part I Standard Enquiries of Local Authority

2002 and CON 29 DW (2002) Standard Drainage and Water Enquiries, but there is no obligation to use these search and enquiry forms.

In addition to the required documents listed above, the HIP must also include the following according to the type of property for sale.

For a leasehold property

☐ The lease (for leasehold property)
☐ Part 2 of the property information questionnaire (for leasehold property)

For new leasehold interests

☐ The lease or the terms of the proposed lease
☐ Estimates of service charges, ground rent and insurance expected for the 12 months following completion

For commonhold property

☐ An official copy of the title register and official copy of the title plan relating to the common parts
☐ An official copy of the commonhold community statement
☐ Any additional rules or regulations made for managing the commonhold which are not included in the commonhold community statement
☐ Any amendments proposed to the commonhold community statement and any amendments to any other rules or regulations for managing the commonhold
☐ Most recent requests for payment of the commonhold assessment, reserve fund, and insurance received in the last 12 months
☐ The name and address of current or proposed managing agents and/or other managers
☐ Summary of current or proposed works affecting the property and/or common parts.

For new commonhold interests

☐ The commonhold community statement or terms of the proposed commonhold community statement
☐ Estimates of commonhold assessment, reserve fund, and insurance payments expected for the 12 months following completion.

2.9.2 Authorised documents

In addition to the 'required' documents and information, the HIP may also include any of the following 'authorised' documents and information listed in regulation 9(a)–(p):

☐ A home condition report which complies with Schedule 9 (this can only be provided by a member of a home inspectors certification scheme which has been approved by the Secretary of State under Part 8 of the Regulations

☐   Any documentary evidence of any safety, building, repair or maintenance work carried out since the date of the home condition report

☐   Any policy, warranty or guarantee for defects in the design, building or conversion of the building

☐   Any information about standards to which the property has been built

☐   An accurate translation in any language of any pack document

☐   An additional version of any document, in any other format such as Braille or large print

☐   A summary or explanation of any pack document, including legal advice on the content of the pack or any pack document

☐   Information identifying the property, e.g. a description, photograph or maps

☐   Information about a pack document, e.g. source of supply, complaints procedures

☐   If the property is or includes a registered estate, official copies of any documents referred to in the individual register

☐   Additional information relating to a commonhold specified in Schedule 4, paragraph 3 and which would be of interest to potential buyers

☐   Additional information relating to leaseholds as specified in Schedule 5, paragraphs 1A to 3A and which would be of interest to potential buyers

☐   Search reports relating to matters such as information held by or derived from a local authority, and dealing with matters supplementary to those contained in the search reports required by regulation 8(j) (search of the local land charges register) or 8(k) (local enquiries), common land, rights of access, ground stability, the effects of mining or extractions or the effects of natural subsidence, environmental hazards and flooding, telecommunication services, utility services, transport services and roads, or liability to repair buildings outside of the property (for example, chancel repairs)

☐   Searches relating to another dwelling-house in the vicinity of the property which contain information of interest to a potential buyer

☐   Any document referred to in a search report included in the pack under regulation 8(j), (k) and (l) or under regulation 9(m) and (n)

☐   Information which relates to the list given in Schedule 10 and which would be of interest to potential buyers.

Note: Where the sale includes the creation of a new interest, for example, the creation of a lease of a newly created flat, the sale statement must be completed as if the interest was already in existence, that is, as if the lease had already been created. The title of the superior estate from which the interest is being created must be deduced to comply with regulation 8(c), (d) and (f).

2.10   CIRCUMSTANCES WHERE HIP NOT REQUIRED

References to regulations below are to the Home Information Pack (No.2) Regulations 2007.

☐   Sale without vacant possession
Section 60 of the Housing Act 2004 provides an exception in relation to residential property that is not available for sale with vacant possession.

☐   Seasonal and holiday accommodation
The duties under sections 155–159 of the Housing Act 2004 do not apply to the sale of seasonal and holiday accommodation (regulation 27).

☐   Mixed sales
Where residential property is being sold with business property and, at the first point of marketing, the seller does not intend to accept an offer to sell the residential property in isolation from the business property, sections 155–159 of the Housing Act 2004 will not apply (regulation 28).

☐   Dual use of a dwelling-house
Where the most recent use of the property was both residential and business use and the property is being marketed on the basis that it is suitable for both uses, a HIP need not be provided (regulation 29).

☐   Portfolios of properties
There is no duty to provide a HIP where a number of residential properties are being sold in a portfolio and the seller does not intend to accept an offer to buy one of the properties in isolation from the others (regulation 30).

☐   Unsafe properties and demolition
Where residential properties are being sold in an unsafe condition in that they pose a serious risk to the health and safety of occupants and visitors, or where properties are being sold as suitable for demolition and redevelopment, there is no duty to provide a HIP (regulations 31 and 32).

☐   Non-residential premises
Non-residential premises are defined in regulation 25 as:
(a) premises where the most recent use is or was primarily non-residential;
(b) a dwelling-house where it is clear from the manner in which it is marketed that the house is due to be converted for primarily non-residential use by the time the sale of the house is completed, and all the relevant planning permissions and listed building consents exist in relation to the conversion.

2.11   ACTING AS AN ESTATE AGENT FOR A BUYER

Neither the solicitor nor the firm may act in the conveyancing for a buyer of any property sold through the estate agency unless the conditions set out below (Rule 21.05(f) of the Solicitors' Code of Conduct 2007) have been complied with:

- ☐ The firm must share the ownership of the estate agency with at least one other business in which neither the individual solicitor nor the firm has any financial interest
- ☐ No person in the firm can have dealt with the sale of the seller's property for the separate business *and*
- ☐ The buyer must give written consent to the firm acting after the firm's financial interest in the sale going through has been explained to the buyer.

2.12   PROPERTY SELLING: WRITTEN AGREEMENT AS TO REMUNERATION

When accepting instructions to act as an estate agent in the sale of a property, a solicitor must give the client a written statement containing the following information:

- ☐ The amount of the solicitor's remuneration, or its method of calculation
- ☐ The circumstances in which the remuneration becomes payable
- ☐ The amount of any disbursements which are to be separately charged, or the basis on which they will be calculated, and the circumstances in which they may be incurred
- ☐ Whether VAT is payable and whether it is included in the estimate or fixed fee
- ☐ Whether or not the solicitor is to be a sole agent
- ☐ The identity of the property to be sold
- ☐ The interest to be sold
- ☐ The price to be sought
- ☐ An explanation of the phrases 'sole selling rights', 'ready willing and able purchaser' (or similar phrases), if used in the agreement.

2.13   ADVERTISING

A solicitor may advertise his practice provided that the advertisement complies with Rule 7 of the Solicitors' Code of Conduct 2007 (publicity):

- ☐ Advertisements must not be misleading or inaccurate
- ☐ Any publicity relating to charges must be clearly expressed
- ☐ Where publicity relates to charges, it must make it clear whether disbursements and VAT are included
- ☐ A solicitor must not publicise his firm or practice by making unsolicited approaches in person or by telephone to a member of the public
- ☐ Unsolicited approaches in person and by telephone may be made to a current or former client, another firm or its manager, an existing or potential professional or business connection, or a commercial organisation or public body (subject to any legal requirements such as those under the Data Protection Act 1998).

2.14   ACTING FOR BOTH PARTIES

A solicitor *must not act* for both seller and buyer in the same transaction:

- ☐ Without the written consent of both parties
- ☐ If a conflict of interest exists or arises
- ☐ If the seller is selling or leasing as a builder or developer (but if a builder or developer acquires a property in part exchange, and sells it on without development, they are not selling as a builder or developer for the purpose of Rule 3)

As exceptions to the above, a solicitor *may act* for both seller and buyer, but only if:

- ☐ Both parties are established clients (the test here is an objective one, i.e. whether a reasonable solicitor would regard the person as an established client. A person who is related by blood, adoption, marriage or who is living with an established client counts as an established client. A seller or buyer who instructs the solicitor for the first time is not an established client. A person who is selling or buying jointly with an established client counts as an established client) *or*
- ☐ The consideration is £10,000 or less and the transaction is not the grant of a lease (the value of any property taken in part exchange must be taken into account in calculating the consideration) *or*
- ☐ The seller and buyer are represented by two separate offices in different localities *and*
- ☐ Different solicitors who normally work at each office, conduct or supervise the transaction for seller and buyer *and*
- ☐ No office of the practice (or an associated practice) referred either client to the office conducting his or her transaction *or*
- ☐ The only way in which the solicitor is acting for the buyer is in providing mortgage-related services *or*
- ☐ The only way in which the solicitor is acting for the seller is in providing property selling services through a SEAL

When a solicitor's practice (including a SEAL) acts in the property selling for the seller and either acts for the buyer on the purchase or provides mortgage-related services to the buyer, the following additional conditions must be met:

- ☐ Different individuals must conduct the work for the seller and the work for the buyer; and if the person conducting the work needs supervision, they must be supervised by different solicitors *and*
- ☐ The solicitor must inform the seller in writing, before accepting instructions to deal with the property selling, of any services which might be offered to a buyer, whether through the same practice or any practice associated with it *and*
- ☐ The solicitor must explain to the buyer, before the buyer gives consent to the arrangement:
  - ☐ The implications of a conflict of interest arising *and*
  - ☐ The solicitor's financial interest in the sale going through *and*
  - ☐ If the solicitor proposes to provide mortgage-related services to the buyer through a SEAL which is also acting for the seller, that the solicitor cannot advise the buyer on the merits of the purchase.

2.15 ACTING FOR LENDERS: OWNERSHIP OF DOCUMENTS AND CONFIDENTIALITY

The following guidance relates to the position where the same firm of solicitors acted for the buyer/borrower and for the lender on a contemporaneous purchase and mortgage and the lender asks to see documents on the 'conveyancing file'.

The documents which the lender will be entitled to see fall into two categories:

☐ Documents prepared or received by the solicitor on behalf of the lender

☐ Documents prepared or received by the solicitor on behalf of the borrower which, it is considered, the lender is nonetheless entitled to see. The rationale is that these documents relate to that part of the solicitor's work where the lender and borrower can be said to have a common interest, i.e. the deduction of title, the acquisition of a good title to the property and ancillary legal issues, such as the use of the property.

Examples of the most common items in these two categories are set out below.

Documents held by the solicitor on behalf of the lender are:

☐ The lender's instructions to the solicitor

☐ Copy mortgage deed

☐ Copy report on title

☐ Any correspondence between the solicitor and the lender or between the solicitor and a third party written or received on the lender's behalf.

Documents held by the solicitor on behalf of the borrower are:

☐ Contract for sale

☐ Property information form/enquiries before contract

☐ Abstract or epitome of title/official copy entries of the title

☐ Requisitions on title

☐ Draft purchase deed

☐ Draft licence to assign (where appropriate)

☐ Land Registry application forms.

2.16 FINANCIAL SERVICES: REGULATED ACTIVITIES

The following activities may involve a solicitor in regulated activities under the Financial Services and Markets Act 2000:

☐ Advising a client about obtaining a regulated mortgage, an insurance contract (e.g. endowment, mortgage protection, defective title, household contents or building policies) an ISA or a pension mortgage

☐ Where a property sale is linked to the sale of a business in the form of a sale of company shares

☐ Where shares in a management company are transferred on completion

☐ Where the sale of a property for a client leads to the client looking for advice on how to invest the proceeds of sale.

2.17 REFERRALS: INFORMATION TO BE GIVEN TO CLIENT

Before accepting instructions to act for a client referred under an agreement under Rule 9 of the Solicitors' Code of Conduct 2007, the solicitor must give the client the following written information concerning the referral. This disclosure is required as soon as the referral is made and the solicitor will normally be expected to write to the client with the information before the first interview. If, due to lack of time, the disclosure is made at the first interview, it should be made at the start of the first interview and confirmed in writing.

☐ The fact that the solicitor has a financial arrangement with the introducer *and*

☐ The amount of any payment to the introducer which is calculated by reference to that referral *or*

☐ Where the introducer is paying the solicitor to provide services to the introducer's customers:

    ☐ the amount the introducer is paying the solicitor to provide those services *and*

    ☐ the amount the client is required to pay the introducer *and*

☐ A statement that any advice given by the solicitor will be independent and that the client is free to raise questions on all aspects of the transaction *and*

☐ Confirmation that any information disclosed to the solicitor will not be disclosed to the introducer unless the client consents; but that where the solicitor is also acting for the introducer in the same matter and a conflict of interests arises, the solicitor might be obliged to cease acting.

2.18 CHECKING THE CLIENT'S IDENTITY

It is always necessary to check the identity of the client at the outset of the transaction. The following guidelines have been extracted from the Law Society's Practice Note Identity Evidence for the Land Registry – 4 December 2008 and should be used in conjunction with the full Practice Note available from **www. lawsociety.org.uk** (where it is updated from time to time).

2.18.1 Natural persons

It is considered good practice to have either:

☐ One government document which verifies either name and address or name and date of birth *or*

☐ A government document which verifies the client's full name and another supporting document which verifies their name and either their address or date of birth.

2.18.2 UK residents

The following sources may be useful for verification of UK-based clients:

☐ Current signed passport
☐ UK identity card
☐ Birth certificate
☐ Current photocard driver's licence
☐ Current EEA member state identity card
☐ Current identity card issued by the Electoral Office for Northern Ireland
☐ Residence permit issued by the Home Office
☐ Firearms certificate or shotgun licence
☐ Photographic registration cards for self-employed individuals and partnerships in the construction industry
☐ Benefit book or original notification letter from the DWP confirming the right to benefits
☐ Council tax bill
☐ Utility bill or statement, or a certificate from a utilities supplier confirming an arrangement to pay services on pre-payment terms
☐ A cheque or electronic transfer drawn on an account in the name of the client with a credit or financial institution regulated for the purposes of money laundering
☐ Bank, building society or credit union statement or passbook containing current address
☐ Entry in a local or national telephone directory confirming name and address
☐ Confirmation from an electoral register that a person of that name lives at that address
☐ A recent original mortgage statement from a recognised lender
☐ Solicitor's letter confirming recent house purchase or Land Registry confirmation of address
☐ Local council or housing association rent card or tenancy agreement
☐ HMRC self-assessment statement or tax demand
☐ House or motor insurance certificate
☐ Record of any home visit made
☐ Statement from a member of the firm or other person in the regulated sector who has known the client for a number of years attesting to their identity.

2.18.3 Persons not resident in the UK

☐ Where you meet the client you are likely to be able to see the person's passport or national identity card. If you have concerns that the identity document might not be genuine, contact the relevant embassy or consulate
☐ The client's address may be obtained from:
☐ An official overseas source
☐ A reputable directory
☐ A person regulated for money laundering purposes in the country where the

person is resident who confirms that the client is known to them and lives or works at the overseas address given
□ If documents are in a foreign language, you must take appropriate steps to be reasonably satisfied that the documents, in fact, provide evidence of the client's identity
□ Where you do not meet the client, the Regulations state that you must undertake enhanced due diligence measures.

2.18.3 Clients unable to produce standard documentation

Consider whether the inability to provide you with standard verification is consistent with the client's profile and circumstances or whether it might make you suspicious that money laundering or terrorist financing is occurring.

Where you decide that a client has a good reason for not meeting the standard verification requirements, you may accept a letter from an appropriate person who knows the individual and can verify the client's identity.

For example:

□ Clients in care homes might be able to provide a letter from the manager
□ Clients without a permanent residence might be able to provide a letter from a householder named on a current council tax bill or a hostel manager, confirming temporary residence
□ A refugee might be able to provide a letter from the Home Office confirming refugee status and granting permission to work, or a Home Office travel document for refugees
□ An asylum seeker might be able to provide their registration card and any other identity documentation they hold, or a letter of assurance as to identity from a community member such as a priest, GP, or local councillor who has knowledge of the client
□ A student or minor might be able to provide a birth certificate and confirmation of their parent's address or confirmation of address from the register of the school or higher education institution
□ A person with mental health problems or mental incapacity might know medical workers, hostel staff, social workers, deputies or guardians appointed by the court who can locate identification documents or confirm the client's identity.

2.18.4 Professionals

Where other professionals use your services, you may consult their professional directory to confirm the person's name and business address. It will not be necessary to then confirm the person's home address. You may consult directories for foreign professionals, if you are satisfied it is a valid directory, e.g. one produced and maintained by their professional body, and you can either translate the information, or understand it already.

2.18.5   Partnerships, limited partnerships and UK LLPs

A partnership is not a separate legal entity, so you must obtain information on the constituent individuals.

- ☐ Where partnerships or unincorporated businesses are:
  - ☐ Well-known, reputable organisations
  - ☐ With long histories in their industries *and*
  - ☐ With substantial public information about them, their principals, and controllers the following information should be sufficient:
    - ☐ Name
    - ☐ Registered address, if any
    - ☐ Trading address
    - ☐ Nature of business
- ☐ Other partnerships and unincorporated businesses which are small and have few partners should be treated as private individuals. Where the numbers are larger, they should be treated as private companies
- ☐ Where a partnership is made up of regulated professionals, it will be sufficient to confirm the firm's existence and the trading address from a reputable professional directory or search facility with the relevant professional body. Otherwise you should obtain evidence on the identity of at least the partner instructing you and one other partner, and evidence of the firm's trading address
- ☐ For a UK LLP, obtain information in accordance with the requirements for companies as outlined below.

2.18.6   Companies

Consider whether the person instructing you on behalf of the company has the authority to do so.

Public companies listed in the UK

- ☐ For a listed company (London Stock Exchange), evidence may simply be confirmation of the company's listing on the regulated market such as:
- ☐ A copy of the dated page of the website of the relevant stock exchange showing the listing
- ☐ A photocopy of the listing in a reputable daily newspaper
- ☐ Information from a reputable electronic verification service provider or online registry
- ☐ For a subsidiary of a listed company you will also require evidence of the parent/subsidiary relationship. Such evidence may be:
- ☐ The subsidiary's last filed annual return
- ☐ A note in the parent's or subsidiary's last audited accounts
- ☐ Information from a reputable electronic verification service provider or online registry
- ☐ Where further client due diligence (CDD) is required for a listed company (i.e. when it is not on a regulated market) obtain relevant particulars of the company's identity.

☐ Verification sources may include:

☐ A search of the relevant company registry (such as Companies House: **www.companieshouse.gov.uk**)

☐ A copy of the company's certificate of incorporation

☐ Information from a reputable electronic verification service provider

Private and unlisted companies in the UK

☐ The standard identifiers for private companies are:

☐ Full name

☐ Business/registered address

☐ Names of two directors, or equivalent

☐ Nature of business

☐ Other sources for verifying corporate identification may include:

☐ Certificate of incorporation

☐ Details from the relevant company registry, confirming details of the company and of the director, including the director's address

☐ Filed audited accounts

☐ Information from a reputable electronic verification service provider

2.18.7 Other arrangements or bodies

Trusts

☐ A trust is not a separate legal entity

☐ The client, whether they are the trustee(s), settlor or beneficiaries, must be identified in accordance with their relevant category, (i.e. natural person, company, etc.). Where you are acting for more than one trustee, it is preferable that you verify the identity of at least two of the trustees.

Charities

☐ Charities may take a number of forms. In the UK, you may come across five types of charities:

☐ Small

☐ Registered

☐ Unregistered

☐ Excepted, such as churches

☐ Exempt, such as museums and universities

☐ For registered charities, you should take a record of their full name, registration number and place of business. Details of registered charities can be obtained from:

☐ The Charity Commission of England and Wales at **www.charity-commission.gov.uk**

☐ The Office of the Scottish Charity Regulator at **www.oscr.org.uk**

☐ For all other types of charities, you should consider the business structure of the charity and apply the relevant CDD measures for that business structure. You can also generally get confirmation of their charitable status from HMRC.

Deceased persons' estates

When acting for the executor(s) or administrators of an estate, you should establish their identity using the procedures for natural persons or companies set out above. When acting for more than one executor or administrator, it is preferable to verify the identity of at least two of them.

Clubs and associations

The following information may be relevant to the identity of the club or association:

- [ ] Full name
- [ ] Legal status
- [ ] Purpose
- [ ] Any registered address
- [ ] Names of all office holders
- [ ] Documents which may verify the existence of the club or association include:
- [ ] Any articles of association or constitutions
- [ ] Statement from a bank, building society or credit union
- [ ] Recent audited accounts
- [ ] Listing in a local or national telephone directory

Government agencies and councils

The following information may be relevant when establishing a public sector entity's identity:

- [ ] Full name of the entity
- [ ] Nature and status of the entity
- [ ] Address of the entity
- [ ] Name of the home state authority
- [ ] Name of the directors or equivalent.

2.19   WARNING SIGNS FOR MORTGAGE FRAUD

The following guidelines have been extracted from the Law Society's Practice Note Mortgage Fraud – 15 April 2009 and should be used in conjunction with the full Practice Note available from **www.lawsociety.org.uk** (where it is updated from time to time).

- [ ] The client or the property involved is located a long distance from your firm
- [ ] The client seems unusually uninterested in their purchase
- [ ] The seller is a private company or they have recently purchased the property from a private company
- [ ] The client does not usually engage in property investment of this scale
- [ ] The current owner has owned the property for under six months
- [ ] The client's credit history is shorter than you would expect for their age

- ☐ There are plans for a sub-sale or back-to-back transactions
- ☐ There is a last minute change of representative on the other side
- ☐ The property has a history of being re-sold quickly or mortgages settled quickly
- ☐ A transfer of title to land is requested with respect to only some of the seller's holdings and the properties are not grouped together
- ☐ Finance is sought after the property has been registered in the buyer's name.
- ☐ The property has been registered to an owner for a significant period of time and the person claiming to be the owner does not appear to be of an age to have held the land for that length of time
- ☐ The other conveyancer or solicitor allegedly involved in the transaction has an e-mail address from a large-scale web-based provider
- ☐ There is a county court judgment against the property
- ☐ The land is transferred following a court order, but the mortgage is sought some time later
- ☐ The property value has significantly increased in a short period of time out of line with the market in the area
- ☐ The mortgage is for the full property value
- ☐ The seller or developer have provided incentives, allowances or discounts
- ☐ The deposit is being paid by someone other than the purchaser
- ☐ The purchaser has paid the deposit directly to the seller or a developer
- ☐ There is money left over from the mortgage after the purchase price has been paid, and you are asked to pay this money to the account of someone you do not know, or to the introducer
- ☐ You are asked to enter a price on the title that is greater than you know was paid for the property
- ☐ There has been a recent transfer of land where no money has changed hands or the price was significantly less than the full market value
- ☐ You receive unusual instructions from your client.

3

Pre-contract procedures

3.1 FACTORS INDICATING NEED FOR STRUCTURAL SURVEY

The need for a full structural survey may be indicated by the presence of one or more of the following factors:

☐ The property is of a high value
☐ The amount of the buyer's intended mortgage represents a low proportion of the purchase price, e.g. less than 70%
☐ The property is more than 100 years old
☐ The buyer intends to alter or extend the property after completion
☐ The property is not of conventional brick and mortar construction
☐ The proximity of the property to features which may cause subsidence or other structural problems, e.g. mines, filled-in gravel pits, rivers, vibration damage from aircraft or railways
☐ The property is not detached (surveyor may also need to inspect adjoining property).

3.2 SURVEYS IN SPECIAL CASES

☐ A property which does not have the benefit of mains drainage will require a separate drainage survey
☐ If the electric wiring system in the property has not been inspected during the past five years, a report on the adequacy and safety of the electrical installations may be desirable
☐ Where environmental issues are relevant, e.g. on purchases of development land, a separate environmental survey may be desirable
☐ In areas affected by radon the Radon Protection Division of the Health Protection Agency provides information on radon, and offers a written report on the radon potential for a property
☐ The client may be advised to obtain a separate survey of the water supply pipes from his water supply company where the pipes supplying the property being surveyed pass through or under adjoining property.

3.3 TRANSFERS ON BREAKDOWN OF MARRIAGE

Special considerations apply to the transfer of property between husband and wife on the breakdown of a marriage. Even in cases where the settlement is amicable and is not made pursuant to a court order in matrimonial proceedings, the parties must be independently advised because of the inevitable risk of conflict of interests which arises in this situation.

3.3.1 Acting for the transferor

☐ Ascertain the extent of existing mortgages over the property to be transferred

☐ Decide whether the property is to be transferred free of the mortgage to the other spouse and, if so, whether the transferring spouse will redeem the mortgage or will continue to make repayments

☐ If the property is to be transferred free of the mortgage, steps must be taken to discharge those charges before completion of the transfer. This may involve advising the transferor about refinancing and taking a new loan secured over another property in order to discharge his indebtedness over the property to be transferred

☐ Obtain the lender's consent to the transfer if either the mortgage deed requires it or if the borrower-spouse is to be released from his or her covenant under the mortgage

☐ Where the mortgage is not to be discharged, arrangements must be made for the continuation of payments under the mortgage

☐ Any life policy taken out in connection with an existing mortgage should be checked to ascertain the name(s) of the person(s) insured under the policy

☐ If the property is to be transferred free of the mortgage to which the policy related, a reassignment of the policy should be effected on discharge of the mortgage

☐ If the benefit of the policy is to be transferred, the consent of the lender should be obtained and the insurance company notified of the change

☐ If the matrimonial home comprises property which had been bought from a local authority and the court makes an order for the sale of the property under Matrimonial Causes Act 1973, s.24A, a proportion of the discount may be repayable if the property is sold within three years after its purchase from the local authority.

3.3.2 Acting for the transferee

☐ Undertake the normal pre-contract searches and enquiries to ensure that no entries exist which might adversely affect the property or its value

☐ Any charge which had been registered to protect the spouse's rights of occupation under the Family Law Act 1996 ceases to be effective on issue of a divorce decree absolute unless an order under section 33(5) of the Act has been made and registered

☐ In appropriate cases, advice should be given in relation to raising finance to purchase the share in the property to be transferred

☐ If the property is to be transferred subject to an existing mortgage, the lender's consent to the transfer must be obtained if the borrower is to be released from the covenant and/or if the mortgage so requires and arrangements made for the continuance of payments under the mortgage

☐   If the benefit of a life policy is to be transferred, the lender's consent may be
    necessary and notice of the transfer must be given to the insurance company
    after completion

☐   Where the transferred property is mortgaged, consideration should be given to
    the protection of the mortgage by either an endowment policy or a mortgage
    protection policy. A lender may also insist that a policy to insure against the
    transferor's subsequent insolvency is acquired.

☐   A transfer of land between spouses for which 'value' is not given (i.e. the
    equivalent of full consideration, in some form), may be set aside by the
    court under Insolvency Act 1986, ss.339–342 at the request of the trustee
    in bankruptcy if the transferring spouse becomes bankrupt within five years
    of the transfer. The solvency of the transferring spouse at the time of the
    transfer may be a material factor in the decision whether the transfer can or
    should be set aside, so the transferee spouse may want to get a declaration
    of solvency from the transferor at the time when the transfer is made. The
    transferee might also want to consider the possibility of insuring against the
    risk of the transferor's becoming bankrupt within five years.

☐   Transfers of shares of property between joint owners are subject to Land
    Registry identity requirements and the applicant for registration will have to
    give details of the conveyancers acting for all the other parties to the transaction
    and, where a party is unrepresented, provide evidence of that party's identity
    (see the Law Society's Practice Note Identity Evidence for Land Registry – 4
    December 2008).

3.4   INTEREST ON CLIENT'S MONEY

If the money is held in a general client account, the duty to pay interest depends
on the amount of money held and the period for which it is held, but there is no
requirement to pay interest if the amount calculated is £20 or less. (See Solicitors'
Accounts Rules (SAR) 1998, Part C, rules 24–27 for more information on interest.)

3.4.1 Table of minimum balances

No interest need be paid if the money held does not exceed the amounts set out in
the table below for times not exceeding the periods shown.

Time in weeks	Amount
8	£1,000
4	£2,000
2	£10,000
1	£20,000

3.4.2   Sums exceeding £20,000

If a sum exceeding £20,000 is held for one week or less, a solicitor is not required
to pay interest unless it is fair and reasonable to do so in all the circumstances.

Although this part of SAR, r.24 allows some discretion to be exercised by the solicitor in deciding whether or not to pay interest, such discretion should be exercised in the client's favour. Thus, if a sum of £1,000,000 were held on behalf of a client for two days, the considerable amount of interest which would accrue during that short time should be paid to the client.

3.5 DEDUCING TITLE

3.5.1 Unregistered titles

☐ Check when the compulsory registration order came into force in the area and that no dealings which would have induced registration have occurred since that date (the date for compulsory registration for each district is set out in Land Registry Practice Guide 51)

☐ If it transpires that the land should have been registered on a previous disposition, an immediate application for late registration must be made by the seller's solicitor, a full disclosure of the situation being made to both the seller and the buyer's solicitor

☐ An index map search should be made to ensure that no part of the land has already been registered without the owner's knowledge and that no caution against first registration affects the land (the result of an index map search is a required document in a HIP)

☐ Make a Land Charges Department search against the name of the seller to ensure that no incumbrances exist other than those revealed by the title deeds.

☐ In most cases, the land will require registration after completion of the current transaction. Although this will primarily be the responsibility of the buyer, this factor should be borne in mind by the seller's solicitor in his pre-contract investigation of title so that any areas of difficulty which might be the subject of a requisition by the Land Registry may be clarified.

3.5.2 Unregistered freeholds

☐ Decide which document is to be used as the root of title, and check the validity of the chain of title forwards from that time

☐ Does the root document refer to any earlier documents which the buyer may be entitled to call for?

☐ Are there any pre-root covenants which need to be disclosed to the buyer?

☐ Are all documents within the chain correctly stamped and executed?

☐ Watch for change of names, e.g. on marriage or change of a company name. Obtain evidence of the changes if necessary

☐ If in doubt as to the effectiveness of restrictive covenants, options or third party rights revealed by the title, a Land Charges Department search should be made to clarify the position

☐ Obtain copies of any necessary death certificates or grants of representation.

3.5.3   Unregistered existing leaseholds

Law of Property Act 1925, s.44 limits the right of an intended lessee or assignee of an existing lease to require production of the reversionary title or titles. This limitation, however, does not apply to:

☐   Registered land or a term of years to be derived out of registered land or
☐   A contract for the grant of a lease to which the compulsory registration provisions apply (Law of Property Act 1925, s.44, as amended by Land Registration Act 2002, Sched.11, para.2).

The following points should be checked:

☐   Is a marked copy of the freehold title available or can it be obtained? If not, check that the contract excludes the buyer's right to deduction of the freehold
☐   Check the chain of title from the lease (or sub-lease) including evidence of surrenders and copies of any necessary consents, e.g. to assignments or alterations
☐   Is consent to this assignment required? If so, obtain the names of referees from the buyer's solicitor and forward them to the landlord's solicitor. Obtain a firm estimate from the landlord's solicitor before giving an undertaking for costs
☐   Is the freehold or superior leasehold title registered? Whether or not this is so can be ascertained by making an index map search. Where the freehold or superior title is registered, official copy entries of the title can be obtained by the buyer. This may overcome the limitation posed by the seller being unable to deliver the freehold or superior leasehold title.

3.6   DISCLOSURE

3.6.1   What must the seller disclose?

As an exception to the *caveat emptor* principle, the seller is under a duty to disclose to the buyer any latent incumbrances and defects in his title. This duty exists irrespective of whether the buyer raises enquiries about such matters. Matters which need to be disclosed include the following:

☐   Latent defects (i.e. those not apparent from physical inspection or the title deeds)
☐   Occupiers
☐   Local land charges
☐   Overriding interests.

3.6.2   Matters falling outside the duty of disclosure

☐   Matters known to the buyer
☐   Matters apparent on inspection

☐ Physical defects
☐ Planning matters.

3.7 DEFECTIVE TITLE INSURANCE

3.7.1 Information needed by insurance company

Before issue of the policy, the insurance company will need to assess the risk involved. The seller's solicitor should be prepared to provide the insurance company with the following information or documents:

☐ The precise nature of the defect
☐ Where relevant, a copy of the document in which the defect appears
☐ The date when the defect arose, or the date when the problem giving rise to the defect occurred
☐ What steps (if any) have been taken to remedy the defect
☐ Whether any third party has taken steps to assert rights against the land because of the defect
☐ An approximate estimate of the amount of cover needed.

3.7.2 Restrictive covenant insurance

Apart from the matters listed in **3.7.1**, the insurance company will also need the following information or documents:

☐ A copy of the document imposing the covenant or, if this is not available, a copy of the exact wording of the covenant
☐ The exact nature of the breach which has occurred or details of the action which is contemplated which will cause the breach
☐ The date when the covenant was imposed
☐ Whether or not the covenant is registered on the charges register of the title (or as a Class D(ii) charge in unregistered land where the covenant was imposed after 1925)
☐ The nature of other properties in the immediate neighbourhood (a plan which shows the property in the context of the surrounding locality is often useful)
☐ A copy of any planning permission which permits the development to be undertaken by the client and copies of any objections which were lodged in respect of the application
☐ What steps have been taken (if any) to trace the person(s) with the benefit of the covenant and the results of those enquiries. The identity of the person who has the benefit of the covenant should be revealed if known, but steps should not be taken to approach that person without the prior consent of the insurance company since such an approach may have an adverse effect on the outcome of the situation and the consequent insurance risk
☐ Details of any complaints which have been received from persons with the benefit of the covenants.

3.7.3 Accepting a defective title insurance policy if acting for the buyer

Consideration should be given to the following matters:

☐ Check that full disclosure of all relevant facts was made to the insurer prior to the issue of the policy

☐ Ensure that the policy enures to the benefit of successors and is not restricted to a named person

☐ Check that the policy covers the defect or breach in question

☐ Check that the amount of cover offered by the policy appears to be adequate

☐ If the policy is already in existence, enquire whether any claims have been made under the policy and the result of those claims

☐ Ensure that the original policy will be handed over on completion. Where the policy has been taken out by a developer to cover the building of several properties, an examined or certified copy of the policy should be handed over on completion

☐ Where a policy already exists, consideration should be given to taking an express assignment of the benefit of the policy from the seller and, after completion, giving notice of the assignment to the insurance company

☐ Obtain any proposed lender's approval to the policy terms and amount of cover.

3.8 CHARITIES

3.8.1 Non-exempt charities

If there is no restriction on the proprietorship register, a buyer may safely deal with the charity as if it were an absolute owner. If there is a restriction on the register, the matters contained in the next paragraph should be considered and reference should also be made to Land Registry Practice Guide 14.

Unless a charity is an exempt charity, no disposition (the term disposition applies to the transfer or conveyance of land and not to the contract for sale – *Osborne and Co. Ltd* v. *Dior; Marito Holdings SA* v. *Borhane* CA [2003] All ER (D) 185 (Jan)) can be made by the charity without an order of the court or the Charity Commissioners unless all the following conditions are satisfied:

☐ The trustees must obtain a written report about the proposed disposition from a qualified surveyor (FRICS, ARICS, SVA or ASVA)

☐ The property is advertised for the period and in the manner advised by the surveyor

☐ The trustees decide that in the light of the surveyor's report they are satisfied that the terms of the disposition are the best that can be obtained

☐ Prescribed words are inserted in both the contract and purchase deed.

3.8.2   Dealing with land owned by a charity

The following points should be checked:

☐ Is the transaction authorised by the statute or deed which governs the charity?

☐ Is the charity exempt? If so, the transaction can proceed without delay

☐ If not an exempt charity:

☐ Can the trustees give the certificate in the prescribed form of wording (see 6.4)?

☐ If not, has an order of the court or the Charity Commissioners been obtained?

3.9   FIDUCIARY RELATIONSHIPS

A fiduciary relationship is deemed to exist in dealings between the following persons:

☐ Solicitor and client

☐ Trustee and beneficiary

☐ Parent and child (where the influence of the parent over the child may be held to have endured beyond the child's majority)

☐ Doctor and patient

☐ Religious advisor and disciple

☐ Teacher and pupil

☐ Fiancé(e)s (but not between husband and wife).

If a solicitor is asked to act in dealings between any of the parties listed above or in any other situation where he feels that the relationship between the contracting parties may be classed as fiduciary, he should ensure that:

☐ An independent valuation of the property is obtained

☐ All the facts pertaining to the transaction are known by and understood by both parties

☐ The parties are separately represented.

3.10   PURCHASE FROM ADMINISTRATIVE RECEIVER

When buying a property from an administrator or an administrative receiver, the validity of the appointment should be checked, including:

☐ The validity of the floating charge under which the appointment was made and that the charge is a qualifying floating charge under paragraph 14 Schedule B1 to Insolvency Act 1986, as amended by Schedule 16 to Enterprise Act 2002

☐ That the charge covered the whole or substantially the whole of the company's property

☐ That the charge is not likely to be invalidated, e.g. for want of registration, or fraudulent preference

- ☐ That the appointment does not exceed any powers in the charge
- ☐ That the administrator or the administrative receiver has power to conduct the transaction in question
- ☐ In a case where two receivers have been appointed, whether they are able to act jointly and severally or jointly only
- ☐ A certified copy of the appointment should be obtained by the buyer since this is one of the documents that will have to be produced to the Land Registry on registration (see Land Registry Practice Guides 35 and 36).

3.11 OVERVIEW OF PRE-CONTRACT SEARCHES AND ENQUIRIES

3.11.1 All transactions

The following searches are regarded as 'usual' and should be undertaken in every transaction:

- ☐ Search of the local land charges register (LLC1)
- ☐ Enquiries of the local authority (CON 29R) and, if appropriate, optional enquiries (CON 29O)
- ☐ Standard drainage and water enquiries of the water service company (CON 29DW)
- ☐ Pre-contract enquiries of the seller (TA6 and, if leasehold, TA7).

3.11.2 Registered land

In addition to the searches and enquiries listed in **3.11.1**, official copy entries of the title must be obtained.

3.11.3 Unregistered title

In addition to the searches and enquiries listed in **3.11.1**, a Land Charges Department search against the name of the seller and prior estate owners whose names appear on the abstract or epitome of title should be undertaken.

3.11.4 Other common searches and enquiries

Other common searches and enquiries in addition to those listed in **3.11.1** are:

- ☐ Coal mining search
- ☐ Index map search if dealing with unregistered title or an unregistered interest in registered land
- ☐ Environmental data search
- ☐ Disadvantaged Areas search (checking relief from SDLT)
- ☐ Any of the less usual searches which may be applicable in the circumstances (see **3.13**).

3.12   USUAL PRE-CONTRACT SEARCHES AND ENQUIRIES

3.12.1   Local land charges search

☐ **When to make**: in every transaction
☐ **Form**: LLC1 in duplicate (LLC1 is a prescribed form provided for by Local Land Charges Rules 1977, Schedule 1, form C)
☐ **Search methods**:
  ☐ National Land Information Service Channel (NLIS)
  ☐ post/DX to local authority
  ☐ electronic search (some authorities only)
  ☐ personal search
☐ **Plan**: needed if land cannot be clearly identified from postal address
☐ **Fee**: yes. Contact the relevant authority for details. Fees will differ between authorities. See the Local Land Charges (Amendment) Rules 2003 (SI 2003/2502) for the fee for a personal search: £11.00 (plus £1.00 for each additional plot of land up to a maximum for additional plots of £16.00)
☐ **Summary of information to be obtained from search**: the most important are: some planning decisions, compulsory purchase orders, financial charges affecting the property, tree preservation orders
☐ **Protection given by search**: none. Search result only shows state of register at time when search is made but warning of impending land charges can sometimes be obtained by making an Enquiries of Local Authority search on Form CON 29R. A third party can take the benefit of a search made by someone else (e.g. a seller can make a search to pass the result to buyer or his lender). Local Land Charges Act 1975, s.10 provides compensation in limited circumstances where there is an error on the search certificate, or where a matter is binding on the land but is not revealed by the search, because it was not registered at the time of the search. An entry is binding on the land whether or not it is revealed by the search
☐ **Personal search facility**: there is a statutory right to make a personal search, but local authorities do not guarantee the accuracy of the result. It should only be undertaken where time does not permit for an official search to be made. Some lenders will not accept personal searches and, if a personal search is undertaken, clients should be warned that it is not guaranteed by the local authority
☐ **Special points**: can be made personally or by agent, but the result is not guaranteed. Insurance may be available if exchange has to take place before the result of the search is received.

3.12.2   Standard and optional enquiries of local authority

☐ **When to make**: standard enquiries in every transaction, optional enquiries where appropriate
☐ **Form**: the enquiry form CON 29 is split into two forms and both should be submitted in duplicate:

☐   CON 29R Enquiries of Local Authority (2007)
☐   CON 29O Optional Enquiries of Local Authority (2007)
☐ **Search methods:**
  ☐   National Land Information Service Channel (NLIS)
  ☐   post/DX to local authority
  ☐   electronic search (some authorities only)
  ☐   personal search

In view of local government boundary changes, care should be exercised to ensure that the search forms are sent to the correct local authority.

☐ **Plan**: always include a plan with search requests. Some local authorities have specific requirements in relation to the submission of forms and plans (e.g. Cornwall County and District Councils). Non-compliance with these procedures may result in delay in receiving the answers to enquiries

☐ **Fee**: yes. Contact the relevant authority for details. Fees will differ between authorities and between standard and optional enquiries. VAT is payable on a personal search but not on one made by post. See also the special points below

☐ **Summary of information to be obtained**: relates only to the property being searched against. Matters which affect neighbouring properties are not disclosed in the search replies

☐ **From standard enquiries**: planning and building regulations; roads; land for public purposes; land for road works; drainage agreements and consents; road schemes; railway schemes; traffic schemes; outstanding notices; infringements of building regulations; notices, orders, directions and proceedings under planning acts; conservation areas; compulsory purchase; contaminated land; radon gas

☐ **From optional enquiries**: road proposals by private bodies; public paths and byways; advertisements; completion notices; parks and countryside; pipelines; houses in multiple occupation; noise abatement; urban development areas; enterprise zones; inner urban improvement areas; simplified planning zones; land maintenance notices; mineral consultation areas; hazardous substance consents; environmental and pollution notices; food safety notices; hedgerow notices; common land and town and village greens

☐ **Protection given by search**: the buyer is bound by matters even if not discovered by search. The authorities 'do not accept legal responsibility for an incorrect reply, except for negligence. Any liability for negligence will extend to the person who raised the enquiries and the person on whose behalf they were raised. It will also extend to any other person who has knowledge (personally or through an agent) of the replies before the time when he purchases, takes a tenancy of, or lends money on the security of the property or (if earlier) the time when he becomes contractually bound to do so' (extract from the notes to Forms CON 29R and CON 29O)

☐ **Personal search facility**: some authorities permit personal searches, but do not guarantee the accuracy of the result; it should only be undertaken where time does not permit for an official search to be made. Even where facilities are granted for personal searches, these may not cover all the matters normally covered by Forms CON 29R and CON 29O and may not be acceptable to the buyer's lender

☐ There are limitations on personal searches and some lenders will not accept them. The accuracy of a personal search depends on the ability and diligence of the searcher. It is not guaranteed by the local authority. If a personal search is undertaken, clients should be told of this and advised of the limitations on personal searches and their possible implications

☐ A personal search may be included in a HIP provided that it meets the requirements of Schedule 6, Home Information Pack (No.2) Regulations 2007 (SI 2007/1667). After 6 April 2009, insurance may not be used to cover those parts of a personal search for which access to local authority data cannot be obtained

☐ **Special points**: can be made personally or by agent, but the result is not guaranteed. Insurance is available if exchange has to take place before the result of the search is received, but check lender's requirements. Where a local authority refuses to answer a question relating to whether or not a property abuts a public highway, consideration should be given to enquiry 22 of Form CON 29O Optional Enquiries of Local Authority, relating to common land and town and village greens and to making an inspection of the property.

Notes:

1. The fee requested from the client in respect of the local land charges search and the enquiries of the local authority must accurately reflect the fee charged by the local authority or the local search agents used by the solicitor. It is not acceptable to charge the client an enhanced fee. It is also not acceptable to charge the client an enhanced fee which is paid to the local search agent in exchange for a commission payment from the local search agent to the solicitor.

2. Both the local search and enquiries of the local authority contain questions relating to planning matters. In most cases, the local authority to whom the search application is submitted will also be the planning authority for the area which will therefore answer the planning enquiries on the standard forms. In a few cases, e.g. new town development corporations, the planning authority is separate from the local authority and planning enquiries have to be separately addressed to the planning authority. If in doubt, telephone the local authority prior to submitting the search application in order to check the position.

3.12.3   Standard drainage and water enquiries

☐ **When to make**: standard enquiries in every transaction
☐ **Form**: CON 29DW (2007) Standard Drainage and Water Enquiries
☐ **Search methods**:
    ☐ National Land Information Service Channel (NLIS)
    ☐ online via relevant company's website
    ☐ post/DX to relevant company
    ☐ fax to the relevant company

Care should be exercised to ensure that the search forms are sent to the correct company. In some cases, enquiries will need to be made of more than one company. The website **www.drainageandwater.co.uk** has a postcode search facility that will return the correct company for a property.

- **Plan**: insisted on by some water service companies, always needed if land cannot be clearly identified from postal address
- **Fee**: yes. Contact the appropriate regional water service company for details or visit **www.drainageandwater.co.uk**. All regional water service companies answer standard drainage and water enquiries (and for a higher fee may answer an expedited standard search). A 'commercial search' is available at a higher fee (except from Welsh Water). Solicitors should be aware that the Law Society has only been involved in approving the form and content of the CON 29DW Standard Drainage and Water Search. Some areas, such as those served by Dee Valley Water plc, may be subject to further administrative charges – always check with the appropriate water service company before sending fees
- **Summary of information to be obtained from search**: location of public sewers within boundaries of the property or its vicinity; whether foul water and surface drainage from property drain to a public sewer; whether any sewers or proposed sewers are adopted; location of public water mains and whether the property is connected; the basis of charging for sewerage and water supply to the property
- **Protection given by search**: The standard drainage and water enquiries were aimed primarily at residential property but were not intended to exclude commercial properties, however, when first launched, the liability was limited to £5,000. Following representations from the profession and discussion between the Law Society and the regional water service companies, an interim measure was agreed in September 2002 – an increase in professional indemnity cover maintained by most water companies to £2 million for commercial property transactions. Some companies do not offer the increased level of cover. Solicitors are advised to check the level of liability cover with individual water service companies before making a search
- **Personal search facility**: none
- **Special points**: protection extends to the person, company or body who is the recipient of the report with an actual or potential interest in the property. The property may be located where two different water companies separately provide water and sewerage services. Check carefully for this before submitting the search form to avoid unnecessary delays.

3.12.4   Pre-contract enquiries of seller

- **When to make**: in every transaction
- **Form**:
  - TA6 Property Information Form (2nd edition)
  - TA7 Leasehold Information Form (2nd edition) (for use in addition to Form TA6 for leasehold property)
  - TA9 Commonhold Information Form (for use in addition to Form TA6 for commonhold property)

☐   Commercial Property Standard Enquiries (CPSEs)

☐   other forms from legal stationers are also available

☐   **Search methods**: send to seller's solicitor

☐   **Plan**: no

☐   **Fee**: no

☐   **Summary of information to be obtained from search**:

  ☐   TA6 Property Information Form: boundaries and boundary features (fences, walls, hedges, ditches or similar); disputes and complaints; notices and proposals; alterations, planning and building control; guarantees and warranties; council tax; environmental matters; formal and informal arrangements; other charges; occupiers; transaction information; services; connection to utilities and services

  ☐   TA7 Leasehold Information Form: the property; relevant documents; management of the building; contact details; maintenance and service charges; notices; consents; complaints; alterations; enfranchisement

  ☐   TA9 Commonhold Information Form: commonhold association; commonhold assessments and reserve fund levies; notices; common parts; insurance; consents; complaints; rights for the developer

  ☐   Commercial Property Standard Enquiries (general – for all transactions): boundaries and extent; party walls; rights benefiting the property; adverse rights affecting the property; title policies; access to neighbouring land; access to and from the property; physical condition; contents; utilities and services; fire safety and means of escape; planning and building regulations; statutory agreements and infrastructure; statutory and other requirements; environmental; occupiers and employees; insurance; rates and other outgoings; capital allowances; VAT registration information; transfer of a business as a going concern; other VAT treatment; standard-rated supplies; exempt supplies; zero-rated supplies; transactions outside the scope of VAT; notices; disputes; SDLT on assignment of a lease; deferred payments of SDLT; commonhold

☐   **Protection given by search**: none. Seller may be liable in misrepresentation for inaccurate replies. There may also be criminal liability under Fraud Act 2006

☐   **Personal search facility**: none

☐   **Special points**: Solicitors making pre-contract enquiries of the seller using the TransAction forms may use Form TA6. Forms TA7 Leasehold Information Form and TA9 Commonhold Information Form may be used in addition to Form TA6, when appropriate:

☐   Explanatory notes for the seller have been added to Forms TA6, TA7 and TA10

☐   If TransAction forms are used to make pre-contract enquiries of the seller, the forms should be completed, signed and dated by the seller

☐   Use of the TransAction forms by solicitors is voluntary and there are currently no standard procedures or good practice guidance recommended by the Law Society in relation to their use by solicitors

☐   There is no requirement for the seller's solicitor to certify the information given on the TransAction Forms TA6 Property Information Form, TA7 Leasehold Information Form or TA9 Commonhold Information Form. However, this does not affect the legal responsibility of the seller's solicitor and checking the answers given is part of the solicitor's duty as a prudent conveyancer. Failure to do this may amount to inadequate professional service and may be professional negligence (*McMeekin* v. *Long* [2003] 29 EG 120). Where questions have been answered in the terms 'not so far as the seller is aware', this will imply that the seller and his solicitor have made investigations and have no actual knowledge of any defect (*William Sindall plc* v. *Cambridgeshire County Council* [1994] 3 All ER 932). To be adequate, these investigations must cover the seller's personal knowledge as well as the contents of such files, deeds, etc., as are in the firm's personal possession and any other reasonable investigations

☐ In addition, solicitors acting for the buyer should not accept a TA6 Property Information Form, TA7 Leasehold Information Form or TA9 Commonhold Information Form if it has not been properly completed. Acceptance of an improperly completed form may amount to a failure to carry out all the usual enquiries and the solicitor will be in breach of his duty to the buyer client and to any lender client for whom he is also acting

☐ Enquiries additional to those on the TransAction forms should only be raised where relevant and necessary to the particular transaction. Do not raise additional enquiries about matters that can be resolved by a survey or personal inspection of the property. Seller's replies should be factual and accurate and not based on statements of opinion. The seller's solicitor must take his client's instructions before answering the enquiries

☐ In commercial property cases where CPSEs are used, it is standard practice for the buyer's solicitor to submit the request form to the seller's solicitors (usually via email) while the CPSEs referred to in the request are available to all parties on the Practical Law Company's website (**www.practicallaw.com**).

3.12.5   Official copies of the title

☐ **When to make**: in every registered land transaction
☐ **Form**:
  ☐ OC1 Application for Official Copies of Register/Title Plan and/or certificate in Form CI
  ☐ OC2 Application for Official Copies of Documents Only
☐ **Search methods**:
  ☐ National Land Information Service Channel (NLIS)
  ☐ Online at **www1.landregistry.gov.uk**
  ☐ post/DX/fax to the Land Registry
  ☐ telephone by credit account holders on 0844 892 0307 (English counties) or 0844 892 0308 (Welsh counties and Welsh speaking)
☐ **Plan**: no (except where the application is for a certificate in Form CI and an estate plan has not been approved)
☐ **Fee**: yes, see Land Registration Fee Order 2009 at **Appendix C1**

☐ **Summary of information to be obtained from search**: up-to-date copy of entries affecting seller's title

☐ **Special points**: the application is usually made by the seller who supplies the results to the buyer. For more information see Land Registry Practice Guide 11.

3.12.6 Land Charges Department search

☐ **When to make**: in all cases when dealing with unregistered land. Strictly not relevant to land registered with an absolute title but sensible for seller's solicitor to make search against his own client's name to ensure no bankruptcy proceedings pending

☐ **Form**:
　☐ Form K15 Application for an Official Search: not applicable to registered land
　☐ Form K16 Application for an Official Search (bankruptcy only)

☐ **Search methods**:
　☐ National Land Information Service Channel (NLIS)
　☐ Online at **www1.landregistry.gov.uk**
　☐ post/DX/fax to Land Charges Department, Plymouth
　☐ personal search at Plymouth address only
　☐ telephone by credit account holders on 0844 892 0307 (English counties) or 0844 892 0308 (Welsh counties and Welsh speaking)

☐ **Plan**: none

☐ **Fee**: £1 per name for written applications, £2 per name for telephone, fax and computer searches

☐ **Summary of information to be obtained from search**: this is the quickest method of checking that no bankruptcy proceedings are registered against a client (although it must be borne in mind that bankruptcy entries are normally cancelled automatically after five years). In addition, in unregistered land, information relating to incumbrances over the land, e.g. post-1925 restrictive covenants, second and subsequent mortgages, estate contracts, and home rights

☐ **Protection given by search: full search**: 15 working days from date of official search certificate provided completion takes place within this period. Where an entry is revealed which appears to be irrelevant to the transaction in hand, the seller's solicitor may be asked to certify that the entry does not apply to the transaction (by endorsing the search certificate to this effect). Such endorsement does not alter the legal significance of the search result, but an unqualified endorsement by the seller's solicitor would commit him to personal liability if loss were subsequently suffered by the buyer resulting from that particular entry

☐ **Personal search facility**: at Land Charges Department, Plymouth only, but no protection given by personal search

☐ **Special points**: the effect of Law of Property Act 1969, s.24 (by displacing the 'registration is notice' rule contained in Law of Property Act 1925, s.198)

is to place the burden of disclosure of incumbrances on the seller and thus renders this search strictly unnecessary at the pre-contract stage of the transaction. Since the search needs to be made against all estate owners of the land whose names are revealed in the evidence of title, it is only possible for a buyer to make proper searches if title is deduced to him before exchange. These points notwithstanding, it is advisable for the buyer to make a search at least against the seller's name at this stage in order to ensure that no bankruptcy or other financial charges are pending against the seller and that no Class F charge protecting the seller's spouse's or civil partner's home rights have been registered at that time. Additionally, if the documentation supplied by the seller reveals the existence of restrictive covenants which, if valid, would impede the buyer's proposed use of the land, a check may be made against the name of the person on whom the burden of the covenants was imposed to check whether the covenants were registered as Class D(ii) land charges (if not, the covenants are not enforceable against a subsequent purchaser if entered into after 1925). To take advantage of the protection period afforded by the search, it will usually need to be repeated shortly before completion. In registered land, bankruptcy entries or a notice protecting a spouse's or civil partner's home rights will be entered on the register and so revealed by official copy entries of the title so long as those copies are up to date. For more information see Land Registry Practice Guide 63.

3.12.7   Commons registration

☐ **When to make**: in any case where the property abuts a village green or common land, where property is newly built on or is to be built on previously undeveloped land, where a verge or strip or other land, not owned by the property, separates the property from the public highway
☐ **Form**: this information is now obtained by making an optional enquiry of local authority, enquiry 22 'Common land, town and village greens', on Form CON 29O Optional Enquiries of Local Authority (2007)
☐ **Search methods**:
    ☐ National Land Information Service Channel (NLIS)
    ☐ post/DX to local authority
    ☐ electronic search (some authorities)
    ☐ personal search
☐ **Fee**: £14
☐ **Summary of information to be obtained**: whether any land is registered under Commons Registration Act 1965 (CRA 1965) or Commons Act 2006 (CA 2006)
☐ **Protection given**: see 3.12.2
☐ **Personal enquiry facility**: see 3.12.2
☐ **Special points**: where land has been registered as a common or as a town or village green under CRA 1965 or CA 2006, generally no development over the land will be possible. Third parties may have rights over land that is registered, e.g. rights to graze cattle. CA 2006 provides for the registration of land as a

town or village green where the land has been used by a significant number of the inhabitants for sports and other pastimes as of right over a period of 20 years and they continue to do so at the time of the application. Section 15 CA 2006 allows the following periods of grace for such applications for registration where the use as of right has ceased before the application is made:

□ two years from the use ceasing *or*
□ five years where the use ceased before 19 July 2006. (The five-year period of grace may not apply where planning permission was granted and construction works commenced before 23 June 2006.)

CA 2006 also contains provisions that enable 'missed' commons to be registered and wrongly registered land to be deregistered.

Section 2 of the Countryside and Rights of Way Act 2000 provides for the right of access to open country or registered common land as shown on the maps issued by the Countryside Agency. The maps can be inspected at **www.openaccess.gov.uk.**

3.12.8 Coal mining and brine subsidence claim search

□ **When to make**: in any case when dealing with land in coal mining and brine subsidence claim areas, known as 'affected areas'. To determine whether a coal mining and brine subsidence claim search is required, conveyancers may consult the Coal Authority's gazetteer at **www.coal.gov.uk/services/miningreports/gazetteer/** or consult the printed gazetteer in *Coal Mining and Brine Subsidence Claim Searches: Directory and Guidance* (Law Society, 2006). This book also contains further guidance from the Law Society and a user guide from the Coal Authority
□ **Form**: CON 29M (2006) Coal Mining and Brine Subsidence Claim Search form
□ **Search methods**:
　□ National Land Information Service Channel (NLIS)
　□ online via the Coal Authority's Property Search Service (**www.groundstability.com**)
　□ fax (an expedited same/next working day service is available for an additional fee)
　□ post/DX to the Coal Authority
　□ telephone to the Coal Authority's customer service team on 0845 762 6848
□ **Plan**: yes
□ **Fee**: Current fees for residential property are £33.91 plus VAT for postal or telephone applications and £27.00 plus VAT for online applications. Fees for non-residential searches up to a maximum extent of 25 hectares are £64.00 plus VAT irrespective of the method of application. An additional fee of £50.00 plus VAT is payable for same/next working day fax service. Fees information is available from the Coal Authority by telephone, 0845 762 6848 and at **www.coal.gov.uk/services/miningreports**
□ **Summary of information to be obtained from search (coal enquiries):**

whether the property is in an area where coal mining has taken or is likely to take place; the existence of underground coal workings and mine entries which may cause problems with subsidence; whether compensation for subsidence has been paid in the past or repairs carried out or any claim is current

☐ **Summary of information to be obtained from search (Cheshire brine subsidence claims)**: whether the property is in the Cheshire Brine Compensation District or within a Consultation Area prescribed by the Brine Board; an indication of whether there have been any claims for damage made by the owner or a previous owner against the Brine Board for past or suspected past damage; whether the Board has made a 'once-and-for-all' payment commuting the property from any further claim for compensation: such a commutation will usually result in the value of the property being reduced and making it difficult to mortgage. If the search result reveals that a claim for compensation has been lodged but not yet adjudicated, the buyer must, after completion, give notice of the change of ownership to the Board

☐ **Protection given by search**: Any liability of the Coal Authority for negligence in giving mining reports shall be for the benefit of not only enquirers but also a person (being a purchaser for the purpose of Local Land Charges Act 1975, s.10(3)) who or whose agent had knowledge before the relevant time (as defined in that section) of the contents of the mining report. Such extension of liability to another (who did not purchase the mining report from the Authority) is limited to a purchaser, lessee or mortgagee of the property and not others (e.g. other recipients of reports on title, etc.). Full terms and conditions and guidance on liability can be found in the book *Coal Mining and Brine Subsidence Claim Searches* (Law Society, 2006) or online at **www. coal.gov.uk/services/miningreports**. All residential reports include insurance cover for the property owner of up to £20,000 in respect of loss of value as a result of there being a material change in the mining information in a subsequent residential report. It is intended to cover loss suffered as a result of changes in the coal mining database at any time during the insured person's ownership of the property. Where the search is obtained by the seller, the buyer will receive the benefit of the insurance cover. Similar cover applies to 'residential-search-not-required' certificates

☐ **Personal search facility**: none

☐ **Special points**: disused mines exist in many areas where coal mining has not been carried on within living memory. The dangers of subsidence exist in any area where mining has at some time taken place. Provisions for compensation for subsidence are complex: in some cases, once a sum has been paid in compensation, no further claim can be sustained despite further subsidence damage to the land

☐ The Coal Authority also offers an interpretive report service for residential property. Under the service, the applicant will be provided with detailed analysis and advice about mine shafts revealed in the initial report, including a risk assessment as to whether, in the opinion of the Coal Authority, the main building of the property is inside the possible zone of ground movement from any reported mine entry. This service will be offered at an additional cost if the initial report discloses a mine shaft

☐ The Coal Authority also promotes a product called the 'ground stability' report. This report reveals information from the British Geological Survey relating to natural subsidence. It also includes replies to the enquiries made in the CON 29M (2006) Coal Mining and Brine Subsidence Claim Search. The Law Society has not participated in the development of the ground stability search. The Law Society recommends that solicitors make a CON 29M Coal Mining and Brine Subsidence Claim Search when dealing with land in areas affected by coal mining and brine subsidence.

3.12.9   Index map search

☐ **When to make**: in all cases when buying an interest in unregistered land. It is also useful when buying an area of land comprised in more than one registered title
☐ **Form**: SIM Application for an Official Search of the Index Map
☐ **Search methods**:
  ☐ National Land Information Service Channel (NLIS)
  ☐ Online at **www1.landregistry.gov.uk**
  ☐ post/DX/fax/telephone to the Land Registry
☐ **Plan**: a suitable plan may be needed, see Land Registry Practice Guide 10
☐ **Fee**: see Land Registration Fee Order 2009
☐ **Summary of information to be obtained from search**: whether the land is already registered or is subject to a pending application or caution against first registration or existence of a registered rentcharge or affecting franchise
☐ **Protection given by search**: none, although if search result is inaccurate, a right to indemnity may arise
☐ **Personal search facility**: not available
☐ **Special points**: if it is discovered that the land is already registered or that a compulsory registration order came into force before the date of the most recent conveyance on sale on the title, the seller must be asked to rectify the situation before this transaction proceeds. For more information, see Land Registry Practice Guide 10.

3.12.10   Environmental data search

☐ **When to make**: there is no professional obligation to undertake an environmental data search in the course of property transactions. Solicitors must, however, consider whether contamination is an issue in every transaction and advise clients of the potential liabilities associated with environmental issues, without overstating them. In all commercial transactions, and in residential cases where contamination is considered a potential issue, solicitors may consider making specific pre-contract enquiries of the seller, and other enquiries of statutory and regulatory bodies and if there is a possibility that the site is contaminated, or the buyer or lender requests one, an environmental data search may be made, see the *Environmental Law Handbook*, 6th edition (Law Society, 2005)

☐   **Form**: there is no standard form
☐   **Search methods**:
   ☐   National Land Information Service (NLIS)
   ☐   online with search providers
   ☐   post to search providers
   ☐   fax to search providers
☐   **Plan**: it is essential to confirm the location of the land by reference to a plan (paper or online) or by grid reference
☐   **Fee**: From £25 to several hundred pounds (differs for residential and commercial)
☐   **Summary of information to be obtained from search**: (depending on provider) all information held by regulatory bodies, a detailed land use survey highlighting current and historic uses, floodplain data, risk assessment
☐   **Protection given by search**: none
☐   **Personal search facility**: none
☐   **Special points**: the purpose of this search is to establish that there is no cause for concern regarding environmental issues or, if there is a concern, to inform further enquiries and advice to the client. For further guidance see the *Environmental Law Handbook* (Law Society, 2005).

3.12.11   Disadvantaged Areas Search (relief from SDLT)

☐   **When to make**: when acting for the buyer or seller of residential property, a search should be made to determine whether a property is located within a designated disadvantaged area. This will be necessary in every purchase of residential property where the purchase price does not exceed £150,000. However, until 31 December 2009, the purchase of a wholly residential property for not more than £175,000 is exempt from SDLT. This temporary increase of the zero-rate band for residential property is above the current Disadvantaged Area Relief threshold of £150,000
   ☐   From 17 March 2005 Disadvantaged Areas Relief is not available for non-residential land transactions
   ☐   The purchase of six or more separate dwellings as a single transaction is classed as a non-residential transaction and SDLT is payable at the appropriate rate. Finance Act 2003, s.116 defines residential, commercial, and mixed-use property. In mixed-use property (part residential and part non-residential) the value has to be apportioned and the £150,000 limit applied to the residential part
   ☐   The scope of the exemption is such that it applies to property which on 7 May 1998 was situated in specified qualifying wards included in the current indices of deprivation for England and Wales (Indices of Deprivation 2000)
   ☐   The exemption will apply to a property falling outside a qualifying ward if, on 27 November 2001, it had the same postcode as land which on 7 May 1998 was within a qualifying ward
   ☐   Where a property is partly inside a qualifying ward, the purchase price must be apportioned and the part outside will be subject to SDLT

- ☐ This complicated definition can give rise to a number of problems, not least that searches currently available to establish whether property falls within a qualifying ward for the purposes of disadvantaged areas SDLT exemption are not always conclusive.
- ☐ **Form**: not applicable
- ☐ **Search method for properties with a postcode**:
  - ☐ Check the postcode lies in a disadvantaged area by using the postcode search on the HMRC website (**www.hmrc.gov.uk/so/dar/dar-search.htm**)
  - ☐ Check in which ward the property was located in England on 7 May 1998 (1 April 1998 for Wales) by visiting **www.neighbourhood.statistics.gov. uk** and searching against the property's postcode
  - ☐ Check the ward is listed on the HMRC website (**www.hmrc.gov.uk/sdlt/ reliefs-exemptions**). There are separate lists for wards in England, Wales, Northern Ireland and Scotland
  - ☐ If the results of these three checks are positive, then the property is exempt
  - ☐ If the postcode search is positive but the ward search shows part or all of the property is outside the relevant ward, the property will still be exempt if the property on 27 November 2001 had the same postcode as land which on 7 May 1998 fell within a qualifying ward
  - ☐ **Warning:** The HMRC postcode search is not complete, and is therefore inconclusive. If the postcode search shows that the property is outside a designated area or no postcode is found, it may be prudent to follow the steps for properties without postcodes below
- ☐ **Search method for properties without a postcode**:
  - ☐ Check with the local authority to find out in which ward the property was located in England on 7 May 1998 (1 April 1998 for Wales). Maps showing wards as at 1998 can be viewed as pdf files on **www. neighbourhood. statistics.gov.uk**
  - ☐ Check whether the ward is listed on the HMRC website (**www.hmrc.gov. uk/sdlt/reliefs-exemptions**)
  - ☐ Obtain a copy of the 7 May 1998 (England) or 1 April 1998 (Wales) boundary ward map from the Ordnance Survey Boundaries Service (Tel. 023 8030 5092) and check that the property is within the boundaries shown. The Neighbourhood Statistics website also holds pdf files of the 1998 ward boundary maps
  - ☐ If the results of these checks above show the property within the ward, it is exempt. Any part outside the ward is subject to SDLT
- ☐ **Alternative search method**:
  - ☐ The procedures to ascertain whether a property qualifies for the relief can be time-consuming and not always conclusive. An alternative may be to submit a good plan of the property together with the relevant transaction document to either HMRC Stamp Taxes Enquiry Line or in writing to the offices in Worthing, Manchester or Birmingham (complex transactions) and seek written advice
  - ☐ However, you are only able to obtain a binding opinion of the SDLT due if you inform HMRC of everything they need to know about the transaction.

If advice is sought, HMRC will assist, but any opinion they give will be an informal opinion and will not bind them

- [ ] Telephone enquiries made on the Stamp Taxes Helpline on 0845 603 0135 may also be of general assistance

- [ ] **Plan**: a copy of the 7 May 1998 (England) or 1 April 1998 (Wales) ward map clearly showing the property within a ward boundary
- [ ] **Fee**: none
- [ ] **Summary of information to be obtained from search**: an indication of whether the property falls within one of the designated areas that qualify for relief
- [ ] **Protection given by search**: none
- [ ] **Personal search facility**: not applicable. Telephone queries may be directed to the Stamp Taxes Helpline on 0845 603 0135
- [ ] **Special points**: Schedule 6 Finance Act 2003 determines how property situated partly within and partly outside a designated disadvantaged area is to be treated for the purposes of the relief (queries may be referred to HMRC Stamp Taxes Office)
- [ ] **Claiming the relief**: For transactions affected by SDLT, relief will be claimed by completing form SDLT1. Box 9 of the form deals with reliefs. No supporting documents or evidence need accompany the return. After the HMRC certificate has been issued, some claims will be checked. At this point the client or solicitor may be asked to provide evidence to substantiate the claim, which may include:
  - [ ] The full postcode for the property being transferred
  - [ ] A full photocopy of the transfer document
  - [ ] A copy of the contract or sale agreement
  - [ ] Evidence that consideration for the transaction did not exceed £150,000
  - [ ] If the document is a lease, a payment in respect of the rent element
  - [ ] If possible, a copy of the ward map with the location of the property clearly marked.

3.13   LESS USUAL SEARCHES AND ENQUIRIES

The buyer's solicitor must in all cases be alert to the need to make additional searches. A summary of some of the less usual pre-contract searches appears below.

3.13.1   Waterways

- [ ] **When to make**: where a river, stream or canal passes through or adjoins the property
- [ ] **Form**: letter
- [ ] **Search methods**:
  - [ ] National Land Information Service Channel (NLIS)
  - [ ] For rivers, streams or brooks post to the Environmental Agency
  - [ ] For canals, post to the British Waterways Board

☐ **Plan**: yes
☐ **Fee**: yes
☐ **Summary of information to be obtained from search**: ownership of river banks and canals; liability for repairs of and maintenance of river banks and canals; fishing rights; licences to abstract water; drainage rights; liability for flooding from rivers; rights of way affecting towpaths along sides of canals
☐ **Protection given by search**: none
☐ **Personal search facility**: none
☐ **Special points**: The local authority may be responsible for smaller waterways within its own area. Although a search may be requested electronically through an NLIS channel, the response will arrive by post/DX.

3.13.2 Underground railways

☐ **When to make**: land adjoins railway, railway passes through land, property built close to underground railway network
☐ **Form**: letter
☐ **Search methods**:
    ☐ National Land Information Service Channel (NLIS)
    ☐ Post to appropriate underground authority
☐ **Plan**: yes
☐ **Fee**: yes
☐ **Summary of information to be obtained from search**: ownership of track, routes of underground tunnels
☐ **Protection given by search**: none
☐ **Personal search facility**: not available
☐ **Special points**: although a search may be requested electronically through an NLIS channel, the response will arrive by post/DX.

3.13.3 Overground railways

There is no statutory basis for response to property enquiries by the railway industry in Great Britain. The main infrastructure controller is Network Rail (formerly Railtrack plc) and a variety of train operators use the track, occupy stations and other railway land. None of these bodies has a system to respond to search letters. Network Rail does not respond to enquiries. Network Rail has answered a series of frequently asked questions at **www.networkrail.co.uk**. Enquiry 3.5 'Nearby Railway Schemes', on Form CON 29R Enquiries of Local Authority (2007) will give details of railways within 200m of the property.

3.13.4 Tin mining

☐ **When to make**: mainly applicable to land to be purchased in West Devon or Cornwall
☐ **Form**: letter

☐ **Search methods**:
  ☐ National Land Information Service Channel (NLIS)
  ☐ Post to Cornwall Consultants
☐ **Plan**: yes
☐ **Fee**: yes
☐ **Summary of information to be obtained from search**: presence of disused underground workings which could cause subsidence damage
☐ **Protection given by search**: none
☐ **Personal search facility**: not available
☐ **Special points**: although a search may be requested through an NLIS channel, the response will arrive by post/DX.

3.13.5   Clay mining

☐ **When to make**: mainly applicable to land to be purchased in Dorset, West Devon or Cornwall. To determine whether a search is required conveyancers can use the online postcode search at **www.kabca.org**
☐ **Form**: letter
☐ **Search methods**:
  ☐ National Land Information Service Channel (NLIS)
  ☐ Post/fax to Imerys Minerals Ltd (for china clay searches in Cornwall and Devon) or to Sibelco UK Ltd (for ball clay searches in Devon and Dorset)
☐ **Plan**: yes
☐ **Fee**: yes
☐ **Summary of information to be obtained from search**: presence of workings which could cause subsidence damage
☐ **Protection given by search**: none
☐ **Personal search facility**: not available
☐ **Special points**: although a search may be requested through an NLIS channel, the response will arrive by post/DX.

3.13.6   Brine subsidence claims

See **3.12.8**.

☐ **When to make**: land to be purchased in Cheshire (check the place name in the printed directory, *Coal Mining and Brine Subsidence Claim Searches* (Law Society, 2006) or online at **www.coalminingreports.co.uk**)
☐ **Form**: CON 29M Coal Mining and Brine Subsidence Claim Search (see **3.12.8**)
☐ **Search methods**:
  ☐ Internet via National Land Information Service Channel or **www.coalminingreports.co.uk**
  ☐ Post or DX to the Coal Authority
  ☐ Telephone to the Coal Authority's customer service team on 0845 762 6848
☐ **Plan**: yes
☐ **Fee**: yes

☐ **Summary of information to be obtained from search**: presence of disused brine extraction workings which could cause subsidence damage; an indication of whether there have been any claims for damage made by the owner or a previous owner against the Brine Board for past or suspected past damage; whether the Board has made a 'once-and-for-all' payment commuting the property from any further claim for compensation: such a commutation will usually result in the value of the property being reduced and making it difficult to mortgage. If the search result reveals that a claim for compensation has been lodged but not yet adjudicated, the buyer must, after completion, give notice of the change of ownership to the Board

☐ **Protection given by search**: none

☐ **Personal search facility**: not available

☐ **Special points**: subsidence due to brine pumping also known to affect properties in Greater Manchester and Droitwich. Separate enquiries of the local authority should be made in these areas.

3.13.7   Limestone

☐ **When to make**: land to be purchased in Dudley, Sandwell, Walsall or Wolverhampton

☐ **Form**: letter

☐ **Search methods**:

   ☐ National Land Information Service Channel (NLIS)

   ☐ Post to local, district or metropolitan council

☐ **Plan**: yes

☐ **Fee**: yes

☐ **Summary of information to be obtained from search**: presence of disused underground workings which could cause subsidence damage

☐ **Protection given by search**: none

☐ **Personal search facility**: not available

☐ **Special points**: although a search may be requested through an NLIS channel, the response will arrive by post/DX.

3.13.8   Rent registers

☐ **When to make**: land to be purchased is subject to a Rent Act 1977 tenancy

☐ **Form**: CON 29E Request for a search of the register kept pursuant to section 79 Rent Act 1977 (in duplicate)

☐ **Search methods**: post to the relevant Rent Assessment Panel

☐ **Plan**: no

☐ **Fee**: £1

☐ **Summary of information to be obtained from search**: the form of enquiry is as follows: 'Are there any, and if so what, subsisting entries in the Register in respect of the above property or any part of it kept pursuant to Section 79 of the Rent Act 1977, as amended by Paragraph 43 of Schedule 25 to the Housing Act 1980?' Such entries will be disclosed by the search

☐ **Protection given by search**: the replies are furnished in the belief that they are correct but on the distinct understanding that neither the President nor any member of his staff is legally responsible, except in negligence

☐ **Personal search facility**: not available

☐ **Special points**: if a rent is registered, it is an offence for the landlord to charge more than the registered rent for the property. Rent charged in excess of the registered amount is recoverable by the tenant. Registration of a revised rent can normally only be made after two years have elapsed since the last registration. There are now five Rent Assessment Panels covering England, and one covering Wales. For details of their coverage, visit the website of the Residential Property Tribunal Service (**www.rpts.gov.uk**). Form CON 29E was agreed between the Law Society and the Department of the Environment; it has not been updated since 1996.

3.13.9   Chancel repair liability

The cost of repairing the chancel of a parish church (Church of England or Church in Wales) is generally met by either the parochial church council, the representative body of the church in Wales, other ecclesiastical bodies, or educational establishments. In some rare instances, however, landowners are liable for the costs of such repair.

Where the liability is not recorded in the title deeds, consideration should be given as to whether it is appropriate to make enquiries.

Enquiries may be made using commercial products that determine if a property is located in a parish where there remains a potential to enforce chancel repair liability, but these products are not property specific.

Property specific enquiries may be made by conducting a personal search or 'FOI paid for search' of the Record of Ascertainments held by the National Archives. For details, see National Archives Legal Records Information Leaflet 33 and 'Information from the Archive L1', both available from **www.nationalarchives. gov.uk**. It is understood, however, that these records are incomplete.

Insurance may be considered as an option following the results of a search, or as an alternative to searching. Insurers may require confirmation that no enquiries of the local church have been made regarding chancel repair liability.

Schedule 1 to Land Registration Act 2002 provides that a right in respect of the repair of a church chancel is an interest which overrides a disposition of a registered title. This liability will retain its overriding status until 13 October 2013. After this date, a purchaser will generally only be bound by the liability if it has been protected by an entry on the register or, in the case of unregistered land, a caution against first registration has been registered or the liability is referred to on the title deeds. See Land Registry Practice Guide 66 as to overriding interests losing automatic protection in 2013.

3.13.10 Search of the index of relating franchises and manors

This search will not be required in most conveyancing transactions but may be appropriate when dealing with agricultural land. The application should be made in form SIF.

For more details see Land Registry Practice Guide 13.

3.13.11 Drains and sewers

Where a property does not have the benefit of mains drainage, consideration should be given to commissioning a separate drainage survey to ensure that the system is in working order and complies with current environmental legislation.

3.13.12 Company search

Where the seller is a private limited company, consider making a company search to ensure that the company exists and is solvent and has no fixed or floating charges which will impinge upon the present transaction.

3.14 CHECKLIST FOR MAKING PRE-CONTRACT SEARCHES AND ENQUIRIES

3.14.1 Making searches

☐ Decide which searches need to be made and which method is most appropriate
☐ Is a plan required, is it accurate, and is it on a sufficiently large scale to identify the property and the surrounding area clearly?
☐ What questions (in addition to those on the printed form) need to be asked?
☐ Correct application form and fee?
☐ Correct address for submission of the search?
☐ Diarise the file and chase up delayed responses.

3.14.2 Search replies

☐ Analyse the answer to each question – does it accord with what you would expect to find and with what the client wants?
☐ If it does: place a tick in the margin against that question
☐ If it does not: place a cross in the margin by the question, pursue the question with the relevant authority until a satisfactory reply is received, then replace the cross with a tick and take the client's further instructions if the ultimate reply is not satisfactory
☐ Where an answer contains information which should be communicated to the client or on which the client's further instructions are needed, place a 'C' in the margin beside that question and contact the client
☐ Do not exchange contracts until all search replies have been received and all answers are marked with a tick

☐   Consider whether the results of any searches require an insurance policy to be taken out to cover potential liabilities. Remember that the negotiation of an insurance policy may constitute 'arranging' within Financial Services and Markets Act 2000.

3.15   RELYING ON SEARCHES MADE BY A THIRD PARTY

☐   Is the search up to date?
☐   Does it cover the correct property?
☐   Have all the relevant questions been asked?
☐   Are its results transferable to the buyer and his lender?
☐   Is the search acceptable to the buyer's lender?

3.16   INSPECTION OF THE PROPERTY

If a physical inspection is carried out, take a plan of the property and look for any of the following matters:

☐   A discrepancy or uncertainty over the identity or boundaries of the property
☐   Evidence of easements which adversely affect the property
☐   The existence and status of non-owning occupiers
☐   Discrepancy between the fixtures and fittings which the client understood to belong to the property and those actually existing.

3.17   AGRICULTURAL LAND: ENQUIRIES OF THE SELLER

Some of the following additional enquiries may be relevant to the purchase:

☐   Planning enquiries concerning agricultural buildings and whether or not they fall within the Agricultural General Development Order
☐   Enquiries concerning listed buildings and scheduling under Ancient Monuments and Archaeological Areas Act 1979
☐   Information should be sought on all grant or subsidy schemes relating to the property ascertaining whether the conditions applicable to them have been properly observed and ensuring no money will become repayable
☐   Enquiries concerning single farm payment entitlement and other quotas which may benefit the property and whether they are transferable to the buyer
☐   Enquiries concerning boundaries and their maintenance
☐   Enquiries relating to services benefiting the property (especially water supplies)
☐   Enquiries relating to sites of special scientific interest or other environmental designations whether or not these come to light in answers to a local search
☐   Enquiries relating to abstraction and discharge licences granted by the Environment Agency under Water Resources Act 1991, Environmental Protection Act 1990 or Environment Act 1995

☐ Enquiries as to the history of the occurrence of notifiable diseases on the property
☐ Specific enquiries relating to sporting rights
☐ Enquiries relating to the existence of standing timber felling licences and grant conditions.
☐ Some or all of the following enquiries may need to be raised in connection with the water supply to the property:
  ☐ Does the property have a mains water supply?
  ☐ If there is a mains water supply, does the mains pipe (which is maintained by the water company) run through the property or immediately adjacent to the property in a public highway?
  ☐ If there is no direct access to the mains water pipe, how is the property connected to the mains, who owns and is liable for the private spur, and does the property have the benefit of private easements for the continued use of the pipe, its maintenance, repair and replacement and the taking of water through it?
  ☐ Where is the mains water meter?
  ☐ If the property has a private water supply, its source should be identified and enquiries raised as to whether the source supplies this property exclusively
  ☐ Are special water uses required, e.g. for spray irrigation?
  ☐ If the property is supplied by a private water source from an adjoining property, enquiries should be raised to ascertain the contractual rights and obligations of the parties.

3.18   BUYING AGRICULTURAL LAND WITH MILK QUOTA: ADDITIONAL PRE-CONTRACT ENQUIRIES

Additional pre-contract enquiries will be necessary to establish:

☐ The exact amount of quota attaching to the land
☐ The composition of the quota (i.e. does it include direct sales, or wholesale quota?)
☐ That the seller is the freehold owner of the whole holding to which the quota attaches
☐ That the quota does not attach to any land outside the land agreed to be sold
☐ That, if the seller is not the freehold owner of the entire holding, all other persons with an interest in the holding, such as landlords or lenders, who will be affected by the disposal of the quota have signified their agreement to the disposal on Form MQ/1
☐ If an apportionment of the quota has been made within the previous six months and notified to the Rural Payments Agency by means of Form MQ/8.

3.19   DISCOVERING EASEMENTS

To discover easements the solicitor needs to:

☐   Inspect the official copy of the register or the title deeds
☐   If the title is unregistered, carry out a search at the Land Charges Department to check whether any Class D(iii) (equitable easement) land charges are registered
☐   If acting for the seller, make enquiries of the seller client as to the rights his neighbours and others enjoy over the property being sold and the rights he enjoys over adjoining property
☐   If acting for the buyer, instruct the buyer to make a personal inspection of the property to look for evidence of any easements, e.g. rights of way, rights to light, drainage, right to park, both enjoyed by the property and exercised over it.

3.20   ENVIRONMENTAL ISSUES: SPECIFIC ENQUIRIES OF THE SELLER

The extent and type of enquiries will depend on whether the land and property to be transferred is for domestic residential or commercial use. The following are examples of some of the enquiries that may be made of the seller in domestic residential transactions:

☐   Whether the seller is aware of any potentially contaminative use of the site or previous accidents, incidents or spillages
☐   Whether the site has been used for landfill or waste disposal purposes
☐   Details of previous owners or occupiers and activities carried out by them
☐   Whether there have been any disputes, or circumstances which may give rise to any disputes with neighbours or regulatory bodies regarding the state of the land
☐   What (if any) planning consents have been issued in respect of the site, what conditions they contained regarding contamination and its remediation, and details of any works carried out to comply with the conditions.

3.21   POWERS OF ATTORNEY

☐   Except in the case of a security power or an enduring or lasting power which has been registered with the Court of Protection, if the power was more than 12 months old at the date it was purportedly exercised, Powers of Attorney Act 1971 provides that when the person who buys from the attorney comes to sell the property he must provide a statutory declaration to his buyer stating that he (the purchaser or the attorney) had no knowledge of any revocation of the power at the time he bought the property (see Powers of Attorney Act 1971, s.5)
☐   In the case of registered land, the fact that the registered proprietor bought the property from an attorney will not be apparent from the register. For

this reason, Land Registration Rules 2003, r.62 provides that any required evidence of non-revocation should be produced when the buyer from the attorney applies to be registered as proprietor

☐ If the Land Registry does call for evidence of non-revocation, it will require the buyer from the attorney to provide either:

    ☐ A statutory declaration stating that the buyer from the attorney was not aware of any revocation of the power at the date of the transaction *or*

    ☐ A certificate in Form 2 (Schedule 3 to the Land Registration Rules 2003) signed by the buyer's conveyancer

☐ The buyer from the attorney must provide the declaration or certificate, not the attorney nor the seller's solicitor

☐ In all cases, the Land Registry will require evidence of the power of attorney which should either be:

    ☐ Form 1 completed by the buyer's conveyancer *or*

    ☐ The original power of attorney *or*

    ☐ A certified copy of the power of attorney

☐ For more details see Land Registry Practice Guide 9.

3.22   LICENSING

3.22.1   Activities requiring a licence

Under the Licensing Act 2003 a single licence – the premises licence – authorises the use of any premises, part of premises or place for any or all of the 'licensable activities'. The licensable activities covered by the Act are:

☐ The sale by retail of alcohol
☐ The supply of alcohol by clubs
☐ The provision of regulated entertainment (including cinemas and theatres)
☐ The provision of late night refreshment.

3.22.2   Premises requiring a licence

A premises licence will be required for a wide range of premises, including:

☐ Pubs and bars
☐ Restaurants
☐ Nightclubs
☐ Supermarkets, off licences and shops making retail alcohol sales
☐ Hotels
☐ Late-night refreshment premises
☐ Non-qualifying clubs
☐ Cinemas
☐ Theatres.

3.22.3   Pre-contract enquiries for licensed premises

The following enquiries should be made of the seller by a buyer who is buying licensed premises:

- ☐ Supply a copy of the premises licence
- ☐ Supply a plan of the premises as incorporated in the licence
- ☐ Supply a copy of any application which has been submitted for a variation of the premises licence
- ☐ Establish that no alterations have been made to the premises since the licence was granted
- ☐ Supply a copy of any provisional statement which has been issued in connection with the property
- ☐ Obtain confirmation that the designated premises supervisor (as specified in the licence) remains on the premises
- ☐ Provide details of all personal licensees currently working on the premises
- ☐ Confirm that no closure orders or applications for closure orders have been made in relation to the premises
- ☐ Ascertain the outcome of any reviews by the licensing authority in relation to the premises licence, or whether any review is pending
- ☐ Confirm any current capacity limit on the premises
- ☐ Specify the number of temporary event notices held at the premises (including their duration) in the current year and to provide copies of any notifications which have been given on future temporary events
- ☐ Provide a copy of the receipt for the current annual fee
- ☐ Confirm the rateable value of the premises
- ☐ Obtain confirmation that the licence holders have complied with the terms of their licence and any mandatory conditions which apply to the premises *and*
- ☐ Require copies of any correspondence between either responsible authorities or interested parties that might indicate the possibility of an application to review the licence.

3.23   UNDERTAKINGS

3.23.1   Guidelines

- ☐ Obtain the client's irrevocable written authority before giving an undertaking
- ☐ Ensure the wording of the undertaking is clear, unambiguous and totally capable of performance
- ☐ Only give undertakings in writing, signed or authorised by a partner
- ☐ Mark the client's file conspicuously to ensure that the undertaking is not overlooked
- ☐ When the undertaking has been fulfilled, obtain a written release from the recipient.

3.23.2 Checklist before giving an undertaking

☐ Do I know the client well enough to feel confident about giving the undertaking?

☐ Have I got the client's irrevocable written authority to give the undertaking?

☐ Has the client disclosed all subsisting mortgages and liabilities which will or might affect the amount of money which will be available to discharge the loan?

☐ Is there sufficient equity to repay the loan with interest?

☐ Are the terms of the undertaking totally acceptable?

☐ Are negotiations for the client's sale sufficiently firm and advanced to make it safe to give the undertaking?

☐ Has the undertaking been authorised by a partner?

☐ Has the cover of the client's sale file been clearly marked to show that an undertaking has been given, to whom, and for what amount?

☐ The Solicitors Regulation Authority has issued a warning card on undertakings which is reproduced at **Appendix A7** and **www.sra.org.uk**.

3.24 LIMITATIONS ON BANK UNDERTAKINGS

☐ A bank's standard form of undertaking should be read carefully in the light of the particular transaction to ensure that the wording is appropriate for those circumstances. If the wording is not wholly appropriate to the circumstances in hand, the undertaking should be amended to reflect the particular requirements of the transaction

☐ The terms of the undertaking should be confined to repayment:

    ☐ of a stated figure, plus interest on that sum if so instructed

    ☐ from a defined source, e.g. the proceeds of sale of a named property

    ☐ of the net proceeds of sale, having defined what is understood by the word 'net', i.e. after deduction of specified loans, estate agents' commission, solicitor's fees, disbursements on the sale and purchase, and any other known and defined liabilities which will reduce the amount available to repay the loan

    ☐ when the proceeds of sale are actually received by the solicitor. This protects the solicitor against having to honour the undertaking in circumstances where the sale of the property is completed but for some reason the funds are never received by him, e.g. the client intercepts the money and absconds with it.

4

Contracts

4.1 DRAFTING THE CONTRACT: OTHER PARTY REPRESENTED BY UNQUALIFIED PERSON

Check that the contract contains clauses to deal with the following matters:

☐ Personal attendance by an unrepresented seller at completion to take up the deeds and purchase price *and either*

☐ Payment of the deposit to an estate agent who is a member of a recognised professional body *or*

☐ Payment of the deposit to the buyer's solicitor in the capacity of stakeholder *or*

☐ Provision for the deposit to be placed in a bank or building society deposit account in the joint names of seller and buyer.

4.2 SUGGESTED FORM OF WORDING FOR RELEASE OF RIGHTS BY NON-OWNING OCCUPIER

Where a non-owning occupier is to release his/her rights in the property, check that an appropriate clause to this effect is included in the contract and that the contract is signed by the party releasing the rights.

Suggested form of wording for release of rights:

☐ 'In consideration of the buyer entering this agreement I [*name of spouse or civil partner*] agree:

    (i)   to the sale of the property on the terms of this agreement; and

    (ii) that I will not register rights in relation to the property, whether under Family Law Act 1996 or otherwise, and that I will procure before completion the removal of any registration made by me; and

    (iii) that I will vacate the property by the completion date.'

    or

☐ 'In consideration of your today entering into a contract with [*name of owning spouse or civil partner*] for the purchase of the property known as [*insert address of property to be sold*], I agree:

    (i)   to release any beneficial interest which I may have in the property (such interest, if any, being transferred to the proceeds of sale of the property), such release to be effective from the date of completion of the sale of this property;

(ii) to procure the cancellation of any registration which may have been effected by me or on my behalf on or before completion, including any registration in respect of rights of occupation which I may have under Family Law Act 1996; and

(iii) to vacate the property by the completion date.'

4.3 SELLER'S TITLE AWAITING REGISTRATION

Where the seller's title is awaiting registration, check that the contract contains clauses:

☐ Requiring the seller to expedite the application and assist the buyer in answering any requisitions which might be raised by the Land Registry in relation to the pending registration

☐ Requiring the buyer to purchase the seller's existing equitable interest in the property (the seller does not have the legal estate until registration is complete). The seller must be required to give an undertaking to transfer the legal estate to the buyer on completion of the seller's registration of title.

4.4 CHECKLIST OF USUAL SPECIAL CONDITIONS

Condition to deal with	Reason for inclusion	Standard Condition
Title	Buyer is entitled to know what title is being offered	SC 4.1 SCPC 6.1
Deposit	No provision at common law, variation of general conditions may be required	SC 2.2 SCPC 2.2
Interest on deposit	Interest is payable under the Solicitors' Accounts Rules	SC 2.2.6
Completion date	Open contract rule and general conditions not satisfactory	SC 6.1 SCPC 8.1
Title guarantee	Defines scope of implied covenants for title	SC 4.6.2 SCPC 6.6.2
Incumbrances	Seller's duty of disclosure	SC 3 SCPC 3
Fixtures and fittings	To create an obligation and to avoid disputes between the parties	SC 10 SCPC 12
Vacant possession	Implied by common law unless stated to the contrary. Normally included for certainty and must deal with requirement for completion to take place at the property if so required	SC Special condition 4 SCPC Special condition 2

4.5   GUIDELINES FOR CONTRACT DRAFTING

☐   Does the contract describe clearly what is to be sold?
☐   Is a plan necessary?
☐   Does the contract accord with the client's instructions as to the conditions on which the property is to be sold?
☐   Are the conditions concise and unambiguous?

4.6   CONDITIONAL CONTRACTS

4.6.1   Use of conditional contracts

Conditional contracts may be considered for use in the following circumstances:

☐   Where the buyer has not had the opportunity before exchange of contracts to make searches and enquiries or to conduct a survey or where his mortgage arrangements have not been finalised
☐   Where the contract is dependent on planning permission being obtained for the property
☐   Where the sale requires the consent of the Charity Commissioners under Charities Act 1993
☐   Where the sale is dependent on permission being obtained from a third party, e.g. ministerial consent, landlord's consent
☐   Where the parties wish to be bound to a contract but there is some other unresolved matter which prevents commitment to an unconditional contract for the time being, e.g. the seller has to get in part of the legal estate.

4.6.2   Guidelines

☐   Consider the precise event(s) on which the contract is to be made conditional
☐   By what time must the condition be fulfilled? (Bear in mind that the specified time limit cannot be extended)
☐   Consider the precise terms on which the party with the benefit of the condition may rescind
☐   Ensure that there are no loopholes which would enable one party to escape from the contract other than for the non-fulfilment of the event(s) contemplated in the first bullet point above
☐   Use an established precedent, tailoring it to fit your exact requirements
☐   Take your time: a condition which is hastily drafted may contain unforeseen errors
☐   Having drafted your 'perfect' condition, leave it on the desk overnight and review the wording objectively in the cold light of day. Does the condition achieve its objectives? Is it clear and certain? Do any unforeseen or unwanted consequences flow from the wording?

4.6.3 Rescission: 'subject to searches'

☐ Which searches?
☐ Which adverse entries will give rise to the right to rescind?
☐ By when must the search result(s) be received?
☐ Can the buyer rescind if he changes his mind and never makes search applications?

4.6.4 Rescission: 'subject to mortgage'

☐ Specify name of lender(s) to whom application made
☐ Specify amount of required advance
☐ Specify acceptable interest rates
☐ Should the buyer be entitled to rescind if the mortgage offer is subject to conditions or a retention – what conditions attached to the offer would be acceptable/unacceptable?
☐ What is the time limit by which application must be determined?
☐ Can the buyer rescind if he changes his mind and never puts in an application for a mortgage?

4.6.5 Rescission - 'subject to survey'

☐ Named surveyor?
☐ What type of survey?
☐ Which defects revealed by survey report will entitle buyer to withdraw?
☐ Should a financial limit be placed on the entitlement to rescind? For example, the buyer can rescind if survey reveals defects which exceed £x in total – if so, who assesses the value?
☐ Time limit for obtaining result of survey
☐ Can buyer rescind if he changes his mind and never instructs the surveyor?

4.6.6 Rescission: 'subject to planning permission'

☐ Form of planning application to be agreed between the parties
☐ What conditions attached to the consent would entitle the buyer to rescind?
☐ Can the buyer rescind if he changes his mind and never puts in a planning application?
☐ Time limit for result of application
☐ Which party is to make the application and pay the fee?
☐ The non-applying party should agree in writing not to oppose the application and to support it
☐ Is the application to be for outline or detailed permission?
☐ Which party is to pay the architect's and other professional fees in connection with the application?

4.7 CHECKLIST FOR DEPOSIT TERMS

☐   How much deposit is required in total?
☐   Has a preliminary deposit been paid – if so, how much and to whom?
☐   Who is to hold the deposit and in which capacity?
☐   Method of payment?
☐   If in cash, provide for payment by banker's draft or equivalent
☐   If less than 10%, provide for balance to be immediately payable on service of a completion notice.

4.8 PLANS

4.8.1 Land Registry guidelines

A Land Registry plan should be prepared having regard to the following guidelines:

☐   It should be drawn to and show its actual scale
☐   Show its orientation (e.g. a north point)
☐   Use preferred scales of 1/1250–1/500 for urban properties
☐   Use preferred scale of 1/2500 for rural properties (fields and farms, etc.)
☐   Not based on a scale of imperial measurement (e.g. 16 feet to 1 inch)
☐   Not reduced in scale
☐   Not marked or referred to as being for identification only
☐   Not show statements of disclaimer used under Property Misdescriptions Act 1991
☐   Show sufficient detail to be identified on the Ordnance Survey map
☐   Show its general location by showing roads, road junctions or other landmarks
☐   Show the land attached to the property including any garage or garden ground
☐   Show buildings in their correct (or intended) position
☐   Show access drives or pathways if they form part of property boundaries
☐   Show the land and property clearly (e.g. by edging, colouring or hatching)
☐   Have edgings of a width that does not obscure any other detail
☐   Show separate parts by suitable plan markings (house, parking space, dustbin space)
☐   Identify different floor levels (where appropriate)
☐   Show intricate boundaries with a larger scale or inset plan
☐   Show measurements in metric units only, to two decimal places
☐   Show undefined boundaries accurately and, where necessary, by reference to measurements
☐   Show measurements that correspond, so far as possible, to scaled measurements.

Note: The Land Registry does not consider it necessary to specify in any deed or on any plan the area of the property described.

4.8.2 Points to note

☐ Markings should be clear and precise

☐ Land to be sold should be outlined or coloured in red

☐ Retained land (if any) should be outlined or coloured in blue

☐ Other land referred to should be coloured or hatched in distinct colours other than red or blue. If possible, it is best to avoid the use of green on a plan where red has already been used since the most common form of colour blindness relates to the inability to distinguish between these two colours. See Land Registry Practice Guide 40 as to its preferred practice for colouring plans

☐ The ownership of boundaries should be indicated by 'T' marks with the 'T' on the side of the boundary line within the land which bears responsibility for the maintenance of the boundary. In the absence of a specific request, the Land Registry will only show 'T' marks on the title plan if referred to in a covenant or other provision in the transfer

☐ Rights of way and routes of services should be tinted or marked with broken or dotted lines of a distinct colour, with each end of the route being additionally identified with separate capital letters

☐ Where the plan is to scale, the scale should be shown

☐ If the plan is not to scale, metric measurements should be shown along each boundary. An imperial measurement can be used in addition to the metric measurement provided that the metric measurement is placed first and the imperial measurement is in characters no larger than the metric figures

☐ A compass point indicating the direction of north should be shown

☐ A key should be included to explain the meaning of the various colours and lines used on the plan.

4.9 FIXTURES AND FITTINGS

In view of the uncertainty of the status of some items in law, it is essential that, in appropriate circumstances, the contract deals expressly with:

☐ Fixtures which the seller intends to remove on or before completion (including, where appropriate, the tenant's right to remove tenant's trade fixtures)

☐ Compensation for the buyer if the seller causes damage in the course of the removal of fixtures

☐ Fittings which are to remain at the property

☐ Any additional price which the buyer is to pay for the fittings

☐ The apportionment of the purchase price to exclude from the total the price paid for the fittings

☐ Deferring the passing of title to fittings until completion because, in the absence of such a condition, Sale of Goods Act 1979, s.18 will provide that title to the fittings passes to the buyer on exchange

☐ A warranty that fittings are free of incumbrances (e.g. subsisting hire-purchase agreements). Although Sale of Goods Act 1979, s.12 will imply such a warranty, its express inclusion in the contract prevents the matter from being overlooked by the seller (see Standard Condition 10).

4.10   PRE-EXCHANGE CHECKLIST

The checklist below largely reflects matters which are of concern to a buyer, although many of the items will also be of concern to a seller. The seller should pay particular attention to those items marked with an asterisk (*).

4.10.1   Searches

☐   Have all necessary searches and enquiries been made?

☐   Have all the replies to searches and enquiries been received?

☐   Have all search and enquiry replies been checked carefully to ensure that the replies to individual questions are satisfactory and accord with the client's instructions?

☐   Have all outstanding queries been resolved satisfactorily?*

4.10.2   Survey

☐   Has a survey of the property been undertaken?

☐   Is the result of that survey satisfactory?

4.10.3   Mortgage arrangements

☐   Has a satisfactory mortgage offer been made and (where necessary) accepted by the client?

☐   Are arrangements in hand to comply with any conditions attached to the advance, e.g. in relation to an endowment policy?

☐   Taking into account the deposit, the mortgage advance (less any retention) and the costs of the transaction (including SDLT, Land Registry fees and other disbursements), has the client sufficient funds to proceed with the purchase?

☐   Have arrangements been made to discharge the seller's existing mortgage(s)?*

☐   If the transaction is a sale of part, has the seller's lender (if any) agreed to release the property to be sold from the mortgage?*

4.10.4   Deposit

☐   How much (if any) preliminary deposit has been paid?*

☐   How much money is needed to fund the deposit required on exchange?*

☐   Has a suitable undertaking been given in relation to bridging finance?

☐   To whom is the deposit to be paid?* (**Note:** Where Formula C is to be used for exchange, the deposit may have to be paid to someone other than the immediate seller.)

☐   Have the deposit funds been obtained from the client and cleared through clients' account? (**Note:** Standard Condition 2.4 requires that payment is to be made only by a cheque drawn on a solicitor's or licensed conveyancer's client account or by direct credit. Standard Commercial Property Condition 2.2 requires payment be made by direct credit.)

4.10.5   The contract

☐   Have all outstanding queries been satisfactorily resolved?*
☐   Have all agreed amendments been incorporated clearly in both parts of the contract?*
☐   Has the approved draft been returned to the seller?*
☐   Is a clean top copy of the contract available for signature by the client?*
☐   Have the terms of the contract been explained to the client?*
☐   Has the list of fixtures and fittings been agreed between the parties?*

4.10.6   Insurance

☐   Have steps been taken to insure the property immediately on exchange?
☐   If the buyer is to rely on the seller's insurance policy, has the buyer's interest been noted on that policy?*
☐   Have steps been taken to obtain any life policy required under the terms of the buyer's mortgage offer?

4.10.7   Completion date

☐   Has a completion date been agreed?*

4.10.8   Method of exchange

☐   Which method of exchange is most suitable to be used in this transaction?*

4.10.9   Synchronisation

☐   Where the client requires a simultaneous exchange on both sale and purchase contracts, are both transactions and all related transactions in the chain also ready to proceed?*

4.10.10   Signature of contract

☐   Has the client signed the contract?*

4.10.11   Occupiers

☐   Has the concurrence of all non-owning occupiers been obtained?*

5

Exchange of contracts

5.1 CHECKLIST FOR EXCHANGE BY TELEPHONE

- ☐ Are both parts of the contract identical and signed?
- ☐ Has the deposit been sent/received?
- ☐ Which formula is to be used?
- ☐ Has the completion date been agreed?
- ☐ Have any final amendments to the contract been authorised and made on both parts of the contract?
- ☐ Make a file note to record exchange including the date and time and name and status of the solicitors effecting exchange
- ☐ Send part contract to the other party by first class post or DX
- ☐ Check that insurance is in place.

5.2 REGISTRATION OF THE CONTRACT

The following is not an exhaustive list of all the circumstances in which registration of the contract is desirable. If there is any doubt, err on the side of caution and register the contract in order to protect the client's interests if:

- ☐ There is to be a long interval (e.g. more than two months) between contract and completion
- ☐ There is reason to doubt the seller's good faith
- ☐ A dispute arises between the seller and buyer
- ☐ The seller delays completion beyond the contractual date
- ☐ The purchase price is to be paid by instalments, the conveyance or transfer to be executed after payment of the final instalment
- ☐ The transaction is a sub-sale.

5.3 INSURANCE

5.3.1 Terms of the policy

The terms of the policy should be checked to ensure that:

- ☐ The amount of cover is adequate
- ☐ The sum insured is index linked
- ☐ The risks insured against are adequate, e.g. is flood damage covered where the property is situated in a low-lying area?

☐ Particular features of the property have been disclosed to the insurance company and are adequately insured, e.g. thatched roofs, garden walls, interior decorative plasterwork

☐ Where the property consists of a flat within a larger building, or is otherwise attached to adjoining property, the insurance cover extends to damage to neighbouring property where practicable.

5.3.2 Property at seller's risk

Where the risk in the property remains with the seller, the buyer need not take out his own policy until completion but should ensure, before exchange, that:

☐ The seller will maintain his policy until completion and the terms of that policy provide sufficient protection for the buyer

☐ The buyer receives written confirmation that his interest has been noted on the seller's policy

☐ The contract contains a provision requiring the seller to transfer the property in substantially the same physical condition as it was in at the time of exchange, failing which the buyer is entitled to rescind the contract (Standard Condition 5.1 contains this type of provision). This type of clause is not necessary where the property is in the course of construction because the contract for such a property will normally contain provisions requiring the seller to complete the building in accordance with specifications, failing which the buyer is under no obligation to complete.

5.4 AFTER EXCHANGE: THE SELLER

☐ Inform the client and estate agent that exchange has taken place and enter completion date in diary or file prompt system

☐ Where, immediately after exchange, the seller is in possession of both copies of the contract, the seller's solicitor should check that both parts of the contract have been dated and bear the agreed completion date. The copy of the contract signed by the seller should immediately be sent to the buyer's solicitor to fulfil any undertaking given in the course of an exchange by telephone

☐ Any deposit received must immediately be paid into an interest-bearing clients' deposit account

☐ If any preliminary deposit has been held by an estate agent, the agent should be asked to remit such sum to the seller's solicitor who is normally required under the contract to hold 'the deposit', i.e. the whole of the amount specified in the contract as the contractual deposit (see Standard Condition 2.2 and Standard Commercial Property Condition 2.2). The agent may be reluctant to part with the money, preferring to hold it on account for any commission due to him

☐ If not already done, the seller should deduce title to the buyer.

5.5 AFTER EXCHANGE: THE BUYER

☐ Inform the client and his lender that exchange has taken place and enter completion date in diary or file prompt system

☐ Where exchange has taken place by telephone, immediately send to the seller (or as directed by him) the signed contract and deposit cheque in accordance with the undertaking given, having first checked that the contract is dated and bears the agreed completion date

☐ Where the buyer is to insure, inform the insurer that exchange has taken place and check that the insurance policy is in force

☐ Where appropriate, protect the contract by registration.

6

Pre-completion procedures

6.1 INVESTIGATION OF TITLE: REGISTERED LAND

6.1.1 Components of investigation of title

This comprises:

- □ An examination of the official copy entries of the title supplied by the seller (including a copy of the lease where the title is leasehold, documents which are referred to on the register and evidence relating to matters as to which the register is not conclusive) (see Standard Condition 4.2.1 and Standard Commercial Conditions 6.3.1)
- □ Checking for evidence of overriding interests as these are not entered on the register but are binding on the buyer irrespective of notice
- □ Pre-completion searches.

6.1.2 Discover overriding interests

The existence of most overriding interests can be discovered through:

- □ Pre-contract enquiries of the seller under which the seller will normally be asked to reveal details of adverse interests and occupiers' rights. A seller who did not disclose such matters might be liable to the buyer for non-disclosure
- □ A local land charges search (local land charges not protected on the register are overriding interests)
- □ Inspection of the property before exchange which may reveal, e.g. occupiers, easements, or adverse possession. The buyer may also be advised to re-inspect immediately prior to completion.

6.1.3 Examining official copies

The following points should be checked:

- □ **On the property register:**
    - □ The description of the land accords with the contract description
    - □ The title number corresponds with that given on the contract
    - □ The estate – is it freehold or leasehold?
    - □ Easements enjoyed by the property (if they are entered on the register)

- ☐ Has any land been removed from the title? If so, does this affect the land being purchased?
- ☐ **On the proprietorship register**:
  - ☐ Is the class of title correct?
  - ☐ Is the seller the registered proprietor? If not, who has the ability to transfer the land?
  - ☐ The existence and effect of any other entries (restrictions, or pre-Land Registration Act 2002 cautions or inhibitions)
- ☐ **On the charges register**:
  - ☐ Are there any incumbrances or other entries?
  - ☐ How do these affect the buyer?
  - ☐ Which of them will be removed or discharged on completion and how will their removal be effected?
- ☐ **On the title plan**:
  - ☐ Is the land being purchased included within the title?
  - ☐ Check any colourings/hatchings which may indicate rights of way, the extent of covenants or land which has been removed from the title
  - ☐ The date of issue of the official copy entries of the title.

6.2 INVESTIGATION OF TITLE: UNREGISTERED LAND

6.2.1 Root of title

The epitome must commence with a good root of title, as specified by a special condition in the contract. A good root of title is a document which, at the date of the contract:

- ☐ Is at least 15 years old (see Law of Property Act 1925, s.44, as amended)
- ☐ Deals with or shows the ownership of the whole legal and equitable interest contracted to be sold
- ☐ Contains an adequate description of the property
- ☐ Contains nothing to cast any doubt on the title.

6.2.2 Documents to be included in the abstract or epitome

From the root of title, all dealings with the legal and equitable interests in the land down to and including the interests of the present seller must be shown, thus constituting an unbroken chain of ownership stretching from the seller named in the root document to the present day. This includes the following:

- ☐ Conveyances on sale and by gift
- ☐ Current leases
- ☐ Evidence of devolutions on death (death certificates, grants of representation, assents)
- ☐ Change of name of an estate owner, e.g. marriage certificate, deed poll or statutory declaration

- [ ] Mortgages and discharge of legal mortgages
- [ ] Documents prior to the root which contain details of restrictive covenants which affect the property
- [ ] Memoranda endorsed on documents of title, e.g. recording a sale of part, assent to a beneficiary, or severance of a beneficial joint tenancy
- [ ] Powers of attorney under which a document within the title has been executed.

6.2.3 Documents which need not be included in the abstract or epitome

Certain documents need not be included in the abstract or epitome, although in some cases their inclusion will be helpful to the buyer and may forestall queries on the title raised by the buyer. They include:

- [ ] Documents of record and Land Charges Department search certificates (but it is good practice to include these)
- [ ] Documents relating to equitable interests which will be overreached on completion of the current transaction (but as a matter of good practice some notice of their existence should be given to the buyer)
- [ ] Leases which have expired by effluxion of time (but if the tenant is still in possession of the property, possibly with the benefit of security of tenure, evidence of the terms on which the tenant enjoys the property should be supplied)
- [ ] Documents which pre-date the root of title except where a document within the title refers to the earlier document (see Law of Property Act 1925, s.45) (note that, where a document within the title has been executed under a power of attorney, the power must be abstracted whatever its date)
- [ ] Documents relating to discharged equitable interests in the land, e.g. receipted equitable mortgages.

6.2.4 Investigation of title

Investigation of title comprises:

- [ ] An examination of the documents supplied in the abstract or epitome to check that:
- [ ] The root document is as provided for by the contract or, if none is specified, complies with Law of Property Act 1925, s.44
- [ ] There is an unbroken chain of ownership beginning with the seller in the root document and ending with the present seller
- [ ] There are no defects in the title which will adversely affect the buyer's title or the interests of his lender
- [ ] Verification, i.e. inspection of the original deeds
- [ ] Checking for evidence of occupiers (this is normally done by inspection of the property)
- [ ] Pre-completion searches

☐ Checking the date when the area became subject to compulsory registration to ensure no event triggering registration has taken place since that date (see Land Registry Practice Guide No. 51 for the relevant date).

6.2.5 Method of investigation

☐ Check each document chronologically starting with the root
☐ Is the root as provided for in the contract?
☐ Is there an unbroken chain of title from the root to the present day?

Then, in each document within the abstract or epitome, check the following points, making written notes of any matter which needs to be clarified or rechecked:

☐ **Date**
A deed is not invalid because it is not dated or is wrongly dated, but the date of the document will:

   ☐ Establish whether a root document is a good root
   ☐ Affect the amount of stamp duty payable
   ☐ Affect its vulnerability under the Insolvency Act 1986 in the case of a voluntary disposition
   ☐ Assist in making a reasoned judgment on an apparent defect in title, e.g. a technical defect in a document which is over 15 years old may be less detrimental to the title than one contained in a more recent document.

☐ **Stamp duty**
☐ For transactions completed under the Stamp Act 1891 regime (as amended) and subject to impress of stamps on documents, ad valorem and Particulars Delivered stamp should be checked. The amount of duty will depend on the nature of the document, the value of the consideration and the date of the document. The seller must be required to rectify any irregularities of this nature. If no certificate of value is included in the document, stamp duty at full rate should have been paid on the conveyance. In the event of doubt, the buyer should insist that the earlier document is adjudicated and any additional duty, penalties and interest paid.

☐ **SDLT**
☐ Assignment of lease exempt from SDLT on grant?
☐ Will the buyer become liable to pay SDLT on remainder of term (as if new grant)?
☐ Has any relief been claimed by seller or connected party? Will this transaction trigger clawback (e.g. group relief or charities relief)?
☐ Does the buyer need seller's warranties in respect of SDLT?
☐ If the transaction is not registrable at the Land Registry, has the last buyer made a self-certificate? Is the certified copy available?

☐ **Parties**
For example, are the seller's names as shown on the previous document?

☐ **Description of the property**
Does it accord with the contract and is it consistent throughout the epitome?

☐ **Acknowledgements for production of earlier deeds**
Is there one where necessary, e.g. where deeds are being retained by the seller on a sale of part?

☐ **Execution**
Have all formalities been observed?

☐ **Powers of attorney**
Is the disposition by the attorney valid and are subsequent buyers protected?

☐ **Endorsements on deeds**
Are those that are necessary present, and are there any adverse memoranda?

☐ **Incumbrances**
☐ What are they?
☐ Are they as expected?
☐ Is there a chain of indemnity covenants where required?
☐ **Easements and rights**
☐ Are these as expected?
☐ Do they follow down the chain?
☐ Have any been added or taken away?
☐ **Receipt clause**
This is evidence (although not necessarily conclusive evidence) that the seller's lien for the unpaid purchase price has been extinguished
☐ **Searches supplied with the abstract**
☐ Have searches against all previous estate owners been abstracted or are there gaps?
☐ Are the names and periods searched against correct?
☐ Did completion take place within the priority period?
☐ **Compulsory registration**
☐ Has there been any conveyance on sale since the area became one of compulsory registration? (The date of the compulsory registration order can be checked from Land Registry Practice Guide 51.)
☐ Has there been any dealing of any kind since 1 April 1998
☐ If necessary, the seller should be required to register before completion.

6.2.6   Right to see pre-root documents

Generally, the buyer cannot require evidence of title prior to the root except:

☐ He is always entitled to a copy of a power of attorney under which any abstracted document is executed
☐ Where an abstracted document refers to an earlier document, he may call for that earlier document, e.g. where an abstracted document refers to restrictive covenants imposed by a pre-root conveyance, the document imposing the covenants may be called for
☐ Where an abstracted document describes the property by reference to a plan which is attached to or referred to in an earlier document, that earlier document may be called for so that the plan may be examined

☐ Any document creating any limitation or trust by reference to which any part of the property is disposed of by an abstracted document may be called for even if dated pre-root.

6.2.7 Conveyance by trustees to themselves

If on the title there is a conveyance by trustees or personal representatives to one of themselves, enquiry must be made into the circumstances of the transaction since, on the face of it, such a conveyance is in breach of trust and is voidable by the beneficiaries without enquiry as to fairness.

Such a transaction can be justified if one of the following situations exists:

☐ There is proof of a pre-existing contract to purchase an option or right of pre-emption in favour of the trustee or personal representative
☐ The personal representative was a beneficiary under the will or intestacy of the seller
☐ The consent of all the beneficiaries being legally competent was obtained to the transaction
☐ The conveyance was made under an order of the court
☐ The transaction was sanctioned by the trust instrument.

6.2.8 The survivor of beneficial joint tenants

To gain the protection of the Law of Property (Joint Tenants) Act 1964 the following three conditions must all be satisfied:

☐ There must be no memorandum of severance endorsed on the conveyance under which the joint tenants bought the property
☐ There must be no bankruptcy proceedings registered against the names of either of the joint tenants
☐ The conveyance by the survivor must contain a recital stating that the survivor is solely and beneficially entitled to the land.

If any of the above conditions is not met, the survivor must be treated as a surviving tenant in common.

6.2.9 Effect of failure to register land charges

☐ Charges of Classes C(i), C(ii), C(iii) and F are void against a purchaser of any interest in the land for valuable consideration (including marriage).
☐ Charges of Classes C(iv) and D are void only against a purchaser of a legal estate for money or money's worth.

6.3 EXECUTION OF DOCUMENTS

The letter which accompanies the purchase deed should:

☐ Explain the purpose and contents of the document
☐ Contain clear instructions relating to the execution of the deed

☐ Specify a date by which the signed document must be returned to the solicitor

☐ Request that the client leaves the document undated.

6.3.1 Attorneys

A person who holds a power of attorney on behalf of another may execute a deed on that person's behalf. The attorney may sign either in his own name or in that of the person on behalf of whom he is acting, e.g. 'X by his attorney Y' or 'Y as attorney on behalf of X'.

6.3.2 Companies

A deed can be executed by a company in one of the following ways:

☐ By affixing its common seal (the company is free to determine by its articles what additional formalities are required), or

☐ By a director and secretary of the company or two directors each signing the deed on behalf of the company and the deed being expressed to be executed by the company, or

☐ By the document being signed on behalf of the company by a director of the company in the presence of a witness who attests the signature and the document being expressed to be executed by the company.

6.3.3 Execution by other bodies

☐ Check the procedure for execution in advance of execution

☐ Attach a copy of the authority of the signatory to sign attached to the deed to prove the validity of its execution.

6.3.4 Execution in special cases

☐ **Trustee in bankruptcy**

A trustee in bankruptcy should sign a contract using the following wording:

'trustee in bankruptcy of XY a bankrupt [without personal liability]'.

The attestation clause of the purchase deed can be expressed in the following way:

'signed as a deed by CD in the presence of [*name*] (trustee of the estate of XY, a bankrupt)'.

Note: Many insolvency practitioners seek to limit their liability by adding the words 'without personal liability' to the attestation clause. It is understood that these words imply that the trustee can still be sued qua trustee, but that liability in him in his personal capacity is excluded. These words do not preclude negligence liability for which most insolvency practitioners will carry indemnity insurance.

☐ **Supervisor of voluntary arrangement**

The company, individual or mortgagee will execute the document in the normal way unless the scheme is such that the land has been vested in the supervisor or trustee. If this occurs, the supervisor must transfer and execute as a trustee.

A contract signed or transfer executed by a supervisor may use the following wording:

> 'Supervisor of XY acting in the voluntary arrangement of XY [without personal liability]'.

Note: The words 'without personal liability' have the same effect as explained above.

☐ **Administrative receiver**

In the absence of any provision to the contrary, section 42 and Schedule 1 to the Insolvency Act 1986 give power to an administrative receiver to execute deeds and other documents in the name of and on behalf of the company using the company's seal.

☐ **Company in administration**

A deed can be executed using the common seal of the company in the presence of the administrator, or by the administrator signing in the name of and on behalf of the company (Insolvency Act 1986, Schedule 1(8)–(9)).

☐ **Law of Property Act receiver**

A Law of Property Act receiver can sign a contract or execute a transfer provided that the appointing lender delegates this power. The authority from the lender should be in writing but under section 1 Law of Property (Miscellaneous Provisions) Act 1989 does not need to be under seal. A receiver signs a contract as agent for the borrower. It is normal practice in these circumstances for the appointing lender to sign the contract and execute the transfer using his power of sale. The capacity in which the lender sells will affect the nature of the implied covenants for title given to the buyer in the purchase deed.

☐ **Debenture holder**

A debenture holder can sign in the name of the company provided that he holds a valid power of attorney from the company. The attestation clause should read as follows:

> Signed as a deed by [*name of company*] acting by [*name of attorney*] duly appointed to execute as an officer of [*name of bank*] pursuant to clause [of a debenture dated …] in the presence of: [*Sign here the name of the company and your own name with details of the resolution appointing you (example: John Smith Ltd by its attorney Jane Brown duly appointed officer of … Bank by a resolution of … Bank plc dated …)*]

☐ **Company in liquidation**

A disposition made by a company in liquidation will be executed by the liquidator, who may either use the common seal, in which case he will sign the document to attest that the seal was affixed in his presence, or the liquidator may sign the deed on behalf of the company.

☐ **Signature of contracts**

To avoid incurring personal liability, any contracts for the disposal of land should be signed by including the extra words 'without personal liability' in order to ensure that a signatory signs as agent and not principal. The following is a suggested example of how agreements should be signed:

Signed as agent for ABC Ltd without personal liability ....

Signature of supervisor/administrator/administrative receiver/liquidator/ trustee..

After winding up, or after the presentation of a winding-up petition, a better wording may be:

Signed in the name of ABC Ltd by its [administrator/administrative receiver] JOHN SMITH ESQ. ....

Without personal liability ....

Signature: ABC Ltd [in liquidation] ....

6.4 PRESCRIBED WORDS TO BE INSERTED IN TRANSFER FROM A CHARITY

Check that the transfer contains wording in one of the following forms:

☐ The land transferred (or as the case may be) is held by [(*proprietors*) in trust for] (*charity*), an exempt charity *or*

☐ The land transferred (or as the case may be) is held by [(*proprietors*) in trust for] (*charity*), a non-exempt charity, but this transfer (or as the case may be) is one falling within paragraphs (a), (b) or (c) (as the case may be) of section 36(9) Charities Act 1993 *or*

☐ The land transferred (or as the case may be) is held by [(*proprietors*) in trust for] (*charity*), a non-exempt charity, and this transfer (or as the case may be) is not one falling within paragraphs (a), (b) or (c) of section 36(9) Charities Act 1993, so the restrictions on disposition imposed by section 36 of that Act apply to the land.

Note: When there is no trust (i.e. the land is the corporate property of the registered proprietor charity) the words 'XXXX in trust for' are omitted.

6.5 PRE-COMPLETION: WHICH SEARCHES TO MAKE

The following searches should be made:

☐ For registered land, search against title number at the Land Registry

☐ For unregistered land, including an unregistered reversion to a lease, search at the Land Charges Department against names of estate owners of the land

☐ If acting for a lender, a bankruptcy search against the name of the borrower

☐ Such other of the searches as are applicable to the transaction (e.g. probate search, company search, enduring and lasting power of attorney search, and local land charges).

6.5.1   Land Registry search

☐ For search of whole of a title use Form OS1
☐ For search of part of a title use Form OS2. If attaching a plan to Form OS2, it must:
　☐ Clearly show the extent of the land to be searched (e.g. by thick black edging, hatching or stippling)
　☐ Be drawn to a stated scale of not less than 1/1250
　☐ Be sufficiently detailed to allow accurate plotting to be undertaken on the title plan
　☐ Include a north point
　☐ Not be endorsed with a statement of disclaimer intending to comply with Property Misdescriptions Act 1991 nor stated to be 'for identification only'.

6.5.2   Land Registry search: application by telephone

Only available using the Telephone Service Centre for a search of whole title:

☐ By an applicant who is or acts for an intending buyer (including lessee or chargee)
☐ Between 8.30am and 6.30pm Monday to Friday excluding Christmas Day, Good Friday and statutory bank holidays and from 8.30am to 1.00pm on Saturday
☐ By credit account holder.

Further information is contained in Land Registry Practice Guide 61.
　On telephoning the Land Registry, the following information must be supplied:

☐ The applicant's key number
☐ Name and address of firm holding the account
☐ If different from the previous bullet point, the name and address to which the result of search is to be sent
☐ Title number of the land
☐ The name of the registered proprietor (or applicant for first registration)
☐ (If requested) the administrative area or local authority district in which the land is situated
☐ Where the land is already registered, the date from which the search is to be made
☐ The applicant's reference (maximum 25 characters)
☐ Whether the search is intended to protect a purchase lease or charge
☐ The name of the applicant on whose behalf the search is being made
☐ The name and telephone number of the person making the search telephone call or the person to be contacted if there is an enquiry.

6.5.3 Unregistered land: use of previous search certificates

Where the seller provides previous search certificates as part of the evidence of title, it is not necessary to repeat a search against a former estate owner provided that the search certificate supplied by the seller reveals no adverse entries and was made:

☐ Against the correct name of the estate owner as shown in the deeds
☐ For the correct period of ownership as shown in the title deeds
☐ Against the correct description of the property as shown in the deeds

and the next disposition in the chain of title took place within the priority period afforded by the search certificate. If any of the conditions outlined above cannot be met, a further search against the previous estate owner must be made.

6.5.4 Unregistered land searches in sub-sale transactions

Where A has contracted to sell to B, and before B completes his purchase he contracts to sub-sell to C, the sub-purchaser (C) will need to make a search against A's title since, at the time of C's search application, B will not be the estate owner of the land. B's name should be included on the search (although B will not be an estate owner in the land within the terms of Land Charges Act 1972) because the search may reveal bankruptcy entries against him. If, however, B does become an estate owner before completing the second sale to C, B's name must also be searched against.

6.5.5 Repeat of local searches prior to completion

These searches should be repeated prior to completion if:

☐ There is to be a period of two months or more between exchange of contracts and completion and the search has not been covered by insurance or replaced by insurance
☐ Information received by the buyer's solicitor suggests that a further search may be advisable in order to guard against a recently entered adverse entry on the register
☐ The contract was conditional on the satisfactory results of later searches
☐ Required under paragraph 5.2 of the Lenders' Handbook.

6.5.6 Unregistered land: unexpected land charges search entries

If an unexpected entry (other than a Class D(ii) protecting restrictive covenants, which cannot generally be removed) is revealed by the search result, the buyer's solicitor should:

☐ Find out exactly what the entry relates to
☐ If the entry appears to adversely affect the property, contact the seller's solicitor as soon as possible to seek his confirmation that the entry will be removed on or before completion

- ☐ In the case of a Land Charges Department search, apply for an office copy of the entry using Form K19. The office copy consists of a copy of the application form which was submitted when the charge was registered and will reveal the name and address of the person with the benefit of the charge who may have to be contacted to seek his consent to its removal
- ☐ Keep the client, his lender and, subject to the duty of confidentiality, other solicitors involved in the chain of transactions informed of the situation since negotiations for the removal of the charge may cause a delay in completion.

6.6 ACTING FOR LENDER (BUT NOT FOR BUYER)

When acting only for the lender, the lender's solicitor should request the buyer's solicitor to send him copies of the following documents as soon as the buyer's solicitor has completed his own investigation of title:

- ☐ All pre-contract searches and enquiries with their results
- ☐ The contract
- ☐ Evidence of title
- ☐ Requisitions on title with their answers
- ☐ The draft and subsequently the approved purchase deed
- ☐ At a later stage, all pre-completion searches with their results
- ☐ Any other documents which are relevant to the acquisition of a good title by the lender or which are specifically required by the lender's instructions.

6.7 SELLER'S PRE-COMPLETION CHECKLIST

- ☐ Ensure purchase deed has been approved and requisitions answered
- ☐ Receive engrossed purchase deed from the buyer
- ☐ Check the buyer has executed the deed (where appropriate) and plan (if used), or that an acceptable undertaking has been given that he will execute after completion
- ☐ Get seller to execute purchase deed and return it to the solicitor in time for completion
- ☐ Obtain redemption figure(s) for the seller's mortgage(s) and check that they are correct. Where the redemption figure relates to a 'flexible mortgage', i.e. one where the borrower's savings and income appear in the same account, it may be necessary to ask for the account to be frozen until the redemption figure has been transferred at completion.
- ☐ Obtain last receipts, etc. where apportionments are to be made on completion
- ☐ Prepare completion statement (where necessary) and send two copies to the buyer in good time before completion
- ☐ Remind the client to organise final readings of meters at the property
- ☐ Prepare forms for discharge of land charges where necessary (unregistered land)
- ☐ Approve any memorandum which the buyer has requested be placed on retained title deeds or grant of representation (unregistered land)

☐ Prepare any undertaking which needs to be given on completion (e.g. for discharge of the seller's mortgage if also acting for the lender)

☐ Contact the lender to confirm final arrangements for discharge of the seller's mortgage, method of payment, certificate of non-crystallisation, etc.

☐ Prepare authority addressed to tenants relating to payment of future rent (tenanted property)

☐ Check through the file to ensure all outstanding queries have been dealt with

☐ Prepare list of matters to be dealt with on actual completion

☐ Locate deeds and documents which will need to be inspected/handed over on completion and prepare certified copies for the buyer of those documents which are to be retained by the seller

☐ Prepare two copies of schedule of deeds to be handed to the buyer on completion

☐ Prepare inventory of chattels and receipt for money payable for them

☐ Check arrangements for vacant possession and handing over keys

☐ Receive instructions from the buyer's solicitor to act as his agent on completion and clarify instructions with him if necessary

☐ Make final arrangements with the buyer's solicitor for time and place of completion

☐ Ensure estate agents are aware of completion arrangements

☐ Prepare bill for submission to the client.

6.8 BUYER'S PRE-COMPLETION CHECKLIST

☐ Ensure purchase deed has been approved and requisitions satisfactorily answered

☐ Engross purchase and mortgage deeds

☐ Get the buyer to execute the mortgage deed, purchase deed and plan (if necessary) and return it to solicitor

☐ Send (executed) purchase deed to the seller's solicitor for his client's execution in time for completion. The submission of the deed should be in escrow subject to the express condition that the buyer may withdraw if the seller fails to complete

☐ Make pre-completion searches and ensure their results are satisfactory

☐ Make report on title to the lender and request advance cheque in time for completion

☐ Receive completion statement (where necessary) and copies of last receipts in support of apportionments and check it is correct

☐ Remind the client of arrangements for completion

☐ Prepare forms for discharge of land charges where necessary (unregistered land)

☐ Obtain the seller's approval to the wording of any memorandum which the buyer has requested be placed on retained title deeds or grant of representation (unregistered land)

☐ Prepare and agree the form of wording of any undertaking which needs to be given or received on completion

- ☐ Confirm with a seller that a certificate of non-crystallisation will be given (if appropriate)
- ☐ Contact the lender to confirm final arrangements for completion
- ☐ Ensure that any life policy required by the lender is on foot and check with the client that any other insurances required for the property (e.g. house contents insurance) have been taken out. Prepare and engross assignments of other insurance policies to the buyer (e.g. for damp treatment) if appropriate
- ☐ Check through file to ensure all outstanding queries have been dealt with
- ☐ Prepare statement of account and bill for the client and submit together with a copy of the completion statement, requesting balance due from the client be paid in sufficient time for the funds to be cleared before completion
- ☐ Receive advance cheque from the lender, pay into clients' account and clear funds before completion
- ☐ Receive balance of funds from the client and clear through clients' account before completion
- ☐ Arrange for final inspection of property if necessary
- ☐ Prepare list of matters to be dealt with on actual completion
- ☐ Check arrangements for vacant possession and handing over keys
- ☐ Instruct the seller's solicitor to act as agent on completion if completion not to be by personal attendance
- ☐ Make final arrangements with the seller's solicitor for time and place of completion
- ☐ Ensure estate agents are aware of completion arrangements
- ☐ Make arrangements for transmission of completion money to the seller's solicitor (or as he has directed).

6.9   COMPLETION STATEMENT

The statement, prepared by the seller's solicitor, should show clearly the total amount due on completion, and how that total sum is made up. Depending on the circumstances, it may be necessary to take account of some or all of the following items:

- ☐ The purchase price, giving credit for any deposit paid
- ☐ Apportionments of outgoings
- ☐ Money payable for chattels
- ☐ Compensation if completion is delayed
- ☐ A licence fee if the buyer has been in occupation of the property.

6.9.1   Completion statement: agricultural land

In addition to the normal requirements for a completion statement, the following may need to be considered on a dealing with agricultural land:

- ☐ VAT on vatable supplies, e.g. farming stock and assets, sporting or fishing rights, entitlement units and quota
- ☐ Apportionment of agricultural rents, cottage rents, wayleave payments, sporting or fishing rents

- ☐ Payment for fittings being purchased
- ☐ Payment for any seeds, cultivations or labour at valuation (plus VAT if applicable)
- ☐ Allowance for any agreed retentions for holdover
- ☐ Where VAT is payable, a separate VAT invoice should be supplied with the completion statement on receipt of the VAT from the buyer.

6.9.2   Financial statement

In addition to the matters dealt with on the completion statement, the financial statement should also take account of such of the following matters as are relevant to the transaction:

- ☐ The mortgage advance and any costs and/or retentions made in respect of it
- ☐ Disbursements, e.g. SDLT, Land Registry fees, fees payable for registration of notices or search fees
- ☐ The solicitor's costs.

6.10   BUYER IN OCCUPATION BEFORE COMPLETION

Some or all of the following conditions may be considered:

- ☐ The occupation shall be a licence and not a tenancy
- ☐ Payment of a further instalment of the purchase price as a precondition of occupation
- ☐ Payment of a licence fee during occupation (frequently this is calculated by reference to the rate at which compensation for late completion is payable under the general conditions of the contract)
- ☐ The licence should be non-assignable
- ☐ Restrictions on who may occupy the property
- ☐ Restrictions on the use of the property during the buyer's occupation (including an obligation to comply with the terms of the lease in the case of leasehold property)
- ☐ Payment by the buyer of all outgoings on the property
- ☐ The buyer to be responsible for insuring the property and/or paying the insurance premium
- ☐ The buyer to be responsible for repairs and maintenance
- ☐ Prohibition of alterations and improvements
- ☐ Provisions for termination of the licence by either party
- ☐ Entitlement to the income of the property (if any).

6.11   DEATH OF CO-OWNER BETWEEN CONTRACT AND COMPLETION

6.11.1   Surviving beneficial joint tenant

Where the sole surviving joint tenant is to transfer registered land, the buyer should:

☐ Check that no restriction is entered on the proprietorship register of the title
☐ Redraft the transfer to reflect the change of parties and capacity of the seller
☐ Require the seller to provide evidence of the death (e.g. an official copy of the death certificate of the deceased co-owner).

Where the land is unregistered, the buyer should:

☐ Check the conveyance under which the co-owners bought the property to ensure that no memorandum of severance of the joint tenancy has been endorsed on it
☐ Redraft the purchase deed to reflect the change in parties. The conveyance should recite the death and state that the sole seller has become solely and beneficially entitled to the property
☐ Make a Land Charges Department search against the names of both the deceased and the survivor to ensure that no bankruptcy proceedings have been registered against either name.

If these conditions are not satisfied, another trustee should be appointed to act with the survivor.

6.12   CERTIFICATES OF TITLE

6.12.1   Examples of situations where a certificate may be appropriate

☐ The purchase of shares in a company
☐ The purchase of assets from a company
☐ Flotation, mortgage, debenture or other security arrangements made by companies
☐ Occasionally on a straightforward house purchase, if required by the mortgage lender.

6.12.2   Contents of certificate of title

The certificate should deal with the following matters:

☐ Ownership of the property
☐ An adequate description of the property
☐ Its tenure with relevant details
☐ The name of the current owner of the estate in land

☐ Whether the title to the land is good, marketable and unencumbered

☐ Whether there are any statutory orders, schemes or provisions detrimental to the property or its use

☐ Where appropriate, provisions relating to planning, highways, public health, etc. should be referred to

☐ Appropriate searches which have been made at the Land Registry, the Land Charges Department and the district council, and other relevant searches

☐ Which searches have not been carried out in order to give the recipient a complete picture of the title which he is accepting.

7

Completion and post-completion

7.1 COMPLETION CHECKLIST

Some or all of the items in the following checklist will need to be attended to on actual completion.

The checklist prepared by the solicitor should contain an itemised list of the documents which need to be inspected/marked/handed over/received at completion.

Documents to be available at completion

☐ Contract
☐ Evidence of title
☐ Copy purchase deed
☐ Answers to requisitions
☐ Completion statement.

Documents to be inspected by buyer

☐ Title deeds where in unregistered land these are not to be handed over on completion (e.g. on a sale of part)
☐ General power of attorney, lasting power of attorney or enduring power of attorney
☐ Grant of administration
☐ Receipts/demands for apportionments if not previously supplied.

Documents, etc. to be handed to buyer on completion

☐ Title deeds
☐ Original lease
☐ Executed purchase deed
☐ Schedule of deeds
☐ Form DS1/discharged mortgage or undertaking in respect of discharge of mortgage(s)
☐ Certificate of non-crystallisation (if appropriate)(company charges)
☐ Receipt for money paid for chattels
☐ Authority addressed to tenants relating to payment of future rent and original tenancy agreements/leases (tenanted property)

☐ Keys of the property (if these are not available, the seller's solicitor should be asked to telephone the key holder to request the release of the keys)

☐ Certified copy of any memorandum endorsed on retained deeds

☐ Landlord's licence.

Documents, etc. to be handed to seller on completion

☐ Banker's draft for amount due on completion (unless remitted by direct credit)

☐ Executed duplicate purchase deed/counterpart lease/licence (where appropriate)

☐ Receipted schedule of deeds received from seller

☐ Release of deposit if held by third party in capacity of stakeholder.

Endorsements on documents if required by buyer

☐ Endorsement of assent or conveyance on grant of representation (unregistered land)

☐ Endorsement of sale on most recently dated retained document of title (sale of part of unregistered land)

☐ Mark up abstract or epitome as compared against the original deeds (unregistered land in respect of any document the original of which is not handed over on completion).

7.2 ATTENDING COMPLETION IN PERSON

The representative from the buyer's solicitors who is to attend completion should take with him to the seller's solicitor's office the following items:

☐ The contract (queries which arise may sometimes be resolved by checking the terms of the contract)

☐ Evidence of title (in order to verify the title)

☐ A copy of the approved draft purchase deed and of any other documents which are to be executed by the seller and handed over on completion (in case there is any query over the engrossments)

☐ Answers to requisitions on title (some queries which arise, e.g. over who has the keys, may be resolved by the answers previously given to requisitions)

☐ The completion checklist and completion statement

☐ Banker's draft (if this method of payment is to be used)

☐ Any documents which are required to be handed over to the seller's solicitor on completion, e.g. release of deposit.

7.3 MARKING AN ABSTRACT OR EPITOME (UNREGISTERED LAND)

☐ Check each document in the abstract or epitome against the original
☐ Ensure all details of each document examined match the abstract or epitome
☐ On the epitome or abstract, write in the margin or at the bottom of each document the following words:

Examined against the original at the offices of [*insert name of seller's solicitors or as appropriate*] signed [*by buyer's solicitor's representative either in his own name or in the name of the firm*] and dated [*insert date of examination*].

7.4 CERTIFYING DOCUMENTS FOR THE LAND REGISTRY

Where a certified copy of a document will be required by the Land Registry, the certification should be carried out by a conveyancer (or such other person as the registrar may permit) by writing on the document clearly and in a conspicuous position the words:

I certify this to be a true copy of the [*insert type of document*] dated [*insert date of document being certified*] signed [*signature of conveyancer*] and dated [*insert date of certification*].

The name and address of the signatory should also be endorsed.
Note: A copy of a power of attorney must be certified on every page.

7.5 EVIDENCE OF IDENTITY FOR THE LAND REGISTRY

The Land Registry requires most applicants to give details of the conveyancers acting for all the other parties to the transaction and, where a party is unrepresented, to provide evidence of that party's identity. The following guidelines have been extracted from the Law Society's Practice Note Identity Evidence for the Land Registry – 4 December 2008 and should be used in conjunction with the full Practice Note available from **www.lawsociety.org.uk** (where it is updated from time to time).

The requirement to include on forms AP1, DS2 and FR1 details of registered conveyancers acting for any other parties to the transaction and any unrepresented parties involved in the transaction apply to the following transactions if the property is worth more than £5,000:

☐ Transfers, whether for the full value or not, including changes of trustee
☐ Registration of leases, whether or not for the full value
☐ Surrender of leases
☐ Registration of charges, whether or not for the full value
☐ Discharge paper (DS1)

- [ ] DS3 releases of part
- [ ] Applications for compulsory first registration
- [ ] Applications for voluntary first registration where the title deeds have been lost or destroyed.

The requirement does not apply to:

- [ ] Transactions where the value is £5,000 or less. Evidence must be provided where this is the case
- [ ] Noting of leases or charges
- [ ] Assents
- [ ] Statutory vestings
- [ ] Voluntary applications for first registration where title deeds are available
- [ ] Transactions where an Electronic Notice of Discharge (END) or an Electronic Discharge (ED) has been transmitted directly from the relevant lender.

Identity evidence is not required for some parties, for example:

- [ ] Receivers
- [ ] Liquidators
- [ ] Mental Capacity Act deputies.

Identifying the conveyancer

You should provide details of any conveyancers acting within the transaction and check that the details given are genuine.

Who is a 'conveyancer'?

A 'conveyancer' is defined by Land Registration Rules 2003, rule 217(1) (as amended) as being one of the following:

- [ ] solicitor
- [ ] licensed conveyancer
- [ ] legal executive
- [ ] notary public
- [ ] barrister
- [ ] registered European lawyer.

The conveyancer may also be from an in-house legal department, for example, those representing a developer, lender or local authority.

Checking professional registers

You may check details against the registers of professional bodies.

You should also check that the information in the directory matches both:

- [ ] The practice details *and*
- [ ] The final destination of documents and funds

You can check the Law Society's roll of registered solicitors by using the Find a Solicitor search.

Identifying unrepresented parties

You must provide certified details of any unrepresented parties. Failure to provide details of unrepresented parties will result in rejection of the application to register the transaction.

You can provide the details in one of the following three ways:

☐ Declare that you are satisfied that sufficient steps have been taken to verify the identity of the unrepresented parties. You should exercise caution in taking this option if you have not supplied the verification yourself and you may choose only to confirm satisfaction where you have evidence that verification has been carried out by another conveyancer
☐ Enclose verified Land Registry forms ID1 or ID2 as evidence of the unrepresented party's identity
☐ Request that unrepresented parties attend the Land Registry in person when the application is made so that an official can complete ID1 or ID2 for them.

Using form ID1 – identity of individuals

The ID1 form is in two parts. Section A must be completed by the individual and provides certain basic information including:

☐ Name
☐ Address
☐ Telephone number
☐ Date of birth.

Section B must be completed by the conveyancer. This requires evidence of identity which may include:

☐ Passport
☐ Photocard driving licence
☐ Utility bills
☐ Mortgage statement
☐ Credit or debit card
☐ Council tax bill.

The individual must also supply a passport size photograph.

A conveyancer must verify that they have seen the evidence provided in the ID1 form and that the photograph is of the person who produced it.

Using form ID2 - identity of corporate bodies

The identity of a corporate body or company is confirmed using form ID2. The company must nominate an individual as their representative who must then provide evidence that:

☐ The corporate body they represent and the registered proprietor, or body entitled to be registered as proprietor, are one and the same
☐ The corporate body still exists
☐ The nominee has authority to act as its representative

Does the corporate body exist?

A company search will provide evidence of this for a UK company.

Overseas companies

Overseas corporations must also provide evidence that they are the same as the registered proprietor of the estate or charge. This may be provided as an opinion letter from a lawyer qualified in the relevant jurisdiction, confirming the corporation still exists and that the representative is authorised to act on its behalf.

Who can verify ID?

Details can be verified by, amongst others, any licensed conveyancer, solicitor or European lawyer who is fully qualified and registered in the UK. This person does not have to be acting in the transaction.

Frauds have been perpetrated using fictitious solicitor's details. If you are not completing the verification information yourself, you should check that:

☐ The solicitor who has provided the information actually exists
☐ They hold appropriate qualifications
☐ They can confirm that that they signed the form you have in your possession.

The seller's lender

The new AP1 form requires details of the lender who is discharging the seller's mortgage. You must state whether the discharging lender was represented, and if not, you must take the steps described above to provide details of their identity.

Banks and building societies

UK banks or building societies which send a DS2 and DS1 discharge or DS3 release direct to the Land Registry do not have to lodge form ID2 as well.

Exemptions

There is a general exemption to the ID requirement for lenders who have submitted details through either:

☐ Electronic discharge (ED)
☐ Electronic notification of discharge (END)

Powers of Attorney

Where neither the donor nor the donee are represented:

☐ You must provide evidence of identity for the donor and the donee
☐ Overseas donors must provide ID1 or ID2 forms verified before a British consular official or by a foreign notary.

Records

You should record the steps you have carried out in relation to checking ID for your own protection. This could include keeping a long-term record of verification details, subject to any data protection requirements.

7.6 COMPLETION: AGRICULTURAL LAND WITH MILK QUOTA

In addition to normal completion requirements, the buyer must ensure that such of the following documents as are relevant to the transaction are handed over:

- ☐ Completed Form MQ/1 (consent to transfer of quota)
- ☐ Any documentation relevant to an apportionment of quota
- ☐ The quota notification from the Rural Payments Agency
- ☐ The seller's records for 1983
- ☐ A direct seller's licence.

7.7 POST-COMPLETION: SELLER'S CHECKLIST

Where appropriate to the transaction, the following steps should be taken by the seller's solicitor as soon as possible after completion has taken place:

- ☐ Where completion has taken place by post, telephone the buyer's solicitor to inform him that completion has taken place
- ☐ Telephone the estate agent to inform him of completion and to direct him to release the keys to the buyer
- ☐ Inform the client that completion has taken place
- ☐ Where completion has taken place by post, send purchase deed, title deeds and other relevant documents to the buyer's solicitor by first class post or DX
- ☐ If part of the proceeds of sale are to be used towards the purchase of another property on the same day, make arrangements for the transmission of these funds in accordance with instructions received
- ☐ Deal with the discharge of the seller's existing mortgage(s) by sending a clients' account cheque for the amount required (as per redemption statement previously obtained) to the lender together with the engrossment of the Form DS1 (or deed of release relating to unregistered land) requesting him to discharge the mortgage and to forward the receipted Form DS1 to you as quickly as possible Alternatively, the mortgage may be discharged by using the END, e-DS1 or ED systems. If the mortgage is over unregistered land, the lender will, instead of using a Form DS1, complete the receipt clause on the reverse of the mortgage deed and forward the receipted deed to the seller's solicitor. If in unregistered land the lender is not a building society, the lender should be requested to date the receipt with the date of completion in order to avoid the risk of a transfer of the mortgage under Law of Property Act 1925, s.115. Where necessary, the reassignment of collateral security, e.g. a life

policy, should also be dealt with, and a lender who has insured the property will also need to be told to cancel the property insurance cover

☐ If instructed to do so, pay the estate agent's commission and obtain a receipt for the payment

☐ Account to the seller's bank for the proceeds of sale in accordance with any undertaking given to them

☐ Account to the client for the balance of the proceeds of sale in accordance with his instructions

☐ If not already done, draft and remit a bill of costs to the client

☐ Where money is being held by the solicitor on account of costs, it may be transferred to office account provided that the client has expressly or impliedly agreed to this being done

☐ If the land is to remain unregistered after completion of this transaction, make application for registration of land charges at the Land Charges Department

☐ On receipt of the completed Form DS1 or receipted mortgage from the lender, check the form or receipt to ensure it is correct, then send it to the buyer's solicitor and ask to be discharged from the undertaking given on completion

☐ Remind the client of the need to notify the local and water authorities of the change of ownership of the property

☐ Remind the client to cancel insurance cover over the property (and associated insurances, if relevant)

☐ Advise the client about the payment of capital gains tax on assessment

☐ Deal with the custody of deeds in accordance with the client's instructions. Most, if not all, original deeds will have been passed to the buyer's solicitor on actual completion, but the seller will have retained custody of such deed on a sale of part, or may have, e.g. an original grant of representation or power of attorney

☐ Check through the file to ensure that all outstanding matters have been dealt with before sending the file for storage.

7.8 POST-COMPLETION: BUYER'S CHECKLIST

Where appropriate to the transaction, the following steps should be taken by the buyer's solicitor as soon as possible after completion has taken place:

☐ Inform client and his lender that completion has taken place

☐ Complete the mortgage deed by insertion of the date and any other information which still has to be completed, e.g. date when first repayment is due

☐ Complete file copies of the mortgage, purchase deed and other relevant documents

☐ Ensure that the SDLT return (Form SDLT1) is completed and submitted to HMRC, together with the payment of any tax due, within the time limit

☐ Register any charge created by a company at Companies House within 21 days of its creation in accordance with Companies Act requirements. This time limit is absolute and cannot be extended without an order of the court. Failure to register within the time limit may prejudice the lender's security and will be an act of negligence on the part of the defaulting solicitor

- ☐ Account to the buyer's bank for any bridging finance in accordance with any undertaking given to them and ask to be released from that undertaking
- ☐ If not already done, draft and remit a bill of costs to the client
- ☐ Where money is being held by the solicitor on account of costs, it may be transferred to office account provided that the client has expressly or impliedly agreed to this being done
- ☐ If the seller's land is to remain unregistered after completion of this transaction, make application for registration of land charges at the Land Charges Department within the period given by the previously lodged priority notice, e.g. new restrictive covenants by the seller on a sale of part
- ☐ On receipt of the completed Form DS1 or receipted mortgage from the seller's lender's solicitor, check the form or receipt to ensure it is correct, acknowledge its receipt and release the sender from the undertaking given on completion
- ☐ Make copies of all documents which are to be sent to the Land Registry to ensure that file copies exist in case requisitions are raised by the Registry or the documents are lost or damaged before registration is complete
- ☐ Make copies of any documents where a request is to be made to the registrar for the original to be returned
- ☐ Certify copy documents which are to be sent to the Land Registry
- ☐ Make application for registration of title within the relevant priority period (land already registered) or within two months of completion (application for first registration)
- ☐ Make diary or file prompt entry recording the approximate date when the title information document may be expected to be received from the Land Registry and send a reminder if the document is not received by that time
- ☐ Send notice of assignment of a life policy to the insurance company and place their acknowledgement of receipt with the title deeds
- ☐ Give notice to the landlord's solicitors of an assignment, mortgage, etc. in accordance with a requirement to that effect in the lease or in the mortgagee's instructions and place their acknowledgement of receipt with the title deeds
- ☐ Notify tenants of the change of ownership of the property
- ☐ Make application for the discharge of any entry which was lodged to protect the contract. In registered land this will be combined with any application for registration
- ☐ On receipt of the title information document from the Land Registry, check its contents carefully and ask the Registry to correct any errors which have been made
- ☐ Deal with the custody of deeds in accordance with the client's instructions
- ☐ Check through the file to ensure that all outstanding matters have been dealt with before sending the file for storage.

Note: Where a separate solicitor has been instructed to act for the buyer's lender, the lender's solicitor will normally have taken custody of the purchase deed and other title deeds on completion and he will assume responsibility for the presentation of the documents for SDLT and registration of title in place of the buyer's solicitor.

8

Mortgages

8.1 CREATION OF NEW MORTGAGE: CHECKLIST

☐ Check instructions to ensure that all conditions attached to the advance can be complied with by both the solicitor and the borrower and that the instructions comply with Rule 3.19 Solicitors' Code of Conduct 2007

☐ If the lender is not a building society, confirm with him the rate of charging for acting for him and who is to be responsible for payment of the solicitor's bill

☐ Check that the terms of the contract to purchase are acceptable – does the purchase price in the contract accord with that shown on the lender's instructions?

☐ If the mortgage is being granted to a sole borrower, what are the lender's instructions relating to non-owning occupiers? Has any relevant consent form been signed? A signed deed or form of consent must be obtained from all occupants aged 17 or over (Lender's Handbook, para.7.3)

☐ Have adequate enquiries been made to ensure that there are no overriding interests over the property which will adversely affect the lender's security?

☐ Inform the lender of exchange of contracts and of contractual completion date if necessary

☐ Check that the property will be properly insured from the moment of exchange or completion (as appropriate)

☐ Has investigation of title been completed satisfactorily (including the results of pre-contract searches and enquiries) – have all the lender's specific requirements been met?

☐ Engross mortgage deed and obtain borrower's signature(s) to it. Where there are joint borrowers, one or more of whom is not known personally to the solicitor, precautions should be taken to verify the signature of the unknown borrower(s) in order to guard against forgery, e.g. by requiring the document to be signed in the presence of the solicitor

☐ Engross and obtain the borrower's signature to assignment of life policy (where appropriate)

☐ Ensure that life policy is in terms which comply with the lender's instructions is in existence

☐ Are results of pre-completion searches satisfactory, including a clear result of a bankruptcy search against the names of the borrower(s) and a company search against a company seller?

☐ Send a report on title/certificate of title to the lender and request the advance cheque

☐ On receipt of advance cheque, pay it into clients' account – ensure funds have been cleared before completion

☐ Make arrangements for completion

☐ If required, arrange for inspection of property immediately before completion to ensure vacant possession will be given

☐ Arrange for transmission of funds on day of completion

☐ Inform lender of completion

☐ Obtain purchase deed and title deeds from borrower's solicitor on completion with cheque for SDLT and Land Registry fees

☐ Date and fill in blanks in mortgage deed and related documents

☐ Send notice of assignment of life policy (in duplicate) to insurance company

☐ Give notice to prior lender(s) (if second or subsequent mortgage)

☐ Attend to payment of SDLT

☐ Submit application for registration of title within relevant priority period

☐ Keep lender informed of the reason for any delays at the Land Registry

☐ Prepare schedule of deeds for lender

☐ Send deeds to lender (or as instructed) and request return of receipted schedule of deeds.

8.2 REDEMPTION OF MORTGAGE: CHECKLIST

☐ Request redemption figure from the lender and title deeds if unregistered. If the seller has a 'flexible mortgage', ask for the account to be frozen until after completion

☐ Make a search to check if there is a subsequent chargee to whom the title deeds should be handed on completion

☐ Check instructions from the lender on their receipt

☐ In the case of a related sale, prepare epitome of title and send to the borrower's solicitor (if unregistered land and the lender's solicitor is not also acting for borrower)

☐ In the case of a related sale, keep in touch the with the borrower's solicitor about arrangements for completion

☐ Prepare Form DS1 or END1 (or receipt in unregistered land)

☐ Prepare reassignment of life policy (where relevant)

☐ Prepare undertaking for discharge of mortgage to be given to the buyer's solicitor on completion

☐ Prepare forms for discharge of land charges entries (second and subsequent mortgages of unregistered land)

☐ Obtain final redemption figure from the lender and inform the borrower's solicitor of the figure

☐ Arrange with the borrower's solicitor for actual payment on completion

☐ On receipt of repayment money, clear draft through clients' account and account to the lender in accordance with redemption statement

☐ Hand over undertaking for discharge of mortgage to the buyer's solicitor

☐ Send Form DS1 or END1 (or receipt in unregistered land) and deed of reassignment of life policy to mortgagee for execution and return. In the case of non-building society lenders, request that documents are dated with the date that completion of the mortgagor's sale took place to avoid problems over inadvertent transfer of the mortgage

☐ On receipt of executed Form DS1 (or receipt), check it before sending to the buyer's solicitor and request to be released from the undertaking given on completion

☐ Return life policy to the borrower.

8.3 MORTGAGE NOT SIMULTANEOUS WITH PURCHASE: CHECKLIST

☐ Obtain official copy entries of the title/title deeds

☐ Make relevant pre-contract searches and enquiries including a search to find out whether prior mortgages exist

☐ Make enquiries about non-owning occupiers and obtain signature of consent form/release of rights in accordance with the lender's instructions

☐ Investigate title to the property

☐ Check the state of the prior mortgage account (if relevant)

☐ Ensure compliance with the Consumer Credit Acts where applicable

☐ Draft, then engross mortgage deed

☐ Send report on title/certificate of title to the lender with request for advance cheque

☐ Explain the effect of and obtain the borrower's signature to mortgage deed

☐ Make pre-completion searches, including bankruptcy search against name of the borrower, and obtain clear results to searches

☐ Ensure any conditions attached to the offer of advance have been complied with

☐ Arrange to complete

☐ On completion, hand advance money to the mortgagor, date and fill in any blanks in mortgage deed

☐ Protect the lender's security by registration

☐ Give notice to a prior lender (where relevant)

☐ Advise the lender of completion of the mortgage.

9

Building estates

9.1 SELLER'S SOLICITOR'S CHECKLIST

- ☐ Has the site been inspected to ascertain the boundaries of each plot and the extent of easements and reservations?
- ☐ Has planning permission been obtained?
- ☐ Has a section 38 agreement and bond been obtained in respect of the roads?
- ☐ Has a section 104 agreement and bond been obtained in respect of sewers?
- ☐ Who is responsible for building regulation control and who will issue the certificate of completion of the building?
- ☐ Is the seller to make (and regularly update) pre-contract searches or will this be each buyer's responsibility?
- ☐ Will the property be covered by structural defects insurance? Has the builder registered and handed to his solicitor the appropriate documentation? Ensure that an unqualified (i.e. unconditional) certificate will be issued
- ☐ Has an estate plan been prepared and approved by the Land Registry?
- ☐ Has the form of transfer been approved by the Land Registry? This is not essential but may save time and requisitions from the Land Registry at a later stage
- ☐ Has all the necessary pre-contract documentation been prepared and duplicated for each plot?
- ☐ Have arrangements been made with the seller's lender to release the plots from the charge?
- ☐ Has the builder complied with the Construction (Design and Management) Regulations 2007 (SI 2007/320) (e.g. the appointment of a planning supervisor)?
- ☐ Has the builder provided a CML Disclosure of Incentives Form, and energy performance certificate and either a sustainability certificate or a nil-rated certificate?

9.2 PRE-CONTRACT PACKAGE

Documents to be prepared and sent to the prospective buyer's solicitor for each plot on receipt of instructions:

- ☐ Pre-contract enquiries with answers (may include Form TA8 New home information)
- ☐ Pre-contract searches with replies (where the seller is to undertake this task)
- ☐ Draft contract in duplicate (with the buyer's name left blank)

☐ Draft transfer in duplicate with plan attached (annexed to contract, buyer's name left blank)
☐ Evidence of title
☐ Requisitions on title with answers
☐ Copies of relevant planning permissions and building regulation approval
☐ Copies of relevant section 104 and section 38 agreements and bonds
☐ Structural defects insurance documentation, where appropriate
☐ A copy of the plan of the property properly marked and coloured in accordance with Land Registry requirements, with a spare copy for search purposes
☐ If desired, a general information sheet for the buyer containing, *inter alia*, address of local authorities and other bodies with whom searches may need to be conducted and an explanation of the contract terms (including arrangements for deposit and completion)
☐ A CML Disclosure of Incentives Form
☐ Covering letter.

Sales of part

10.1 MATTERS TO BE CONSIDERED ON SALE OF PART

10.1.1 Easements in the buyer's favour

☐ To what extent will Law of Property Act 1925, s.62 and/or the rule in *Wheeldon* v. *Burrows* imply easements in the buyer's favour?

☐ Is it necessary to extend the implied easements by granting express rights to the buyer?

☐ What does the buyer need? For example:
   ☐ Rights of way
   ☐ Right to lay new cables/pipelines/drains
   ☐ Right to use/maintain existing or new pipelines/cables/drains.

10.1.2 Rights of way

☐ Will the right be to pass over the land in both directions or should it be restricted to one way only?

☐ Should the right be restricted, e.g. to a particular class of user, such as pedestrian only?

☐ Is the exercise of the right to be restricted, e.g. use only for a particular purpose or only at a specified time of day?

10.1.3 All easements

☐ Is the route of the right of way/drain, etc. specified on the plan?

☐ Who is liable for maintenance/repairs?

☐ Will it be necessary for the buyer to enter the seller's land to inspect the state of repair and/or to maintain?

☐ Should the buyer's access to inspect be restricted, e.g. a right to inspect on 24 hours' notice except in case of emergency?

☐ Should the buyer be under an obligation to cause no unnecessary damage and to make good any damage done while inspecting/maintaining?

☐ Where the buyer is to construct a new pipeline/cable, etc., should he be required to finish the construction works within a specified period after completion?

10.1.4   Reservations

☐ Remember the seller generally gets nothing under the implied grant rules
☐ After completion, will the seller need to continue to use a right of way/drain/pipeline/cable passing through the land being sold?
☐ If so, express reservations must be included in the contract by way of special condition
☐ Additionally, to protect the seller, it may be considered necessary to include a general reservations clause in his favour dealing with all easements, quasi-easements, etc. presently enjoyed by the land as a whole
☐ Should rights of light and air be expressly reserved in order to preserve the seller's freedom to use the retained land in the future?

10.1.5   Existing covenants

☐ Is an indemnity clause required?

10.1.6   New covenants

☐ Should new restrictive covenants be imposed?
☐ If so, what type of restrictions will serve to protect the seller's land without imposing unnecessary constraints on the buyer?
☐ Consider:
    ☐ Erection of new buildings on the land
    ☐ Use of the land
    ☐ Repair/maintenance of buildings or land
    ☐ General covenant against nuisance
    ☐ Will the covenants be negative in nature?
    ☐ Do the words used ensure that the covenants will create an enforceable obligation?

10.1.7   Description of the property in the contract

☐ Does the wording of the particulars accurately describe the land being sold?
☐ Has the seller's retained land been precisely defined?
☐ Is there reference in the particulars to a plan?
☐ Is the plan of sufficient size and scale to be able to delineate accurately both the area of land being sold and the routes of easements, etc.?
☐ Does the plan comply with the Land Registry's requirements?

10.1.8   Seller's lender

☐ Will it be necessary to obtain the lender's consent to the sale? If so, has this been obtained?
☐ How will the lender deal with the release of the land being sold from the mortgage?

Leaseholds

11.1 GRANT OF A LEASE: LANDLORD'S CHECKLIST

The landlord's solicitor should normally send to the tenant's solicitor the following documents:

- ☐ Draft contract with draft lease annexed
- ☐ Evidence of the freehold title
- ☐ Any relevant planning and building regulation consents
- ☐ Answers to pre-contract searches and enquiries (including, where these are used, Forms TA6 Property Information Form and TA7 Leasehold Information, or in the case of a complex commercial property, it may be convenient to send replies to the Commercial Property Standard Enquiries)
- ☐ Where appropriate, evidence of the lender's consent to the grant of the lease
- ☐ The memorandum and articles of any management company.

11.2 COMPLETION AND POST-COMPLETION

On completion, in addition to or in substitution for the matters relevant to a freehold transaction the landlord will receive:

- ☐ The counterpart lease executed by the tenant
- ☐ Any premium payable for the grant (less any deposit paid on exchange of contracts)
- ☐ An apportioned sum representing rent payable in advance under the lease and interim service charge.

The landlord should give to the tenant:

- ☐ The lease executed by him
- ☐ If not already done, properly marked or certified copies of the freehold title deeds (unregistered land)
- ☐ Where relevant and if not already done, a certified copy of the consent of the landlord's lender to the transaction
- ☐ Where relevant, the share certificate relating to the management company
- ☐ After completion, the landlord may receive notice in duplicate from the tenant, in accordance with the tenant's covenant to do so in the lease, of the tenant's mortgage of the property. One copy of the notice should be placed with the landlord's title deeds, the other receipted on behalf of the landlord and returned to the tenant's solicitor.

11.3 CHECKING THE LEASE: TENANT'S CHECKLIST

Particular attention should be paid to the provisions relating to the following matters:

- ☐ The property to be demised
- ☐ Easements and reservations (particularly in the case of flats or other non-detached property)
- ☐ Repairing obligations
- ☐ Rent and rent review provisions
- ☐ Provisions relating to service charges
- ☐ Insurance:
    - ☐ Who is to insure: landlord or tenant?
    - ☐ Do the insurance provisions accord with the tenant's mortgagee's instructions?
    - ☐ What is covered by the policy both in terms of premises, amount of cover and risks insured against?
- ☐ Forfeiture clauses
- ☐ Covenants restricting alienation of the property
- ☐ Covenants restricting the use of the property
- ☐ Provisions relating to a management company or residents' association:
    - ☐ Is the tenant required to become a member of a management company which is limited by guarantee?
    - ☐ Will his liability to the management company terminate on assignment of the lease?
- ☐ Requirements for a surety or rent deposit scheme
- ☐ Are any of the covenants onerous?
- ☐ Do the covenants adequately protect the tenant and his lender?
- ☐ Are covenants for title being offered?
- ☐ Requirements of the CML Lenders' Handbook
- ☐ The proper completion of the prescribed clauses where it is a Prescribed Clauses Lease.

11.4 LAND REGISTRY PRESCRIBED CLAUSES

Set out below is an outline of the prescribed clauses:

- ☐ LR1. Date of lease
- ☐ LR2. Title number(s)
- ☐ LR2.1. Landlord's title number(s)
- ☐ LR2.2. Other title numbers. Here it is necessary to insert any existing title numbers against which entries of matters referred to in LR9, LR10, LR11 and LR13 are to be made
- ☐ LR3. Parties to the lease
- ☐ LR4. Property. Note that in the event of discrepancy between the contents of LR4 and the rest of the lease, the Land Registry will rely solely on the contents of LR4 for registration purposes

☐ LR5. Prescribed statements etc.

☐ LR5.1. Statements in leases required by certain statutes. It is necessary to insert here statements prescribed where dispositions are made to a charity, by a charity or where a lease is granted under Leasehold Reform, Housing and Urban Development Act 1993

☐ LR5.2. Lease made under certain statutes. Certain statements must be inserted where the lease is made under, or by reference to, provisions of Leasehold Reform Act 1967, Housing Act 1985, Housing Act 1988 or Housing Act 1996

☐ LR6. Term for which the property is leased

☐ LR7. Premium

☐ LR8. Prohibitions or restrictions on disposing of the lease. It is only necessary to include a statement as to whether or not the lease contains a provision that prohibits or restricts dispositions

☐ LR9. Rights of acquisition etc.:

☐ LR9.1. Tenant's contractual rights to renew the lease, to acquire the reversion or another lease of the property, or to acquire an interest in other land

☐ LR9.2. Tenant's covenant to (or offer to) surrender the lease

☐ LR9.3. Landlord's contractual rights to acquire the lease

☐ LR10. Restrictive covenants given in this lease by the landlord in respect of land other than the property

☐ LR11. Easements. In the relevant sub-clause below a reference must be made to the relevant clause, schedule or paragraph of a schedule in the lease where easements are either granted or reserved as appropriate:

☐ LR11.1. Easements granted by this lease for the benefit of the property

☐ LR11.2. Easements granted or reserved by this lease over the property for the benefit of other property

☐ LR12. Estate rentcharge burdening the property

☐ LR13. Application for standard form of restriction. Note the full text of the standard form restriction must be entered

☐ LR14. Declaration of trust where there is more than one person comprising the tenant.

Full details can be obtained from Land Registry Practice Guide 64.

11.5   LENDER'S REQUIREMENTS (LEASEHOLD PROPERTY)

The tenant's lender will frequently be concerned to see that the following conditions have been satisfied:

☐ The consent of the landlord's lender to the transaction has been obtained (where relevant)

☐ The length of the term to be granted provides adequate security for the loan

☐ The lease contains adequate insurance provisions relating both to the premises themselves and (where relevant) to common parts of the building and that the insurance provisions coincide with the lender's own requirements for insurance

☐ Normally, title to the freehold reversion should be deduced. This will enable the lease to be registered with an absolute title at the Land Registry (where appropriate)

☐ The lease contains proper repairing covenants in respect both of the property itself and (where relevant) the common parts of the building

☐ In the case of residential leases, that there is no provision for forfeiture on the insolvency of the tenant

☐ Where the lease is of part of a building or is, e.g. of one house on an estate comprising leasehold houses all owned by the same landlord, that the lease provides for mutual enforceability of covenants as between the tenants

☐ Where appropriate, the landlord is giving the relevant covenants for title

☐ Where the lender's solicitor's instructions are governed by the CML Lenders' Handbook the requirements of the Handbook must be complied with.

11.6 EXCEPTIONS TO ASSURED TENANCIES

All new assured tenancies granted on or after 28 February 1997 (other than those granted pursuant to a contract made before that date) will be shortholds, subject to certain exceptions which will take effect as ordinary assured tenancies. These include:

☐ Tenancies excluded by notice. The landlord may serve a notice on the tenant either before or after the grant of the tenancy stating that the letting is not to be a shorthold

☐ Tenancies containing a provision stating that the tenancy is not to be a shorthold

☐ Lettings to existing assured tenants.

11.7 DUTY OF LANDLORD TO PROVIDE A STATEMENT OF THE TERMS OF A SHORTHOLD TENANCY

Under the Housing Act 1988, s.20A (as inserted by Housing Act 1996), the landlord is placed under a duty in certain circumstances to provide a tenant with written details of the following terms provided that they are not already evidenced in writing:

☐ The commencement date of the tenancy
☐ The rent payable and the dates on which it is payable
☐ Any terms providing for rent review
☐ The length of a fixed-term tenancy.

The tenant must make a request to the landlord in writing for this information.

11.8   TERMINATION OF AN AGRICULTURAL TENANCY

The following apply to termination:

☐   A fixed-term agreement for two years or less will expire automatically
☐   Common law rules apply to periodic tenancies except that a yearly tenant needs to be given not less than one year's notice, expiring at the end of a year
☐   For a fixed-term tenancy of more than two years, not less than 12 months' notice to terminate on the term day must be given (otherwise the tenancy continues as a tenancy from year to year)
☐   Notices must be in writing.

11.9   LEASES OF FLATS

The lease should consider and deal with the following points:

☐   What is the structure of the building composed of? Repairing covenants must be drafted appropriately so that a covenant, e.g. 'to repair main walls and timbers' will be inappropriate where the building is of concrete construction
☐   Access: the lease must deal with easements of access, e.g. is there a right of way over the drive from the public highway to the entrance of the flats, how does each tenant get from the door of the building to the door of his own flat, is there to be a lift, does each tenant require access to the dustbin area, etc.?
☐   Where do the mains services run? Which tenants need easements for pipes, cables, etc., to pass through another flat or common parts on the way to or from their own flat?
☐   Amenities: who is to have a garage or parking space, are these to be a part of the demise (i.e. a specific allocated space) or is there to be just a licence to use a garage/parking space (with no guarantee that a space will actually be available), use of gardens, is there communal central heating, is there an entry-phone system, is there a communal television or satellite aerial, are individual aerials to be permitted, is there a caretaker's flat?
☐   Service charges: what services are to be included in the charge, will all tenants have the benefit of all the services supplied, should the service charge be split equally between all the tenants or should some pay a greater proportion than others or should different proportions apply to different services?
☐   Check site and floor plans against the physical extent of the building both in relation to the whole building and individual flats, are they accurate, which tenants need which plans, and do they comply with Land Registry requirements?

11.10   FLAT LEASES: CHECKLIST OF ITEMS TO BE SENT TO BUYER'S SOLICITOR

Note: Not all of the following will be relevant in every transaction:

- [ ] Draft contract in duplicate
- [ ] Draft lease in duplicate
- [ ] Copy head lease
- [ ] Other evidence of superior and reversionary titles
- [ ] Draft agreement between landlord and management company for transfer of reversion to management company
- [ ] Copy memorandum and articles of management company
- [ ] Copy local authority search and enquiries with replies
- [ ] Copy planning permissions and building regulation consents
- [ ] Copy indemnity insurance policy covering defects in title, restrictive covenants, etc.
- [ ] Copy approved estate layout plan as deposited at the Land Registry
- [ ] Copy replies to enquiries before contract
- [ ] Copy insurance policy and schedules
- [ ] Copy guarantees, e.g. for repairs to structure
- [ ] Documentation relating to insurance against structural defects
- [ ] Estimated service charge calculation
- [ ] Audited accounts of the management company
- [ ] Replies to local searches
- [ ] Energy efficiency assessment.

11.11   LENDER'S REQUIREMENTS

The CML Lenders' Handbook provides comprehensive instructions for solicitors and licensed conveyancers acting on behalf of lenders in conveyancing transactions. Part 1 of the Lenders' Handbook is reproduced in **Appendix B**.

A lender is usually concerned with the following matters:

- [ ] To ensure that the lease contains proper provision for the mutual enforceability of covenants between tenants (Lenders' Handbook para.5.10.6)
- [ ] To ensure that the property is leasehold and that the lease contains adequate repairing covenants relating to the flat itself, the exterior structure and the common parts of the building (Lenders' Handbook para.5.10.4)
- [ ] That the lease contains adequate provision for the insurance of the whole building (Lenders' Handbook paras.5.10.4. and 5.10.5)
- [ ] That the length of the term of the lease (or unexpired residue in the case of an assignment) is sufficient to permit a resale of the premises on the open market. A common period required by lenders is 55 years unexpired from completion and 30 years unexpired at the end of the mortgage term. Notification may be required if the minimum period is less than 70 years. A term which will have less than 20 years unexpired after the end of the mortgage term may be considered inadequate in the context of normal residential conveyancing

☐ That the lease contains no provision for forfeiture on the insolvency of the tenant (Lenders' Handbook para.5.10.2)

☐ That the lease contains no restrictions on alienation which may hinder a sale on the open market (Lenders' Handbook para.5.10.3)

☐ That the lease is, or will be, registered at the Land Registry with an absolute leasehold title, (a lesser title, e.g. good leasehold title, may be acceptable in certain circumstances (Lenders' Handbook para.5.4))

☐ Where the tenant is to become a member of a management company, the lender sometimes requires that a blank form of share transfer (signed by the borrower) and the tenant's share certificate is deposited with the lender to enable the lender to transfer that share to a buyer should he need to exercise his power of sale. A copy of the management company's memorandum and articles may also have to be deposited with the lender (Lenders' Handbook para.5.11.2)

☐ That notices have been given to the landlord of the mortgage (Lenders' Handbook para.5.10.11)

☐ That the lease reserves an appropriate ground rent and that receipts are provided for rent and service charge payments (Lenders' Handbook paras.5.10.7 and 5.10.10)

☐ If the property being purchased is held under a sub-lease (so that the landlord's own interest is leasehold), it is desirable that the aggregate ground rents payable by the flats in the block should exceed the amount of rent payable by the landlord to the freeholder. If this is not the case, the landlord will have little incentive to pay his own rent, and thus the sub-tenants of the flats would be put at risk from forfeiture of the head-lease. For this reason, it is desirable that in any situation where sub-letting is permitted, the tenant should be required to enter a covenant with his landlord not to sub-let the whole at a rent lower than that payable under his own lease.

11.12   BUSINESS TENANCIES: EXCLUSIONS FROM LANDLORD AND TENANT ACT 1954

These include:

☐ Agricultural holdings
☐ Mining leases
☐ Written service tenancies
☐ Tenancies at will
☐ Fixed-term tenancies not exceeding six months unless the tenancy contains provision for renewing the term or for extending it beyond six months from its beginning. This exception also does not apply if the tenant has been in occupation for a period which, together with any period during which any predecessor in the carrying on of the business carried on by the tenant was in occupation, exceeds 12 months
☐ Tenancies for a term certain where the statutory procedure has been followed to exclude the security of tenure provisions of the Act prior to the commencement of the tenancy.

11.13 STATUTORY PROCEDURE FOR EXCLUSION OF TENANCY UNDER LANDLORD AND TENANT ACT 1954

The procedure is as follows:

☐ A notice in prescribed form containing a warning must be served on the tenant before the tenant 'enters into the tenancy to which it applies, or (if earlier) becomes contractually bound to do so'. This procedure must therefore be followed before a contract to enter into an excluded lease is made unless these provisions are construed as permitting a conditional agreement for a lease.

☐ Either:

   ☐ Not less than 14 days must elapse before the tenant enters into the tenancy. The tenant must then sign a simple, prescribed declaration that he has received the required warning notice and has accepted the consequences of entering into the agreement *or alternatively*

   ☐ The tenant, or a person duly authorised by him to do so, must, before the tenancy or contract is entered into, make a prescribed statutory declaration

☐ A reference to the notice and the simple declaration or (if applicable) the statutory declaration must be contained in or endorsed upon the instrument creating the tenancy

☐ The agreement to exclude the security of tenure provisions of the Act must be contained in or endorsed upon the instrument creating the tenancy.

Note: The forms of notice and declaration are set out in Schedules to the Regulatory Reform (Business Tenancies)(England and Wales) Order 2003 (SI 2003/3096).

11.14 LANDLORD'S GROUNDS FOR OPPOSING NEW TENANCY UNDER LANDLORD AND TENANT ACT 1954

The landlord's grounds for opposing the grant of a new tenancy are contained in Landlord and Tenant Act 1954, s.30 and are briefly as follows:

☐ Breach of repairing obligations by the tenant
☐ Persistent delay in paying rent
☐ Substantial breaches of other obligations under the tenancy
☐ Alternative accommodation
☐ Possession of whole property required where tenant has a sub-tenancy of part
☐ Landlord's intention to demolish or reconstruct the property
☐ Landlord requires possession for his own occupation.

11.15   ASSIGNMENT OF BUSINESS LEASE: ASSIGNEE'S CHECKLIST

A prospective assignee (purchaser) should (in addition to the usual matters to be considered on the assignment of a lease) pay careful attention to the following matters:

☐ The rent review provisions contained in the lease
☐ The repairing obligations imposed by the lease
☐ Any service charge provisions in the lease
☐ The VAT implications of the transaction
☐ Whether the existing tenant has committed any breach of covenant which would give the landlord the right to determine the lease or to refuse a renewal of it
☐ The likelihood of a lease renewal being opposed by a landlord on other grounds, e.g. redevelopment
☐ The provisions relating to alienation of the lease.

11.16   ENFRANCHISEMENT UNDER LEASEHOLD REFORM (HOUSING AND URBAN DEVELOPMENT) ACT 1993

To exercise rights under the Act, the Right to Enfranchise (RTE) company (company specifically set up to manage the property after enfranchisement) must serve an initial notice on the reversioner under section 13 of the Act. The notice must be in writing and may be served by post. The Act prescribes the contents of the notice but not its form. Printed forms are available from law stationers. The notice must:

☐ Specify the premises with a plan
☐ Contain a statement of the grounds on which eligibility rests
☐ Specify other freehold or leasehold interests (if any) to be acquired
☐ State which flats (if any) are subject to mandatory leaseback provisions
☐ Specify the proposed purchase price of the freehold and any other interest specified in the notice
☐ Give the full names of all the qualifying tenants together with details of their leases
☐ Specify which tenants satisfy the residence qualification and how this is achieved
☐ Give the name and address of the RTE company
☐ Specify a date by which the landlord must respond with his counter-notice (not less than two months).

11.17 ENFRANCHISEMENT: ACTING FOR A BUYER OF AN INDIVIDUAL FLAT

When acting for a buyer who is buying an existing lease which potentially qualifies under the Leasehold Reform (Housing and Development) Act 1993, consideration should be given to raising enquiries of the seller to establish:

- ☐ Whether the flat and the lease qualify under the Act
- ☐ How many qualifying flats and qualifying tenants there are in the block
- ☐ Whether and when any initial notice has been served by an RTE company and, if so, how far negotiations have reached (a copy of the notice should be requested if not already supplied by the seller's solicitor)
- ☐ Whether any steps have been taken by the seller to acquire an extension of his lease under the Act.

11.18 EXAMPLES OF SOME LANDLORDS WHO ARE EXEMPT FROM THE LANDLORD AND TENANT ACT 1987

- ☐ Local authorities
- ☐ Urban development corporations
- ☐ Registered housing associations
- ☐ Resident landlords, where the following three conditions are satisfied:
    - ☐ The premises are not a purpose-built block of flats
    - ☐ The landlord occupies a flat in the premises as his only or principal residence
    - ☐ The landlord has been in occupation for the last 12 months.

11.19 LANDLORD AND TENANT ACT 1987: QUALIFYING TENANTS: EXCLUSIONS

A tenant of a flat (including a company tenant) is a qualifying tenant unless his tenancy is:

- ☐ A protected shorthold tenancy
- ☐ A business tenancy within Part II Landlord and Tenant Act 1954
- ☐ An assured tenancy or an assured agricultural occupancy
- ☐ A tenancy terminable on the cessation of the tenant's employment
- ☐ Of the flat and by virtue of one or more non-excluded tenancies he is also the tenant of at least two other flats contained in the same building
- ☐ A sub-tenancy and his landlord is a qualifying tenant of the flat in question.

11.20   LANDLORD AND TENANT ACT 1987: RELEVANT DISPOSALS: EXCLUSIONS

By Landlord and Tenant Act 1987, s.4, the following are excluded from the definition of a relevant disposal:

- ☐ A disposal:
  - ☐ Of an interest of a beneficiary in settled land
  - ☐ By way of the creation of a mortgage
  - ☐ Of any incorporeal hereditament
- ☐ A disposal to a trustee in bankruptcy or liquidator
- ☐ A disposal in pursuance of an order under Matrimonial Causes Act 1973, ss.24 or 24A, or Inheritance (Provision for Family and Dependants) Act 1975, s.2 or similar legislative provisions
- ☐ A disposal in pursuance of a compulsory purchase order or agreement in lieu
- ☐ A disposal of any interest by virtue of Leasehold Reform, Housing and Urban Development Act 1993
- ☐ A gift to a member of the landlord's family as defined in section 4(5) or to a charity
- ☐ A disposal of functional land by one charity to another as defined in section 60
- ☐ A disposal of trust property in connection with the appointment or discharge of a trustee
- ☐ A disposal between members of the same family provided that at least one of the original owners still retains an interest
- ☐ A disposal in pursuance of a contract, option or right of pre-emption which was entered into by the landlord before the tenant's right of first refusal arose
- ☐ A surrender of a tenancy in pursuance of any obligation contained in it
- ☐ A disposal to the Crown
- ☐ Where the landlord is a body corporate, a disposal to an associated company which has been an associated company of that body for at least two years.

11.21   LANDLORD'S OFFER UNDER LANDLORD AND TENANT ACT 1987

The landlord must serve notice on the qualifying tenants of the flats in the premises. Different types of proposed disposals require different prescribed information to be inserted into the notice as set out in section 5A (normal sale by contract), section 5B (sale at auction), section 5C (grant of options and pre-emption rights), section 5D (sale proceeding to completion without contract) and section 5E (wholly or partly for non-monetary consideration).

In outline, a notice served under section 5A must:

- ☐ Set out the principal terms proposed including the property and the estate or interest to be disposed of (the 'protected interest') and the consideration required

☐ State that it constitutes an offer to dispose of the property on those terms which may be accepted by the requisite number of qualifying tenants (the offer is deemed by the Act to be 'subject to contract')

☐ Specify a period for acceptance being at least two months beginning with the date of service

☐ Specify a further period of at least two months beginning with the end of the period of acceptance within which a person or persons may be nominated to take the landlord's interest.

11.22 ACTING FOR THE PURCHASER OF A REVERSIONARY INTERESTS IN FLATS

A person who intends to purchase a reversionary interest directly from a landlord must check before exchange of contracts:

☐ Whether or not the premises fall within the scope of Landlord and Tenant Act 1987 *and if they do*

☐ Whether the landlord and any relevant previous owners have served notice on the qualifying tenants as required by the Act *and if so*

☐ That either the tenants have rejected the landlord's offer or that the time limits for acceptance have expired and the purchase transaction to the buyer can be completed within 12 months of the expiry of the acceptance period *and*

☐ The terms on which the buyer is buying are similar to the terms of the offer which was made to the tenants.

The Standard Commercial Property Conditions contain optional provisions covering these points.

11.23 PROSPECTIVE BUYER'S NOTICE UNDER LANDLORD AND TENANT ACT 1987

Section 18 enables a prospective buyer to serve notice on tenants to ensure that rights of first refusal do not arise where it appears to the buyer that the disposal might be a relevant disposal of premises to which the Act applies. The notice must:

☐ Set out the principal terms of the proposed disposal

☐ Invite the recipient to serve a notice stating:

    ☐ Whether an offer notice has been served

    ☐ If not, whether he is aware of any reason why he is not entitled to such a notice *and*

    ☐ Whether he would wish to exercise any right of first refusal

☐ Set out the effect of section 18(3) which says that, provided notices have been served on at least 80% of the tenants, and not more than 50% have replied within two months, or more than 50% have indicated that they do not regard themselves as entitled to an offer notice or would not wish to exercise a right of first refusal, the premises shall be treated as premises to which the Act does not apply.

11.24   ASSIGNMENT OF LEASE: SELLER'S SOLICITOR'S CHECKLIST

☐   The seller's solicitor should obtain from his client or, if not available from the client, from the landlord:
  ☐   The receipt for the last rent due under the lease
  ☐   Where relevant, evidence of payment of service charge over the past three years including the receipt for the last payment due
  ☐   Details of the insurance of the property including the receipt for the last premium due
  ☐   Details of any fee payable to a management company on the transfer of the lease (mainly applicable to retirement schemes)
  ☐   A copy of the memorandum and articles of association of any management company together with a copy of the seller's share certificate
  ☐   Copies of any side letters made between landlord and tenant which affect the terms of the lease.
☐   Does the seller's solicitor have in his possession:
  ☐   Evidence of the freehold title?
  ☐   Licence permitting the current assignment and/or use of the property?
  ☐   Insurance policy?
  ☐   Latest rent review memo?
☐   What consents are needed:
  ☐   From landlord?
  ☐   From lender?
☐   Consider what statutes affect the current letting and the proposed sale. What impact does this legislation make on the proposed transaction?
☐   Consider the terms of the existing lease, e.g. as to repairs, user, alterations, alienation, forfeiture, because the buyer's solicitor may raise points on these clauses
☐   Will it be necessary to obtain a release of the current sureties' liability from the landlord, or to obtain a deed of variation of the lease to reflect the current situation as between landlord and tenant?
☐   If the lease to be assigned commenced before 1 January 1996, the assignor should be reminded of his continuing liability under the covenants in the lease
☐   If the lease to be assigned commenced after 1 January 1996, its terms should be checked to see whether the landlord requires the outgoing tenant to enter into an authorised guarantee agreement on assignment.

11.25   ASSIGNMENT OF LEASE: BUYER'S SOLICITOR'S CHECKLIST

☐   Check the lease and lease plan carefully and advise the client about his or her responsibility under the various covenants in the lease. The lease may require an assignee to enter into direct covenants with the landlord which will create a contractual relationship between the landlord and the assignee and, in the case of 'old tenancies' (as defined by the Landlord and Tenant (Covenants) Act 1995), will make the assignee liable on all of the lease covenants for the remainder of the term, notwithstanding subsequent assignment of the lease to a third party

☐ Check whether the lease, or rights granted by it, has been registered at the Land Registry (e.g. a lease for over seven years, or a lease of part for less than seven years which grants an easement) where registration was required

☐ Check whether the circumstances surrounding the payment of SDLT by the original tenant may require the buyer to file a subsequent return during the term, e.g. on a rent review within five years from the grant.

11.26   LANDLORD'S CONSENT

If the landlord's consent to the transfer or assignment will be needed, the buyer should be asked to supply his solicitor with the names and addresses of potential referees so that this information may be passed on to the seller's solicitor as quickly as possible in order to avoid any delay in obtaining the licence. References are commonly required from all or some of the following sources:

☐ A current landlord
☐ The buyer's bankers
☐ The buyer's employer
☐ A professional person, e.g. accountant or solicitor
☐ A person or company with whom the buyer regularly trades
☐ Three years' audited accounts in the case of a company or self-employed person.

11.27   ASSIGNMENT OF LEASE: THE PRE-CONTRACT PACKAGE

The seller's solicitor should generally supply the buyer's solicitor with the following documents or information:

☐ The draft contract
☐ A copy of the lease/sub-lease being purchased
☐ A plan of the property (where appropriate)
☐ Evidence of the seller's title
☐ Replies to pre-contract searches
☐ Details of the insurance of the property (including the receipt for the last premium due)
☐ Details of any management company, including copies of the memorandum and articles of association
☐ Service charge accounts for the last three years including the receipt for the last sum payable (where appropriate)
☐ Information about what steps have been taken to obtain the landlord's consent to the transaction (where appropriate)

- [ ] A request for references or such other information about the buyer as the landlord has indicated that he requires (where appropriate)
- [ ] Answers to pre-contract enquiries (e.g. TA6 Property Information Form and TA7 Leasehold Information Form, or in the case of complex commercial property, the Commercial Property Standard Enquiries).

11.28 COMPLETION OF ASSIGNMENT

The procedure on completion follows closely that in a freehold transaction.

The seller will hand to the buyer such of the following documents as are relevant to the transaction in hand:

- [ ] The lease/sub-lease
- [ ] The purchase deed
- [ ] The landlord's licence
- [ ] Marked abstract or other evidence of superior titles in accordance with the contract (lease not registered or not registered with absolute title)
- [ ] Form DS1 or END or an appropriate undertaking in respect of the seller's mortgage
- [ ] Certificate of non-crystallisation (where appropriate)(company charges)
- [ ] Copies of duplicate notices served by the seller and his predecessors on the landlord in accordance with a covenant in the lease requiring the landlord to be notified of any dispositions
- [ ] Insurance policy (or copy if insurance is effected by the landlord) and receipt (or copy) relating to the last premium due
- [ ] Rent and service charge receipts
- [ ] Management company memorandum and articles
- [ ] Seller's share certificate and completed stock transfer form.

The buyer should hand to the seller such of the following items as are appropriate to the transaction:

- [ ] Money due in accordance with the completion statement
- [ ] Duly executed counterpart licence to assign
- [ ] A release of deposit.

11.29 VARIATION OF LONG LEASES

Any party to a long lease of a flat may apply to the Leasehold Valuation Tribunal under Part IV Landlord and Tenant Act 1987 (as amended by Commonhold and Leasehold Reform Act 2002) for an order for the variation of the lease where the lease fails to make satisfactory provision for:

- [ ] Repair or maintenance of the flat or building
- [ ] Insurance of the premises
- [ ] Repair or maintenance of installations
- [ ] The provision of services

- [ ] Recovery by one party to the lease from another party of expenditure incurred for the benefit of the other party
- [ ] Computation of service charges under the lease.

11.30 BUYING TENANTED PROPERTY: BUYER'S CHECKLIST

The matters the buyer's solicitor should check include:

- [ ] The terms of the lease(s) or agreement(s) supplied by the seller's solicitor
- [ ] The effect of any security of tenure legislation on the tenant(s)
- [ ] Details of the landlord's obligations under the lease(s) or agreement(s), and in particular, whether or not the seller has complied with such obligations
- [ ] Whether the tenant has complied with all his obligations under the lease or agreement (e.g. as to payment of rent and service charge) and, if not, what steps the seller has taken to enforce the agreement against the tenant
- [ ] What variations have been made to the agreements and/or licences granted
- [ ] Details of any renewal applications or the exercise of an option made by the tenant
- [ ] Whether the tenants have a right of first refusal. This is also an important consideration for the seller's solicitor, since it is the seller who will be guilty of an offence if he fails to comply with the Landlord and Tenant Act 1987.

11.31 COMPLETION OF TENANTED PROPERTY

In addition to the usual requirements on completion of the purchase of a freehold property, the buyer should receive:

- [ ] The original lease(s) or tenancy agreement(s)
- [ ] An authority signed by the seller and addressed to the tenant(s), authorising the tenant(s) to pay future rent to the buyer.

11.32 TENANTED PROPERTY: AFTER COMPLETION

- [ ] The new landlord (the buyer) must give written notice of the assignment and of his name and address to the tenant not later than the next day on which rent is payable, or if that is within two months of the date of the assignment, the end of the period of two months
- [ ] Send two copies of the notice to the tenants and ask for one to be signed by the tenant and returned to the landlord as proof of receipt
- [ ] Also send a copy of the notice (with a covering letter) to the seller who otherwise remains liable for breaches of covenant occurring until written notice of the assignment is given to the tenant by either the seller or the buyer.

Remedies

12.1 CHECKLIST FOR BREACH OF CONTRACT

The following is a checklist of the main points to be considered:

- ☐ Has there been a breach of contract?
- ☐ If so, what type of breach, i.e. of condition or warranty?
- ☐ What remedy does the client want, e.g. damages or specific performance?
- ☐ Is there a valid exclusion clause which might prevent the claim?
- ☐ When did the limitation period start to run?
- ☐ What (approximately) is the total of the client's financial loss?
- ☐ How much of that loss would be recoverable, bearing in mind the rules on remoteness of damage?
- ☐ Would the costs of an action be justified?
- ☐ Who should be sued, e.g. other party to the contract, solicitor, surveyor?
- ☐ If a claim cannot be made in contract, is there a viable alternative action, e.g. in tort or for misrepresentation?

12.2 CIRCUMSTANCES WHERE SPECIFIC PERFORMANCE WILL NOT BE AWARDED

As an equitable remedy, the award of a decree of specific performance is subject to the usual principles of equity. It will not therefore be awarded where:

- ☐ An award of damages would adequately compensate for the loss sustained by the breach
- ☐ One of the contracting parties lacks full contractual capacity
- ☐ The contract contains a vitiating element, e.g. mistake, fraud, illegality
- ☐ The enforcement of the order would require the constant supervision of the court
- ☐ A third party has acquired an interest for value in the property
- ☐ The award would cause exceptional hardship to the guilty party
- ☐ The seller cannot make good title.

12.3 INDEMNITY FROM THE LAND REGISTRY

Subject to the exceptions contained in Land Registration Act 2002, a person is entitled to be indemnified by the registrar if he suffers loss by reason of:

- A rectification of the register
- A mistake whose correction would involve rectification of the register
- A mistake in an official search
- A mistake in an official copy
- A mistake in a document kept by the registrar which is not an original and is referred to in the register
- The loss or destruction of a document lodged at the registry for inspection or safe custody
- A mistake in the cautions register
- Failure by the registrar to perform his duty under section 50 Land Registration Act 2002 (duty of notification of overriding statutory charges).

12.4 COVENANTS FOR TITLE: FULL TITLE GUARANTEE

Where the full guarantee is given, the seller warrants that:

- He has the right to dispose of the property in the manner purported
- He will at his own cost do all he reasonably can to give his transferee the title he purports to give
- He disposes of his whole interest where that interest is registered
- He disposes of the whole lease where the interest is leasehold
- He disposes of a freehold where it is unclear from the face of the documents whether the interest is freehold or leasehold
- In the case of a subsisting lease, he covenants that the lease is still subsisting and that there is no subsisting breach which might result in forfeiture
- In the case of a mortgage of a property which is subject to a rentcharge or lease, that the borrower will observe and perform the obligations under the rentcharge or lease
- That the person giving the disposition is disposing of it free from all charges and encumbrances (whether monetary or not) and from all other rights exercisable by third parties, not being rights which the transferor does not and could not reasonably be expected to know about.

12.5 COVENANTS FOR TITLE: LIMITED TITLE GUARANTEE

Where limited title guarantee is given, all the warranties in **12.4** apply except for the final one, which is replaced with the following:

- That the transferor has not charged or encumbered the property by a charge or encumbrance which still exists, that he has not granted any third party rights which still subsist and that he is not aware that anyone else has done so since the last disposition for value.

The seller therefore warrants that he has not encumbered the property but he does not warrant that his predecessor has not done so.

12.6   ACTION TO BE TAKEN BY SOLICITOR WHERE NEGLIGENCE SUSPECTED

If a solicitor discovers an act or omission which would justify a claim by a client (or third party) against him he should:

☐   Contact his insurers
☐   Inform the client (or third party) in order to enable him to take independent legal advice
☐   Seek the advice of his insurers as to any further communication with the client (or third party) and
☐   Confirm any oral communication in writing.

12.7   NON-CONTENTIOUS COSTS

Article 3 of the Solicitors' (Non-Contentious Business) Remuneration Order 2009 (SI 2009/1931) provides that the remuneration must be fair and reasonable having regard to all the circumstances of the case and in particular to:

☐   The complexity of the matter or the difficulty or novelty of the questions raised
☐   The skill, labour, specialised knowledge and responsibility involved
☐   The time spent on the business
☐   The number and importance of the documents prepared or considered, without regard to length
☐   The place where and the circumstances in which the business or any part of the business is transacted
☐   The amount or value of any money or property involved
☐   Whether any land involved is registered land within the meaning of the Land Registration Act 2002
☐   The importance of the matter to the client and
☐   The approval (express or implied) of the entitled person or the express approval of the testator to:
  ☐   The solicitor undertaking all or any part of the work giving rise to the costs *or*
  ☐   The amount of the costs.

12.8   AGREEMENT WITH CLIENT FOR NON-CONTENTIOUS COSTS

Solicitors Act 1974, s.57 allows a solicitor to make an agreement with a client for costs in a non-contentious matter.

In order to be enforceable under the Act, the agreement must fully comply with the provisions of s.57. Thus, the agreement must:

☐   Be in writing
☐   Embody all the terms of the agreement

☐ Be signed by the party to be charged or his agent, i.e. the client
☐ Be reasonable in amount and be in lieu of ordinary profit costs.

12.9   SOLICITOR'S BILL OF COSTS

A solicitor's bill must:

☐ Be in writing (and may also be in electronic form)
☐ Be signed by the solicitor or on his behalf by an employee authorised by him to do so (a form of signature such as, e.g. 'signed A. Smith, a partner in A. Smith & Co.' is recommended)
☐ Contain sufficient information to identify the matter to which it relates, the work being charged for and the time period covered by the bill
☐ Itemise disbursements separately
☐ Identify the VAT element of costs
☐ Contain a notice setting out the information in **12.10** below.

12.10   NOTICE CONTAINED IN SOLICITOR'S BILL OF COSTS

A solicitor must not sue unless he has first informed the client in writing that sections 70, 71 and 72 of the Solicitors Act 1974 set out the client's rights in relation to having the bill assessed by the court, and that the solicitor is entitled to charge interest on the outstanding amount of the bill in accordance with article 5 of the Solicitors' (Non-Contentious Business) Remuneration Order 2009.

Before deducting costs (other than disbursements) from money held for or on behalf of a client or estate in satisfaction of a bill and an entitled person objects in writing to the amount of the bill within the prescribed time, a solicitor must inform the client or other entitled person in writing of their rights in relation to having the bill assessed by the court under sections 70, 71 and 72 of the Solicitors Act 1974 and that the solicitor is entitled to charge interest on the outstanding amount of the bill in accordance with article 5 of the Solicitors' (Non-Contentious Business) Remuneration Order 2009. For this purpose, the 'prescribed time' is three months after delivery of the bill or notification to a client or entitled third party, or a lesser time specified in writing to the client or entitled third party at the time of delivery of the bill or notification (but this period cannot be less than one month).

12.11   COSTS: COURT OF PROTECTION WORK

Fixed costs are payable for all conveyancing matters authorised by the Office of the Public Guardian.

Two elements will be allowable, as follows:

☐ A fixed sum in every case to cover correspondence with the Office of the Public Guardian, the preparation of the certificate or affidavit of value, and all other work solely attributable to the Court of Protection together with
☐ A value element of a percentage of the consideration.

As well as a fee for both the above elements, VAT and disbursements will be allowed.

Fixed costs will apply to conveyancing of all types of property. If solicitors wish, they may choose to have their costs assessed by the Supreme Court Costs Office, rather than to accept fixed costs. It should, however, be emphasised that agreed costs will not be an option, save in exceptional circumstances.

13

SDLT, VAT and other tax matters

13.1 SDLT RATES: RESIDENTIAL FREEHOLD PROPERTY

SDLT is calculated as a percentage of the whole of the consideration paid:

Not more than £175,000	0%
More than £175,000 but not more than £250,000	1%
More than £250,000 but not more than £500,000	3%
More than £500,000	4%

From (and including) 1 January 2010, the following rates apply:

Not more than £125,000	0% (outside a DA)
Not more than £150,000	0% (within a DA)
More than £125,000 but not more than £250,000	1%
More than £250,000 but not more than £500,000	3%
More than £500,000	4%

Where the property is partly within a DA, the zero-rate band threshold applicable to the part within the DA is £150,000.

13.2 SDLT RATES: NON-RESIDENTIAL OR MIXED FREEHOLD PROPERTY

SDLT is calculated as a percentage of the whole consideration paid:

Not more than £150,000	0%
More than £150,000 but not more than £250,000	1%
More than £250,000 but not more than £500,000	3%
More than £500,000	4%

13.3 DEFINITION OF RESIDENTIAL PROPERTY FOR SDLT PURPOSES

It is important to distinguish between residential and non-residential property because different rates of SDLT apply (Finance Act 2003, s.116):

☐ A residential property is property which is used or has been adapted for use as a single dwelling, even if the single dwelling is part of a larger building

- ☐ Amenity land forming part of the garden or grounds of the building, a garage (detached or integral), parking space and (domestic) garden shed are all included within the definition of residential property
- ☐ A single transaction involving six or more dwellings is not residential
- ☐ Institutional property used as residential accommodation for school pupils, students, the armed forces or as a principal residence for more than 90% of the occupants is residential property
- ☐ Institutional property used as accommodation for higher education halls of residence, children's homes, care and/or treatment and psychiatric homes, hospitals, prisons and hotels is not residential
- ☐ Where land is used for residential purposes, no account shall be taken of any other use
- ☐ Where land is not used, but is suitable for a particular residential or non-residential use, it will be treated as within that class.

13.4   SDLT RATES ON MIXED USE LAND

- ☐ Mixed use land is land which combines both residential and non-residential property
- ☐ Where that land is situated outside a DA, non-residential tax rates apply (Finance Act 2003, Sched.6)
- ☐ When mixed use land is within or partly within a DA, a just and reasonable apportionment has to be made as between the use and as to the location.

When land is outside a DA and is either wholly non-residential or mixed use, the whole property is treated as non-residential and the £150,000 zero-rate threshold applies.

13.5   SDLT: NOTIFIABLE TRANSACTIONS

The following land transactions are notifiable:

- ☐ The grant, for a chargeable consideration, of a lease for a term of seven years or more (running from the date of the grant)
- ☐ As from 12 March 2008, there is no requirement to notify HMRC of the grant of such a lease if the chargeable consideration (other than rent) is less than £40,000, and the annual rent is less than £1,000
- ☐ The grant of a lease for less than seven years (running from the date of the grant) where the chargeable consideration (either in the form of rent or a premium) would, ignoring the availability of any relief, be chargeable to tax at 1% or higher
- ☐ An acquisition of a freehold interest that is not exempt
- ☐ As from 12 March 2008, there is no requirement to notify HMRC of such an acquisition if the chargeable consideration for the acquisition is less than £40,000
- ☐ An acquisition of a leasehold interest that is not exempt where the lease was originally granted for seven years or more. An acquisition of a leasehold interest includes a surrender

☐ As from 12 March 2008, there is no requirement to notify HMRC of such an acquisition if the chargeable consideration for the acquisition is less than £40,000

☐ An acquisition of a leasehold interest that is not exempt where the lease was originally granted for less than seven years, but only if the chargeable consideration for the acquisition would, ignoring the availability of any relief, be chargeable to tax at 1% or higher. As above, an acquisition of a leasehold interest includes a surrender

☐ An acquisition of a chargeable interest other than a freehold or leasehold interest (e.g. the grant or release of an easement, the release of a restrictive covenant, or the grant of an option) where the chargeable consideration for the acquisition would, ignoring any relief, be chargeable to tax at 1% or higher.

13.6 SDLT: WHERE TAX DUE BEFORE COMPLETION

The charge to SDLT arises when the purchaser has 'substantial benefit of the contract'. In the following circumstances, this will give rise to a charge to tax before actual completion:

☐ Payment of (normally) at least 90% of the purchase price
☐ The purchaser or a connected person having the right to occupy the land, including under a licence
☐ The purchaser or a connected person having the right to receive rents
☐ Payment by the purchaser or a connected person of rent.

13.7 KEEPING RECORDS FOR SDLT PURPOSES

There is a duty to keep and preserve records to enable a complete and correct land transaction return or claim to be made and delivered. The documents which should be retained include:

☐ All materials relating to valuation and/or price
☐ All documents and information relating to apportionments for chattels
☐ Accounts records for funds received and disbursed
☐ Documents demonstrating allowable costs
☐ Calculations for assessment of SDLT.

13.8 DOCUMENTS AND INFORMATION WHICH DO NOT HAVE TO BE PRODUCED TO HMRC AS PART OF THEIR SDLT ENQUIRIES

Documents and information outside the scope of an HMRC notice (Finance Act 2003, Sched.13, Part 4) include:

☐ Personal and journalistic material
☐ Documents relating to a pending tax appeal

- ☐ Documents more than six years old at the date of the notice
- ☐ Documents subject to legal privilege
- ☐ Auditors' and tax advisers' own papers in connection with acting under a statutory appointment.

13.9 CGT LIABILITY

When taking instructions from an individual in relation to the sale of a dwelling-house, the answers to the following four questions will indicate to the solicitor whether there is likely to be a CGT liability on the property. If the client's answers to all the questions set out below match the suggested answers, there is unlikely to be a CGT liability arising out of the transaction. If any of the client's answers differ from those suggested, further enquiries should be raised with the client.

- ☐ Question: Did you move into the house immediately after you bought it?
  Answer: Yes.
- ☐ Question: Have you lived anywhere else since moving into this house?
  Answer: No.
- ☐ Question: Does the house and the garden cover more than 0.5 hectare?
  Answer: No.
- ☐ Question: Do you own another house?
  Answer: No.

13.10 VAT EXEMPTIONS

The sale of an existing building (i.e. not new) which is a dwelling or is used for a qualifying residential purpose or qualifying charitable purpose is generally exempt from VAT. However, zero-rating may apply if it:

- ☐ Has been empty for 10 years or more and has just been renovated
- ☐ Has just been converted from a non-residential building
- ☐ Is a protected building and has undergone a substantial reconstruction
- ☐ It is a first grant of a major interest (freehold or lease if over 21 years) in a new dwelling, or a building for use for 'qualifying residential purposes' or 'qualifying charitable purposes'.

The detailed conditions for zero-rating must be met.

13.11 VAT ON FREEHOLD SALES OF NEW COMMERICAL BUILDINGS: TAKING INSTRUCTIONS

Every freehold sale of a new commercial property (including civil engineering works), before it is completed and within the first three years after its completion, attracts VAT at standard rate unless a sale as a transfer of a property letting business as a going concern can be arranged.

The following should be considered when taking instructions:

☐ Will the sale be a standard-rated supply so that VAT will be chargeable (whether as a 'new' commercial building or as a result of the option to tax having been exercised)?

☐ If not, what evidence (if any) is needed to satisfy HMRC that the sale will be an exempt or zero-rated supply or a transfer of a going concern?

☐ If the sale is exempt from VAT, is the building subject to the Capital Items Scheme (was the building purchased, constructed, renovated or fitted out by the seller, or predecessor, within the last 10 years at a cost in excess of £250,000 plus VAT)?

13.12 VAT ON FREEHOLD SALES OF NEW COMMERCIAL BUILDINGS: MAKING ADDITIONAL ENQUIRIES

If the contract requires the buyer to pay VAT, he will want to be certain that VAT is chargeable and will also wish to have evidence to establish whether or not there is a mandatory charge to VAT on a subsequent sale. If the contract does not require the buyer to pay VAT he may be inclined not to raise the issue with the seller, but he should still ensure that the supply is, in fact, an exempt supply and that he has sufficient evidence to establish that a future sale by him will be exempt.

☐ Why does the seller consider that the sale is a standard-rated supply?

☐ Please provide a copy of the architect's certificate of practical completion

☐ When was the building first fully occupied?

☐ What evidence is available to verify the date when the building was first fully occupied?

☐ Please confirm that, if VAT is paid on completion, the seller will at that time deliver a VAT invoice to the buyer

☐ Has the seller previously opted for tax or does he intend to do so before completion?

☐ If the answer to the previous question is 'yes', please confirm that the exercise of the option to tax has been or will be notified to HMRC within 30 days of its being made. The buyer's solicitor should request a copy of the option to tax document and of the letter of notification to ascertain the extent of the land to which the option will apply and to check that it is valid. It should also be noted that it is HMRC's policy to acknowledge receipt of an option to tax and this can therefore be acceptable evidence

☐ If the purchase is by way of a transfer of a going concern, is the building subject to the capital items scheme? If so, please provide details of the initial deduction on subsequent adjustments, if any.

Note: if the seller agrees not to charge VAT, the contract should either specify that the price stated is inclusive of any VAT or should expressly provide that the seller has not opted to tax in respect of the property and agrees not to do so.

13.13   VAT ON LEASES

If the tenant of a lease makes exempt supplies he will be seriously disadvantaged by having to pay VAT on his rent (since he will not be able to recover some or all of that VAT). An exempt tenant in a market dominated by taxable tenants should consider taking a valuer's advice about the consequences of the VAT implications in his lease.

13.13.1   'Options to tax' checklist for landlords

Consider:

- ☐ How much irrecoverable VAT has the landlord incurred/does the landlord incur?
- ☐ The VAT status of tenants/potential tenants/purchasers
- ☐ The short- and long-term consequences of exercising an option which is only revocable in limited circumstances (generally, within six months, provided that no input tax has been recovered or output tax charged, or after 20 years with the written permission of HMRC – with effect from 1 June 2008 the option to tax will automatically be revoked if a relevant interest in the land or property has not been held within the last six years)
- ☐ The consequences of agreeing a premium rent with an exempt tenant
- ☐ The costs of any additional administration which would be incurred in collecting VAT and issuing VAT invoices.

Reminders for tenants:

- ☐ Check whether or not VAT is included in the rent
- ☐ Remember that, if the lease is silent Value Added Tax Act 1994, s.89 could apply
- ☐ If the tenant makes taxable supplies only, the main adverse consequence of paying VAT on his rent may be a cash flow disadvantage, set against which there may also be cash benefits for the tenant, e.g. the recovery of VAT on his service charge payments
- ☐ If the tenant makes exempt or mainly exempt supplies, he may be seriously disadvantaged by having to pay VAT on his rent since he will not be able to recover some or all of that VAT.

13.13.2   Purchases subject to leases

The leases to which the property is subject should be checked to discover whether the buyer will be able to charge VAT should he wish to exercise his option to tax. The following matters should also be considered:

- ☐ Does the lease expressly provide that VAT is payable in addition to rent and other payments made or consideration given by the tenant or, if not, will Value Added Tax Act 1994, s.89 apply?
- ☐ Will the landlord be able to recover from the tenant VAT on supplies received from a third party? or

☐ Is the landlord under an obligation to attempt to recover VAT from HMRC before he can look to the tenant for indemnity?

☐ Are all other sums referred to in the lease expressed to include any VAT which will be chargeable?

☐ Are the rent review provisions adequate if the landlord decides to opt to tax?

13.14 SUMMARY CHECKLIST OF APPLICATION OF VAT TO PROPERTY TRANSACTIONS

Type of dealing	Rate of tax
A. Freehold sales	
Buildings designed as dwellings built or converted and sold by developer	Zero
Communal residential buildings sold by developer	Zero
Non-business charitable buildings sold by developer	Zero
Domestic and other non-commercial buildings sold by others	Exempt
New commercial buildings	Standard
Other commercial buildings	Exempt subject to option
B. Leases	
New dwellings or dwellings converted from non-residential buildings, communal residential buildings or non-business charitable buildings if for more than 21 years where built by and granted by developer	Zero on premium or first payment of rent, exempt thereafter
Similar to above but lease for 21 years or less	Exempt
Domestic and non-commercial buildings granted by other than developer	Exempt
New commercial buildings	Exempt subject to option
Other commercial buildings	Exempt subject to option
Assignments	Exempt subject to option
Surrenders	Exempt subject to option
Reverse surrenders	Exempt subject to option
C. Listed buildings	
Approved alterations to dwellings, communal residential and non-business charitable buildings	Zero
Other work on similar buildings	Standard or 5%
Freehold sales by developer of substantially reconstructed similar buildings	Zero
Leases for more than 21 years from developer of substantially reconstructed similar buildings	Zero on premium or first payment of rent, exempt thereafter
Any works to commercial listed buildings	Standard

Sales and leases of substantially reconstructed commercial listed buildings	Exempt subject to option

D. Building land

Sales and leases	Exempt subject to option

E. Refurbished buildings

Sales and leases of residential buildings	Exempt
Sales and leases of non-residential buildings	Exempt subject to option

F. Conversions

Freehold sale by developer of conversion from non-residential building into dwelling or communal residential building	Zero
As above but grant of lease for over 21 years	Zero on premium or first payment of rent, exempt thereafter
Construction services supplied to registered housing association on conversion of non-residential building into a dwelling or communal residential building	Zero
Conversion of a property into a different number of dwellings (e.g. house into flats or vice versa) or of a dwelling into residential communal homes	5%

G. Building services

Construction of new buildings designed as dwellings (including sub-contractors' services)	Zero
Construction of communal residential and non-business charitable buildings provided an appropriate certificate is obtained from the customer, and the customer is the person using the building for qualifying purposes	Zero
Construction of new commercial buildings	Standard
Repairs and alterations	Standard
Demolition	Standard unless part of a single zero-rated construction for new build dwellings, etc.
Professional services	Standard
Renovations of dwellings which have been empty for at least three years	5%

H. Civil engineering work

New work	Standard (zero-rated for dwellings)
Repairs, maintenance and alteration of existing buildings	Standard (zero-rating may apply to alterations for listed dwellings)

I. Options

Option to undertake a transaction which itself is chargeable to VAT	
	Standard on option fee

14

Registered land

14.1 REGISTRABLE DISPOSITIONS

The Land Registration Act 2002 sets out the dispositions that must be completed by registration if they are to operate at law (s.27(1)). These are:

- ☐ A transfer
- ☐ The grant of a term of years absolute of an estate in land:
  - ☐ For a term of more than seven years from the date of the grant
  - ☐ Taking effect in possession after the end of the period of three months beginning with the date of the grant
  - ☐ Under which the right to possession is discontinuous
  - ☐ In pursuance of Part 5 Housing Act 1985 (the right to buy)
  - ☐ In circumstances where section 171A of that Act applies (disposal by landlord which leads to a person no longer being a secure tenant)
- ☐ The grant of a lease of a franchise or manor
- ☐ The express grant or reservation of an easement or other right falling within Law of Property Act 1925, s.1(2)(a), other than one which is capable of being registered under the Commons Registration Act 1965
- ☐ The express grant or a reservation of a rentcharge or right of re-entry falling within Law of Property Act 1925, s.1(2)(b) or (e)
- ☐ The grant of a legal charge
- ☐ The transfer or sub-charge of a registered charge (Land Registration Act 2002, s.27(3)).

The requirement for registration also applies to transfers by operation of law except for:

- ☐ A transfer on the death or bankruptcy of an individual proprietor
- ☐ A transfer on the dissolution of a corporate proprietor
- ☐ The creation of a legal charge which is a local land charge (Land Registration Act 2002, s.27(5)).

14.2 SITUATIONS WHEN NOTICES CANNOT BE USED

A notice is used to protect interests that will not be overreached on a disposition (e.g. restrictive covenants and equitable easements) and will therefore continue to affect the land. A notice may either be an agreed notice or a unilateral notice.

Certain interests are excluded from protection by way of notice (Land Registration Act 2002, s.33). The main excluded interests are:

- ☐ An interest under a trust of land
- ☐ A lease for a term of three years or less which is not required to be registered
- ☐ A restrictive covenant between lessor and lessee so far as it relates to the property leased.

Where an interest protected by a notice is valid, then the notice will protect the priority of that interest. The notice itself does not confer any priority.

14.3   COMPULSORY REGISTRATION

14.3.1   Disposals under Land Registration Act 2002

Registration is compulsory on specified types of transfers, leases and mortgages of a qualifying estate, which is defined as either a legal freehold estate or a legal lease with more than seven years to run. Under Land Registration Act 2002, s.4(1) they are:

- ☐ A transfer:
    - ☐ For valuable or other consideration, by way of gift or in pursuance of a court order *or*
    - ☐ By means of an assent
- ☐ The grant of a legal lease:
    - ☐ For a term of more than seven years *and*
    - ☐ For valuable or other consideration, by way of gift or in pursuance of a court order
- ☐ The grant of a legal lease to take effect in possession more than three months after it is granted
- ☐ The creation of a first legal mortgage where the mortgage is protected by the deposit of documents.

14.3.2   Certain disposals under Housing Act 1985

The following disposals under Housing Act 1985 also trigger compulsory registration:

- ☐ The transfer or grant of a legal lease of an unregistered estate where Housing Act 1985, s.171A applies (a disposal by a landlord which leads to a person no longer being a secure tenant) *or*
- ☐ The grant of a 'right to buy' lease under Housing Act 1985, Part 5.

14.4 TRANSFERS NOT SUBJECT TO COMPULSORY REGISTRATION

The compulsory registration provisions do not apply to:

☐ A transfer by operation of law, e.g. the vesting of land in personal representatives (Land Registration Act 2002, s.4(3))

☐ An assignment of a mortgage term

☐ A surrender of a lease where the term is to merge into the reversion (Land Registration Act 2002, s.4(4)).

14.5 REGISTRATION OF LEGAL ESTATES

The following legal estates and interests may be registered under their own title numbers:

☐ A freehold estate

☐ A lease for a term of which more than seven years are unexpired

☐ A lease for a discontinuous term whatever its length

☐ A franchise

☐ A profit à prendre in gross.

14.6 APPLICATIONS FOR FIRST REGISTRATION

The application for first registration must be made to the proper Land Registry office. The application must be made in Form FR1 (Land Registration Rules 2003 (SI 2003/1417), r.23). It must be accompanied by (r.24(1)):

☐ Sufficient details, by plan or otherwise, so that the land can be identified clearly on the Ordnance Survey map

☐ Where the land is leasehold, the lease, if in the control of the applicant, and a certified copy

☐ All deeds and documents relating to the title in the control of the applicant

☐ A list in duplicate in Form DL of all the documents delivered.

14.7 INVESTIGATION OF TITLE ON FIRST REGISTRATION

The registrar needs to investigate title on an application for first registration in order to decide which class of title can be allocated to the title. He therefore needs to have access to all the documents which form the evidence of title to the land. The documents should be individually listed and numbered in chronological sequence in Form DL. They should include:

☐ All the documents which formed the evidence of title supplied by the seller's solicitor

☐ All the buyer's pre-contract searches and enquiries with their replies (including any variations or further information contained in relevant correspondence)

- ☐ The contract
- ☐ Requisitions on title with their replies
- ☐ All pre-completion search certificates
- ☐ The purchase deed
- ☐ The seller's mortgage, duly receipted
- ☐ The buyer's mortgage
- ☐ Where the transaction is leasehold, the original lease and a certified copy
- ☐ A land transaction return certificate where required.

14.8   TRANSFER OF WHOLE

The application for registration of a transfer of the whole of the seller's title (whether freehold or leasehold) should be lodged at the proper office within the 30 business-day priority period conferred by the applicant's pre-completion official search certificate. The period of protection under the search cannot be extended (although a second search conferring a separate priority period can be made). The application should be accompanied by:

- ☐ The transfer in Form TR1 (or TR2 if the transfer is under a chargee's power of sale)
- ☐ The appropriate fee under the current Land Registration Fee Order
- ☐ In appropriate circumstances:
    - ☐ A completed Form DS1 (or reference in Form AP1 to the use of the END, e-DS1 or ED systems) in respect of the seller's mortgage
    - ☐ Where the seller was the personal representative of a sole deceased proprietor, an office copy or certified copy of the grant of representation (Land Registration Rules 2003, rr.163(2) and 214)
    - ☐ Where the transfer has been executed under a power of attorney, the original or a duly certified copy of the power, or a certificate by a conveyancer in Form 1 (Land Registration Rules 2003, r.61(1) and Sched. 3); and where the transfer is not made within one year of the power, appropriate evidence of non-revocation by statutory declaration or in Form 2 (Land Registration Rules 2003, r.62 and Sched. 3)
    - ☐ A land transaction return certificate or a submission receipt when one is required.

PART B
Standard letters

Sale

15.1 LETTER TO THE CLIENT REQUESTING CONFIRMATION OF INSTRUCTIONS

[John Smith
27 Acacia Avenue
Southtown
SX9 4BQ]
[*date*]
Our ref: [JB/rh/3200.1]
Dear [*name*]
Re: Sale of [*property*]

I have today received notification from [*insert name of estate agent*] of your proposed sale of the above property to [*insert name of buyer*] at the price of [*insert price*].

Can you please telephone me to confirm instructions.

Yours sincerely,

15.2 LETTER TO THE CLIENT TO CONFIRM INSTRUCTIONS AND ENCLOSE FORMS

I have today received notification from [*insert name of estate agent*] of your proposed sale of the above property to [*insert name of buyer*] at the price of [*insert price*].

I confirm having written to [*insert name of lender*] to obtain the Title Deeds so that I can prepare and submit a Contract to the Buyer's Solicitors. In addition to the Contract, further information is required and I therefore enclose a Fixtures, Fittings and Contents Form together with a Property Information Form [and a Leasehold Information Form] for completion and return to me as soon as possible in the stamped addressed envelope enclosed. I also enclose a Sale Instruction Form for completion and return.

I confirm that the legal costs will amount to £ [   ], calculated as follows:

Legal Fees	£ [ ]
VAT	£ [ ]
Official Copies	£ [ ]
TOTAL	£ [ ]

Once I have all documentation to hand, I will be able to ascertain whether or not the property is leasehold. If the property is leasehold, there may be an additional disbursement to be paid to the freeholder for Notice of Discharge of Mortgage (if any) and once I know who the freeholder is, I can write to them to obtain a note of their fee.

Yours sincerely,

15.3   CLIENT CARE LETTERS

Note: There follows a basic client care letter and draft paragraphs. The draft paragraphs are adapted from the Law Society's Practice Note Client Care Letters – 19 May 2009. The Practice Note is available from **www.lawsociety.org.uk** where it is updated from time to time.

15.3.1   Basic client care letter

Following our discussion today, I am writing to you, as promised, to confirm the various matters which we talked about and also to give you some additional information.

Thank you for your instructions to act on your behalf in your sale of the property at [insert address] which is a leasehold/freehold property. [Please telephone me to let me know the name of your current lender and your mortgage account number so that I can obtain the Deeds.]

I advised you that [confirm any advice given with particular reference to any time limits or steps to be taken by the client].

Our approximate charges for the work are as follows:

Costs £ [   ] plus VAT

In addition, the following disbursements will be payable:

Official Copies   £ [   ]

If you have any queries about our charges please contact me to discuss.

I shall be dealing with the work personally except for [specify areas to be delegated] which will be dealt with by [insert name] who is a trainee solicitor with this firm. I am a solicitor but not a partner. The partner with overall responsibility for this department is [insert name]. If you are unhappy about the work or any aspect of our work, then please contact me in the first instance. If you are unwilling to do this or feel that the matter is too serious, then you should contact [insert name of partner].

We pride ourselves on giving our clients the very highest level of service but if there is anything you are not happy about, the firm would rather you let us know straight away.

If there is any aspect of our service you are unhappy with, I will either meet with you to discuss the difficulties or your complaint or write to you offering an explanation and try to resolve the difficulty. If you do make a complaint, I will write to you with details of our client's complaint procedure.

Please note that if this matter does not proceed to completion, we reserve the right to charge an abortive charge on your transaction of not more than £ [   ].

Please sign and return to me in the enclosed stamped addressed envelope one copy of this letter as an acceptance of our terms as set out in this letter.

Yours sincerely

15.3.2   Complaints

[*Insert practice name*] is committed to high quality legal advice and client care. If you are unhappy about any aspect of the service you have received, please contact [*insert name*] on [*insert phone number and e-mail*] or by post to our [*insert place*] office.

15.3.3   Service standards

- We will update you [by telephone/in writing] with progress on your matter [*insert as appropriate* – regularly/fortnightly/monthly/following agreed events] – the Law Society believes this should occur at least every six weeks, unless agreed to the contrary.
- We will communicate with you in plain language.
- We will explain to you [by telephone/in writing] the legal work required as your matter progresses.
- We will update you on the cost of your matter [*insert as appropriate* – regularly/ fortnightly/monthly/following agreed events] – the Law Society believes this should occur at least every six months.
- We will update you on whether the likely outcomes still justify the likely costs and risks associated with your matter whenever there is a material change in circumstances.
- We will update you on the likely timescales for each stage of this matter and any important changes in those estimates.
- We will continue to review whether there are alternative methods by which your matter can be funded.

15.3.4   Equality and diversity

[*Insert practice name*] is committed to promoting equality and diversity in all of its dealings with clients, third parties and employees. Please contact us if you would like a copy of our equality and diversity policy.

15.3.5   Data protection

We use the information you provide primarily for the provision of legal services to you and for related purposes including:

- updating and enhancing client records
- analysis to help us manage our practice
- statutory returns
- legal and regulatory compliance.

Our use of that information is subject to your instructions, the Data Protection Act 1998 and our duty of confidentiality. Please note that our work for you may require us to give information to third parties such as expert witnesses and other professional advisers. You have a right of access under data protection legislation to the personal data that we hold about you.

We may from time to time send you information which we think might be of interest to you. If you do not wish to receive that information, please notify our office in writing.

15.3.6   Storage of documents

After completing the work, we will be entitled to keep all your papers and documents while there is still money owed to us for fees and expenses.

We will keep our file of your papers for up to [x] years, except those papers that you ask to be returned to you. We keep files on the understanding that we can destroy them [x] years after the date of the final bill. We will not destroy documents you ask us to deposit in safe custody.

If we take papers or documents out of storage in relation to continuing or new instructions to act for you, we will not normally charge for such retrieval. However, we may charge you both for:

- time spent producing stored papers that are requested
- reading correspondence or other work necessary to comply with your instructions in relation to the retrieved papers.

15.3.7   Outsourcing

Sometimes we ask other companies or people to do [insert as appropriate – typing/photocopying/other work] on our files to ensure this is done promptly. We will always seek a confidentiality agreement with these outsourced providers. If you do not want your file to be outsourced, please tell us as soon as possible.

15.3.8   Vetting of files and confidentiality

External firms or organisations may conduct audit or quality checks on our practice. These external firms or organisations are required to maintain confidentiality in relation to your files.

15.3.9   Limiting liability

Our liability to you for a breach of your instructions shall be limited to £ [   ], unless we expressly state a higher amount in the letter accompanying these terms of business. We will not be liable for any consequential, special, indirect or exemplary damages, costs or losses or any damages, costs or losses attributable to lost profits or opportunities.

We can only limit our liability to the extent the law allows. In particular, we cannot limit our liability for death or personal injury caused by our negligence.

Please ask if you would like us to explain any of the terms above.

15.3.10   Draft paragraphs relating to applicable law

Any dispute or legal issue arising from our terms of business will be determined by the law of England and Wales, and considered exclusively by the English and Welsh courts.

15.3.11   Terminating the retainer

You may end your instructions to us in writing at any time, but we can keep all your papers and documents while there is still money owed to us for fees and expenses.

We may decide to stop acting for you only with good reason, e.g. if you do not pay an interim bill or there is a conflict of interest. We must give you reasonable notice that we will stop acting for you.

If you or we decide that we should stop acting for you, you will pay our charges up until that point. These are calculated on [an hourly basis plus expenses/by proportion of the agreed fee] as set out in these terms and conditions.

15.3.12   Money laundering

The law requires solicitors to get satisfactory evidence of the identity of their clients and sometimes people related to them. This is because solicitors who deal with money and property on behalf of their client can be used by criminals wanting to launder money.

To comply with the law, we need to get evidence of your identity as soon as possible. Our practice is to [insert your standard practice]. The fee for these searches is £ [   ] and will appear on your bill under expenses.

If you cannot provide us with the specific identification requested, please contact us as soon as possible to discuss other ways to verify your identity.

We are professionally and legally obliged to keep your affairs confidential. However, solicitors may be required by statute to make a disclosure to the Serious Organised Crime Agency where they know or suspect that a transaction may involve money laundering or terrorist financing. If we make a disclosure in relation to your matter, we may not be able to tell you that a disclosure has been made. We may have to stop working on your matter for a period of time and may not be able to tell you why.

15.3.13   Mortgage fraud

We are also acting for your proposed lender [insert name of bank/building society] in this transaction. We have a duty to fully reveal to your lender all relevant facts about the purchase and mortgage. This includes:

- any differences between your mortgage application and information we receive during the transaction
- any cash back payments or discount schemes that a seller is giving you.

15.3.14   Introductions and referrals

We have a financial relationship with [*insert firm name*] regarding your case/transaction. As a result of this relationship we:

- (Option A) Pay [*insert practice name*] £[   ] for them to refer your case/transaction to us,
- (Option B) Receive £[   ] from [*insert practice name*] to provide you with [*service(s)*]. You will be required to pay £[   ] to [*insert practice name*] for these services.

Despite this financial relationship with [*insert practice name*], we will provide you with independent advice and you are able to raise questions with us about any aspect of your case/transaction.

Any information you provide to us during your case/transaction will not be shared with [*insert practice name*] unless you agree. However, because we are acting both for you and [*insert practice name*] in your case/transaction, we may have to stop acting for both of you if there is a conflict of interest.

15.3.15   Payment of interest

Any money received on your behalf will be held in our client account. Interest will be calculated and paid to you at the rate set by [*insert name of bank and relevant accounts*]. That, of course, may change. The period for which interest will be paid normally runs from the date(s) when funds are received by us until the date(s) on the cheque(s) issued to you. The payment of interest is subject to certain minimum amounts and periods of time set out in the Solicitors' Accounts Rules 1998.

15.3.16   Distance selling

We have not met with you, so the Consumer Protection (Distance Selling) Regulations 2000 apply to this file. This means you have the right to cancel your instructions to us within seven working days of receiving this letter. You can cancel your instructions by contacting us by post or by fax to this office.

Once we have started work on your file, you may be charged if you then cancel your instructions. If you would like us to commence work on your file within the next seven working days, please:

- sign these terms and conditions;
- tick the box marked 'commence work now';
- return it to this office by post or fax.

15.3.17   Financial arrangements with clients

Our practice's policy is [not to accept cash from clients/to only accept cash up to £ [ ]].

If you try to avoid this policy by depositing cash directly with our bank, we may decide to charge you for any additional checks we decide are necessary to prove the source of the funds.

Where we have to pay money to you, it will be paid by cheque or bank transfer. It will not be paid in cash or to a third party.

15.3.18   Providing exempt financial services

We are not authorised by the Financial Services Authority. If, while we are acting for you, you need advice on investments, we may have to refer you to someone who is authorised to provide the necessary advice.

However, we may provide certain limited investment advice services where these are closely linked to the legal work we are doing for you. This is because we are members of the Law Society of England and Wales, which is a designated professional body for the purposes of the Financial Services and Markets Act 2000.

The Solicitors Regulation Authority is the independent regulatory arm of the Law Society. The Legal Complaints Service is the independent complaints-handling arm of the Law Society. If you are unhappy with any investment advice you receive from us, you should raise your concerns with either of those bodies.

15.3.19   Providing exempt insurance mediation

We are not authorised by the Financial Services Authority. However, we are included on the register maintained by the Financial Services Authority so that we may carry on insurance mediation activity, which is broadly the advising on, selling and administration of insurance contracts. This part of our business, including arrangements for complaints or redress if something goes wrong, is regulated by the Solicitors Regulation Authority. The register can be accessed via the Financial Services website at **www.fsa.gov.uk/register**.

The Law Society of England and Wales is a designated professional body for the purposes of the Financial Services and Markets Act 2000. The Solicitors Regulation Authority is the independent regulatory arm of the Law Society. The Legal Complaints Service is the independent complaints-handling arm of the Law Society. If you are unhappy with any insurance advice you receive from us, you should raise your concerns with either of those bodies.

15.4   LETTER TO THE CLIENT REQUESTING THE RETURN OF FORMS

I refer to my letter to you of the [*insert date*]. Please can you return the completed forms as soon as possible so that this matter can be progressed.

15.5   LETTER TO THE CLIENT ACKNOWLEDGING FORMS

Thank you for returning the forms enclosed with my letter of the [*insert date*].

I have now prepared and submitted draft Contract documentation to the Buyer's Solicitors. I will keep you advised of developments.

15.6   LETTER TO ESTATE AGENT REQUESTING PARTICULARS

We have been instructed by [*name of client*] in connection with the sale of the above property. We understand you are acting as Agents and that a sale has been agreed. Please send us copies of the Memorandum and Particulars of Sale and Home Information Pack.

15.7   LETTER TO ESTATE AGENT ACKNOWLEDGING PARTICULARS

Thank you for your letter of the [*insert date*], the contents of which are noted. We will advise you as soon as contracts have been exchanged.

15.8   LETTER TO BUYER'S SOLICITOR CONFIRMING INSTRUCTIONS

We act on behalf of the Seller , [*insert name(s)*] and understand you are instructed by the Buyer [*insert name(s)*] who have agreed, subject to Contract, to purchase the above property at the price of £ [   ]. We understand that your client has already received a Home Information Pack from the estate agents.

We are at present awaiting our client's Title Deeds and will let you have a draft Contract for approval as soon as possible together with Protocol documentation. [You must, however, effect your own Searches. The local authority is [*insert council*] District Council and the correct address of the property for search purposes is [*insert address*].]

15.9   LETTER TO LENDER REQUESTING TITLE DEEDS

Note: the letter should be referenced with the seller's Roll number, name and the address of the property.

We have been instructed by the above named to act in the sale of the above property which we understand is at present in Mortgage to yourselves. Please send us the Title Deeds on the usual undertaking so that this matter may proceed.

15.10   LETTER TO LENDER TO ACKNOWLEDGE TITLE DEEDS

We acknowledge receipt of the Title Deeds and accordingly enclose your form signed as requested.

15.11   LETTER TO SELLER'S SOLICITOR ENCLOSING CONTRACT DOCUMENTATION

We refer to previous correspondence and now enclose the following:

1.   Draft Contract in duplicate for approval
2.   Official Copies
3.   Answers to pre-contract enquiries.

We await hearing from you with your approval of the terms of the contract.

15.12   LETTER TO CLIENT ENCLOSING CONTRACT FOR SIGNATURE

I now enclose the Contract for Sale in this matter for your signature. Can you please sign this where indicated with an 'X' and then return it to me in the stamped addressed envelope enclosed. Please do not date the document. Can you also please let me have your suggestions for a completion date.

15.13   LETTER TO CLIENT REQUESTING APPOINTMENT TO SIGN CONTRACT

The Contract in this matter is now ready for signature. Can you please telephone to arrange a mutually convenient appointment so that we can explain the Contract to you and you can sign it.

15.14   LETTER TO CLIENT REQUESTING THE RETURN OF THE SIGNED CONTRACT

I refer to my letter of the [*insert date*] enclosing the Contract. Please can you return the signed Contract as soon as possible so that we can proceed to exchange of contracts.

15.15   LETTER TO BUYER'S SOLICITOR REQUESTING APPROVED CONTRACT

We refer to previous correspondence and wonder whether you are yet in a position to return to us an approved Contract.

15.16   LETTER TO BUYER'S SOLICITOR ADVISING OF READINESS TO EXCHANGE

We refer to previous correspondence. We now have a signed Contract on our file ready to exchange. May we please hear from you as soon as possible.

15.17   LETTER TO BUYER'S SOLICITOR CONFIRMING EXCHANGE

Further to our telephone conversation of [*date*] when exchange of Contracts was effected under Law Society Formula [*insert as appropriate*], at [*insert as appropriate*] for completion on the [*completion date*] we enclose our Client's signed Contract.

We look forward to receiving your Client's signed part of the Contract together with your cheque in respect of the deposit.

We also look forward to receiving the draft Transfer for approval together with your Requisitions on Title.

15.18   LETTER TO BUYER'S SOLICITOR REQUESTING CONTRACT AND DEPOSIT

We refer to exchange of Contracts in this matter, effected on the [*date*] and shall be pleased to receive your Client's signed part of the Contract together with the deposit as soon as possible.

We also look forward to receiving the draft Transfer for approval together with your Requisitions on Title.

15.19   LETTER TO BUYER'S SOLICITOR ACKNOWLEDGING TRANSFER AND REPLYING TO REQUISITIONS

Thank you for your letter of the [*date*]. We enclose the draft Transfer approved together with replies to your Requisitions on Title. Thank you for the copies provided for our use.

We await the engrossed Transfer signed by your client for signature by our client in readiness for completion.

15.20   LETTER TO CLIENT CONFIRMING EXCHANGE

I am writing to confirm that Contracts for the sale of your property have today been exchanged and completion will take place on the [*completion date*] as arranged. If you have not already done so, you may now wish to make final arrangements for moving on the completion date and to contact the utilities suppliers so that the meters can be read on that day.

15.21   LETTER TO CLIENT ENCLOSING TRANSFER FOR SIGNATURE

I enclose the Transfer deed in this matter which requires your signature. Can you please sign the document where indicated between the pencil crosses. Your signature should be witnessed by an adult person who should first of all sign their name followed by their printed name, address and occupation, again where indicated. Please do not date the document. Can you please do this immediately and return the document to me in the stamped addressed envelope enclosed.

15.22   LETTER TO CLIENT REQUESTING AN APPOINTMENT TO SIGN THE TRANSFER

The Deed of Transfer in this matter is now ready for your signature. Can you please telephone me to arrange a convenient appointment to come in and sign the document.

15.23   LETTER TO CLIENT REQUESTING THE RETURN OF THE SIGNED TRANSFER

I refer to my letter of the [date] enclosing the Transfer Deed. Please could you return the document to us as soon as possible as the completion date is now approaching.

15.24   LETTER TO ESTATE AGENT REQUESTING THEIR ACCOUNT

Completion of this matter is being arranged for the [completion date]. May we please have your account as soon as possible so that we may obtain our client's approval to the same.

15.25   LETTER TO THE LENDER REQUESTING A REDEMPTION STATEMENT

Completion of the sale of the above property has been arranged for the [completion date]. May we please have a redemption statement as at that date including a daily adjustment rate in case completion is delayed.

15.26   LETTER TO CLIENT ADVISING OF COMPLETION

I am writing to confirm that the sale of your property was completed today as arranged.

I now enclose our receipted Bill of Charges and Completion Statement for your information. As you will see from the Completion Statement, after taking all matters into consideration, there is a final balance due to you of £ [   ]. Our cheque for that sum is enclosed and I shall be obliged if you would acknowledge safe receipt [*or* This sum has been paid into your account at [*bank or building society*] as instructed by you].

I would like to take this opportunity of thanking you for your kind instructions and if I can be of any assistance to you in the future please do not hesitate to contact me.

15.27   LETTER TO THE LENDER REDEEMING THE MORTGAGE

We enclose Form DS1 for sealing together with our cheque in the sum of £ [   ] being the amount required to redeem the above account.

We look forward to receiving sealed Form DS1 as soon as possible.

15.28   LETTER TO THE ESTATE AGENT SETTLING THEIR ACCOUNT

We enclose your account in this matter together with our cheque for £ [   ] in settlement. Can you please receipt and return the account to ourselves in due course.

15.29   LETTER TO THE BUYER'S SOLICITOR FOLLOWING COMPLETION

We acknowledge receiving from you the balance of purchase monies. We now enclose:

1.   Transfer to your client dated [*date*]
2.   Miscellaneous papers as per the attached schedule (in duplicate).

In consideration of your today completing the purchase of [*property*] we hereby undertake forthwith to pay over to [*name of lender*] the money required to redeem the mortgage/legal charge dated [*date*] and to forward the [receipted mortgage/ legal charge/sealed Form DS1] to you as soon as it is received by us from the Building Society.

Please acknowledge safe receipt of the enclosures and sign and return to us one copy of the schedule of deeds.

15.30 SUGGESTED DRAFT UNDERTAKING FOR USE BY SOLICITORS ON THE REDEMPTION OF A BUILDING SOCIETY MORTGAGE USING EDS

In consideration of your today completing the purchase of [*property*], we hereby undertake forthwith to pay over to [*name of building society*] the money required to discharge the mortgage/legal charge dated [*date*] and either to forward to you a copy of the lender's letter confirming successful redemption of their charge and lodgement of an electronic discharge at the Land Registry as soon as we receive it from the Lender or, if Form END1 is required, to forward to you a copy of the notice of confirmation from the lender that an electronic notification of discharge of the charge has been sent to the Land Registry as soon as we receive it from the lender.

15.31 ALTERNATIVE DRAFT UNDERTAKING FOR USE BY SOLICITORS ON THE REDEMPTION OF MORTGAGE USING EDS

In consideration of your today completing the purchase of [*property*], we hereby undertake forthwith to pay over to [*name of building society or bank*] the money required to discharge the mortgage/legal charge dated [*date*] and either to forward a copy of the lender's letter confirming successful redemption of their charge and lodgement of an electronic discharge at the Land Registry as soon as we receive it from the Lender or, if Form DS1 is required, to forward it to the lender for execution as soon as requested by them and to forward the executed form to you as soon as we receive it from the lender.

15.32 LETTER TO LIFE ASSURANCE COMPANY ENCLOSING NOTICE OF REASSIGNMENT OF LIFE POLICY

We enclose Notice of Reassignment in duplicate. Please receipt and return the copy Notice to us as soon as possible.

15.33 LETTER TO THE FREEHOLDER GIVING NOTICE OF DISCHARGE

We enclose Notice of Discharge of Mortgage in duplicate for registration together with our cheque in the sum of £ [   ] in respect of the fee. Please receipt and return one copy of the Notice to us as soon as possible.

15.34   NOTICE TO COMPLETE

As Solicitors for the Seller, we:

1. Refer to the Contract dated [*date*] by which your Client, [*name of buyer*], agreed to buy from our Client, [*name of seller*], the property known as [*address of property*];
2. State that the sale of the property was not completed on the date fixed in the Contract and that our Client is ready, able and willing to fulfil their own outstanding obligations under the Contract;
3. Give you, on behalf of your Client, notice under condition 6.8 of the Standard Conditions of Sale, 4th Edition, to which the Contract was made subject to requiring completion of the Contract in conformity with that condition; and
4. Draw attention to the consequences set out in condition 7.5 of the Standard Conditions of Sale, 4th Edition, which will attend your Client's failure to complete the Contract within 10 working days after service of this notice (exclusive of the day of service).

15.35   LETTER TO THE LENDER REQUESTING SEALED DISCHARGE

We refer to our letter of the [*date*] and shall be pleased to receive sealed Form DS1 as soon as possible.

15.36   LETTER TO BUYER'S SOLICITOR ENCLOSING SEALED DISCHARGE

Further to our undertaking dated [*date*], we now enclose sealed Form DS1. Please acknowledge receipt and confirm our undertaking is now discharged.

15.37   LETTER TO BUYER'S SOLICITOR ENCLOSING RECEIPTED NOTICE FROM THE FREEHOLDER

We now enclose Notice of Discharge registered with the Freeholders. Please acknowledge receipt.

15.38 UNDERTAKING BY SOLICITOR: DEEDS HANDED TO SOLICITOR RE SALE OR MORTGAGE OF PROPERTY, OR PART OF IT, AND TO ACCOUNT TO BANK FOR NET PROCEEDS

[*date*]

To [*insert name*] Bank plc

I/We hereby acknowledge to have received from you the title deeds and/or documents together with a charge to the Bank [*delete if no charge form has been taken*] relating to [*insert name*] in accordance with the schedule hereto for the purpose of the sale/mortgage of this property.

I/We undertake to hold them on your behalf and to return them to you on demand in the same condition in which they now are, pending completion of such transaction. If the transaction is completed I/we undertake:

(a) to pay to you the amount of the purchase/mortgage money, not being less than £ [   ] gross subject only to the deduction therefrom of the deposit (if held by the estate agent(s)), the estate agents' commission and the legal costs and disbursements relating to the transaction, and

(b) if the title deeds and/or documents also relate to other property in addition to that referred to above, to return same to you suitably endorsed or noted.

[*Signature*]

Note: if there are likely to be any deductions from the purchase price other than those shown above, these must be specifically mentioned.

16

Purchase

16.1 LETTER TO THE CLIENT REQUESTING CONFIRMATION OF INSTRUCTIONS

I have today received notification from [*estate agent*] of your proposed purchase of the above property from [*seller*] at the price of £ [   ].

Can you please telephone me to confirm your instructions?

16.2 LETTER TO THE CLIENT TO CONFIRM INSTRUCTIONS AND ENCLOSE FORMS

I have today received notification from [*estate agent*] of your proposed purchase of the above property from [*seller*] at the price of £ [   ].

I have written to the Seller's Solicitors requesting a draft Contract and documentation and when that is to hand I will contact you. Please let me know if you have received a Home Information Pack from the estate agents and, if so, let me have a copy of it.

I now need to send a Local Search Application to [*local authority*] which will cost approximately £ [   ]. Would you please therefore let me have your cheque in the sum of £ [   ] (payable to [*name*]) as soon as possible so that the Search can be sent off. Can you also please complete and return the enclosed Purchase Instruction Sheet in the stamped addressed envelope enclosed.

I confirm that the legal costs will amount to £ [   ] calculated as follows:

Legal Fees	£ [ ]
VAT	£ [ ]
Local Search Fee	£ [ ]
Mining Search Fee	£ [ ]
Environmental Search (optional)	£ [ ]
Bank Charges to transfer funds	£ [ ]
Bankruptcy Search Fee	£ [ ]
Land Registry Search Fee	£ [ ]
Land Registry Fee to register title	£ [ ]
Stamp Duty Land Tax	£ [ ]
TOTAL	£ [ ]

Once I have the draft documentation from the Seller's Solicitors, I will be able to ascertain whether or not the property is Leasehold. If the property is Leasehold, there may be an additional disbursement to be paid to the Freeholder for Notice of Transfer and Mortgage and once I know who the Freeholder is, I can write to them to obtain a note of their fee.

16.3 CLIENT CARE LETTER

Following our discussion today, I am writing to you, as promised, to confirm the various matters which we talked about and also to give you some additional information.

Thank you for your instructions to act on your behalf in your purchase of the property at [address] which is a leasehold/freehold property.

I advised that [confirm any advice given with particular reference to any time limits or steps to be taken by the client].

Our approximate charges for the work are as follows:

Costs £ [   ] plus VAT

In addition, the following are the disbursements payable and payments to others in the matter:

Local Search Fee	£ [ ]
Drainage Search Fees	£ [ ]
Environmental Search (optional)	£ [ ]
Mining Search Fee	£ [ ]
Bank Charges to transfer funds	£ [ ]
Bankruptcy Search Fee	£ [ ]
Land Registry Search Fee	£ [ ]
Land Registry Fee to register title	£ [ ]
Stamp Duty Land Tax	£ [ ]

I hope this letter adequately sets out our charges and disbursements but if you have any queries please contact me to discuss.

I shall be dealing with the work personally except for [specify areas to be delegated] which will be dealt with by [name] who is a trainee solicitor with this firm. I am a solicitor but not a partner. The partner with overall responsibility for this department is [name]. If you are unhappy about our work, then please contact me in the first instance. If you are unwilling to do this or feel that the matter is too serious, then you should contact [name of partner].

We pride ourselves on giving our clients the very highest level of service but if there is anything you are not happy about, we would rather you let us know straight away.

If there is any aspect of our service you are unhappy with, I will either meet with you to discuss the difficulties or your complaint or write to you offering an explanation and try to resolve the difficulty. If you do make a complaint, I will write to you with details of our client's complaint procedure.

I also confirm that, if your purchase does not proceed to completion, we reserve the right to charge an abortive charge on your transaction of not more than £ [   ].

Please sign and return to me in the enclosed stamped addressed envelope one copy of this letter as an acceptance of our terms as set out in this letter.

Yours sincerely

[Note: See **15.3** for a selection of draft paragraphs relating to money laundering which can be used in a client care letter.]

16.4   DRAFT PARAGRAPHS RELATING TO ENVIRONMENTAL SEARCH FOR CLIENT CARE LETTER OR TERMS OF ENGAGEMENT

Option 1: Policy of the practice

For your protection, and the protection of your lender, it is our policy to undertake an environmental search. This examines whether the property is situated on or near land that might be contaminated by, for example, past industrial processes or waste disposal. The purpose of this search is to ensure that any current and potential contamination risks are identified prior to your purchase because you could be responsible for the costs for cleaning up the site in the future. It will also identify any other environmental risks that could spoil the use or enjoyment of your new property such as whether the property lies in a flood plain. The cost of an environmental report is £ [   ] (plus VAT).

We can also offer a search informing you of planning applications and land use issues which could potentially affect the value of your property in the future.

To guard against risks identified or unknown when the search is undertaken, insurance can be obtained which provides cover toward the cost of clearing the site from contamination. This can be used when the site is subject to a remediation order by the local authority, or to prevent it from becoming the subject of an order.

Option 2: Recommendation

For your protection, and the protection of your lender, we recommend that we undertake an environmental search on your behalf. This examines whether the property is situated on or near land that might be contaminated by, for example, past industrial processes or waste disposal. The purpose of this search is to ensure that any current and potential contamination risks are identified prior to your purchase because you could be responsible for costs for cleaning up the site in the future. It will also identify any other environmental risks that could spoil the use or enjoyment of your new property such as whether the property lies in a flood plain. The cost of an environmental report is £ [   ] (plus VAT).

We can also offer a search informing you of planning applications and land use issues which could potentially affect the value of your property in the future.

We will undertake this search as a matter of course, unless you do not require us to do so and specifically instruct us to the contrary. If you do not wish us to undertake this search, please would you confirm this in writing by return and bear in mind that I will not then be in a position to advise you about these issues in this transaction.

To guard against unknown risks at the time of the search, or risks identified within the report, insurance can be purchased at the same time of ordering the search. This will cover you for the costs of clearing contamination if your site is subject to a remediation order by the local authority, or to prevent it becoming the subject of an order.

16.5 LETTER TO CLIENT REQUESTING SEARCH FEES

I refer to my letter of the [date] and shall be pleased to receive your cheque in respect of the Search fees so that this matter can be progressed.

16.6 LETTER TO CLIENT ACKNOWLEDGING RECEIPT OF SEARCH FEES

Thank you for returning the form enclosed with my letter of the [date] together with your cheque in respect of the Search fees. I have now sent a search application to [local authority].

I will keep you advised as to developments.

16.7 LETTER TO THE ESTATE AGENTS REQUESTING PARTICULARS

We have been instructed by [name of buyer] in connection with the purchase of the above property. We understand you are acting as Agents and that a sale to our Client has been agreed. Please provide us with copies of the Memorandum and Particulars of Sale and a copy of the Home Information Pack.

16.8 LETTER TO ESTATE AGENTS ACKNOWLEDGING PARTICULARS

We thank you for your letter of the [date] enclosing particulars of the above property. We will keep you advised of the progress of this matter.

16.9   LETTER TO SELLER'S SOLICITOR CONFIRMING INSTRUCTIONS AND REQUESTING DRAFT CONTRACT

We act on behalf of the Buyer, [*insert name(s)*] and understand you are instructed by the Seller, [*insert name(s)*] who has agreed, subject to Contract, to sell the above property to our Client at the price of £ [   ].

We look forward to receiving the draft Contract for approval as soon as possible.

Can you please advise us by return whether or not you intend to adopt the Law Society Protocol in this matter.

16.10   LETTER TO SELLER'S SOLICITOR WITH FURTHER REQUEST FOR THE DRAFT CONTRACT FOR APPROVAL

We refer to previous correspondence.

We now have our Client's Mortgage Offer and satisfactory result of Local Search. May we please hear from you with the draft Contract documentation as quickly as possible.

Can you please advise us by return whether or not you intend to adopt the Law Society Protocol in this matter.

16.11   LETTER TO LENDER IF LENDER'S INSTRUCTIONS APPEAR TO GO BEYOND THE LIMITATIONS OF RULE 3.19

Thank you for your instructions of [*date*] related to this matter, in accordance with which we shall be pleased to act.

As you will be aware, as solicitors we are bound by the requirements of the Solicitors' Code of Conduct 2007, rule 3.19 which limits the duties which we can undertake to a lender in cases (such as this one) where we are also acting for the borrower.

Although you have certified that your mortgage instructions are subject to the limitations contained in rule 3.19, we are concerned that your instructions may fall outside the terms of the rule in certain respects which we mention in this letter.

We draw to your attention that, since this is a residential property, the certificate of title will be in the form set out in the annex to rule 3.

You will understand that we are professionally bound by the requirements of this rule and are unable to depart from the same. Accordingly, we respectfully point out that the instructions referred to below appear to us to conflict with rule 3. The contractual effect of your certificate is to exclude any obligation (even if it is specifically stated in your instructions) which goes beyond the limitations of the rule. The certificate of title will be accordingly given subject to such exclusion.

List of offending conditions:
[*Offending conditions*]

16.12   LETTER TO SELLER'S SOLICITOR ACKNOWLEDGING RECEIPT OF THE DRAFT CONTRACT

Thank you for your letter of the [*date*] together with enclosures on which we are taking our client's instructions.

16.13   REPORT TO CLIENT (FREEHOLD)

Of the property known as
[15 High Hill, Harkley, Herts]
prepared for [Mr and Mrs Harvey Hart]

1.   The Property

The Property is known as [15 High Hill, Harkley, Herts HH1 2ZZ]. A copy of the Land Registry entries and title plan is attached [*not produced in this book*] showing the extent of the property edged in red.

Land Registry title plans are to a small scale and are not intended to show the precise location of each boundary; these should be checked on site and any significant discrepancies referred to us so that we can seek clarification from the sellers.

2.   Title

The Property is freehold. The title number is [HH123456]. It is registered at the Land Registry with 'absolute' title, which means that ownership is guaranteed by the Registry. You should inspect the property to ensure that it is only occupied by the seller and his immediate family and let us know if this is not the case. The property is being sold to you with full vacant possession on completion.

3.   Rights passing with the Property

The Property has the benefit of a right of way over the alleyway at the rear of the Property, marked in brown on the Land Registry plan, leading to the road known as Hall Hollow. This right is on foot only, so there is no right to drive vehicles (or ride bicycles or horses) along it. The deeds do not make provision for any person to be responsible for maintaining or clearing the alleyway but do provide for the owner of the Property to pay a fair contribution towards any expenditure on such matters. The sellers state that they are not aware of anyone carrying out such works and have not been asked to pay anything in this regard. If the alleyway needs maintaining so that you can walk along it, as a matter of general law the right of way would give you the right to do necessary maintenance, but wholly at your own cost.

4.   Rights over the Property

The owner of the property known as 13 High Hill has a right of way on foot across the south-west corner of the rear garden of the Property, to enable him to pass between the end of his garden and the alleyway. The route is marked in blue on the Land Registry plan. This right was apparently granted because the alleyway stops level with the west boundary of the Property and does not run behind the garden of number 13. The sellers state that the neighbour has never exercised this right during their eight years of ownership of the Property; however, this does not mean that the right has legally lapsed.

5.   Covenants

A number of restrictive covenants were imposed on the owner of the Property when the plot was sold to the original house builder in 1898. It appears that similar covenants were imposed on all the plots in the street, and these covenants may still be enforceable by one house owner against another; if you purchase the Property, you may be obliged to observe them, and you may be entitled to require the neighbouring owners to observe them. The following is a summary of those that may still be relevant:

(1) not to park any caravan or similar vehicle on the Property;
(2) not to erect more than one single house on the Property, apart from a greenhouse or other usual outbuilding;
(3) not to use any house for business use but only as a private dwelling;
(4) not to cause nuisance or annoyance to neighbours.

Even if these covenants are not strictly enforceable in law, planning restrictions imposed by the local authority may, in practice, have a similar effect.

A positive covenant was also imposed in 1898, requiring the owner of the Property to maintain the fence on the east boundary of the Property. We have marked this fence with the letter 'T' on the attached copy of the Land Registry plan. Whilst it is unlikely that anyone could legally enforce compliance with this covenant, in practice, you should be prepared to maintain this fence, and the other fences bounding the Property, at your own cost.

6.   Information from the sellers

The solicitors acting for the sellers, Henry and Hetty Hodgson, have supplied us with a number of documents and we enclose copies of those which you need to look at.

(a) Pre-contract enquiries

This gives information about boundaries, disputes, notices, guarantees, services, rights and other matters. Our comments are:

(1) the information on boundaries must be read subject to our comment about the eastern fence, in paragraph 5 of this Report;
(2) the building work mentioned in reply to question 10.3 of the Form did not need planning permission, but future enlargement of the building might.

(b) List of Fixtures, Fittings and Contents

This indicates which items at the Property are included in the sale and which are not. Please let us know if anything stated to be excluded was, in fact, supposed to be included, or if you reach agreement with the sellers to buy any of the excluded items.

We understand that this sale is dependent upon the sellers buying another property, but their solicitors tell us that this is progressing well and they hope to be in a position to exchange contracts on both transactions at the end of next month.

7. Information from the local authority, etc.

We have made a search in the Register of Local Land Charges and have raised enquiries with the local council, and have obtained the following information which relates to the property which you are intending to buy. A separate search would be needed to obtain information relating to neighbouring properties:

(1) High Hill and Hall Hollow are publicly maintained roads, but the rear alleyway is not;
(2) there are no current plans for road improvements or new roads within 200 metres of the Property;
(3) foul drainage is believed to be connected to the public sewer but the means of connection is not known (a drain running between a house and the public sewer is not maintained at public expense and you should consult your surveyor as to the likelihood of your having to repair or maintain any drain connected to the property).

None of the other replies by the council to our enquiries need to be drawn to your attention.

Because of the location of the Property, we have also made a search with the Coal Authority in order that you or your surveyor can assess the risk of future subsidence due to coal extraction beneath the Property. A statutory compensation scheme is available if you suffer damage as a result of mining works. The Coal Authority has given the following response:

(1) Two seams of coal have been mined at an approximate depth of 200 metres under or near the Property, the last working being in 1990.
(2) There are presently no workings taking place within influencing distance of the Property.

(3) Although coal exists unworked, the Coal Authority states that the possibility of future working is considered unlikely.

8.   Outgoings

The Property is in band F for council tax purposes. The annual water charge (currently £ [   ]) is payable to Hartford Water Company. The water supply at the Property is not metered.

9.   The Purchase Contract

This is in a form incorporating the Standard Conditions of Sale, which are widely used for this type of transaction. The main provisions of the contract are:

(1) The purchase price is £[   ] (no VAT will be payable on this). The price includes the items shown on the list attached to the contract, which corresponds with the list of Fixtures, Fittings and Contents mentioned above.

(2) On exchange of contracts, you must pay a deposit of £ [   ]. If we cannot complete your purchase of the Property due to the Hodgsons' default, you will become entitled to the return of the deposit (and may be able to claim damages for your loss). However, under the Standard Conditions of Sale, all or part of the deposit money can be used by Mr and Mrs Hodgson to pay the deposit on their new property, and only the remainder, if any, will be retained by their solicitors as 'stakeholder' until we satisfactorily complete the purchase. Whilst this arrangement has become common practice, we must warn you that, in the event of the matter not completing, it may be more difficult to obtain repayment of deposit money which has been used by the Hodgsons in that way than if the whole deposit was retained by their solicitors until completion; on the other hand, very few house purchases totally fail to complete (though completion is occasionally delayed), and you may be prepared to take this risk rather than insisting that the Hodgsons incur the expense of obtaining separate bridging finance for the deposit on their new property. Please discuss this with us if you are concerned about it.

(3) The completion date will be inserted just before contracts are exchanged. We will discuss it with you at that time so that a date acceptable to both you and the Hodgsons can be fixed. This date will then be the date on which the transaction is to be completed: the Hodgsons must vacate the Property on that date, if they do not vacate earlier, and we must send the completion money to their solicitors to reach their bank account by 2 p.m. that afternoon. You will be liable to pay daily interest at [   ] % per year above bank base rate if cleared funds are not made available to us in time to remit the completion money early enough, so we will need to receive the funds (other than the loan from your Building Society, mentioned below) from you either by cheque in favour of this firm reaching us at least five working days before the completion date, or by bank transfer into this firm's bank account preferably on the day before the completion date. Nearer the time, we will let you know how much we require;

this will include a sum to cover our fees, disbursements paid or payable by us (including stamp duty land tax of £ [   ] and registration fees of £ [   ]) and VAT.

(4) You are buying the Property in its actual state and condition. You must be satisfied about this from your own inspection of the Property and from your surveyor's report. If you expect the sellers to remedy (or pay for the remedy of) any defects, this will have to be agreed with them before contracts are exchanged and special provisions added to the contract. Your lender has asked us to point out to you that the valuation undertaken by their surveyor may not reveal all the defects in the Property.

(5) The Property remains at the sellers' risk until completion, and the sellers must hand it over in its present condition, except for fair wear and tear. You would be entitled to withdraw from the transaction, with the return of your deposit, if the Property was so badly damaged before the completion date as to make it unusable, and the sellers would have a similar right if the damage was caused by a risk against which they could not have been expected to insure.

10.   Mortgage

We have received instructions from the Highland Building Society to act for them on a mortgage loan to assist you in buying the Property. We have to report to them on the result of our investigations about the Property and also on any discrepancies between the details of the transaction known to us and the details you gave the Society with your mortgage application (e.g. as to the purchase price). So far, the documents supplied to us do not show any such discrepancies.

The main terms of the proposed mortgage are:

(1) The loan will be £ [   ].

(2) Interest is variable at the discretion of the Society, but will initially be at the rate of [   ]% per year.

(3) The loan is repayable, with interest, over [   ] years, by monthly instalments comprising a mixture of capital and interest. Initially, the instalments will be £ [   ] per month, but this is variable and the Society will recalculate the amount as a result of changes in the rate of interest. You will be required to pay the instalments by bank standing order. Failure to pay any instalments will entitle the Society to call for immediate repayment of the entire loan.

(4) The loan will be to both of you, and you will both be individually legally responsible for ensuring that the instalment payments are duly made and that the other provisions of the mortgage, mentioned below, are observed.

(5) The loan and interest will be secured on a first legal mortgage over the Property. This will give the Society various rights if you fail to pay the instalments, including the right to apply to the court to evict you and your family so that the Society can sell the Property in order to recoup the outstanding loan and any unpaid interest. If the sale proceeds exceed the amount due to the Society, the surplus will be paid to you (or to any second lender), but if there is a shortfall the Society can sue you for it.

(6) The mortgage will impose a number of standard obligations and restrictions, the most important being:
    (a) you must keep the Property in good repair;
    (b) you must insure the Property with insurers agreed between you and the Society;
    (c) you must not alter the Property, or change its use, without the Society's prior consent;
    (d) you must not let any part of the Property without the Society's prior consent;
    (e) no second or subsequent mortgage must be taken out without the Society's prior consent.
(7) The mortgage will be security for any future loans you may borrow from the Society, as well as for the loan mentioned above.

The full text of the mortgage terms are set out in the enclosed book from the Society, and we recommend that you read them.

11.   Environmental matters

We [have/have not] made enquiries relating to environmental matters affecting the property. [Our enquiries revealed the following information [set out details].]

Please ask us if you have any queries about this report or on any other aspect of this transaction.

12.   Joint purchase

[Where there are two or more buyers, explain the difference between joint tenancy and tenancy in common and request the buyers to confirm their choice to you.]
    [Name of solicitors]

16.14   REPORT TO CLIENT (LEASEHOLD)

We enclose a copy of the Lease affecting this property, details of which are as follows:

1. The lease is dated [date] and made between [parties]
2. The current Landlord is [name] of [company/address]
3. The current Landlord's Agents who collect the Ground Rent/Rent are [agents]
4. The term is [term length] from [date]. There are therefore [number] years left unexpired.
5. The rent is £ [   ] per annum payable in advance/arrears on the [date] in each year, the next payment date being the [date].

    The rent will be apportioned on completion between Seller and Buyer and you will be responsible for payment of the next rent following completion which will be due on [date]. Failure to pay the rent on the rent days can lead to the Landlord taking proceedings to forfeit the Lease. It is most important to pay rent on the rent days and we suggest you set up a direct debit with your bank to do this. The Landlord may issue a rent demand but it is the Tenant's responsibility to pay the rent regardless of whether a rent demand is issued or not.

6. The following are brief details of covenants in the Lease. You have a copy of the original in your possession and should read the same carefully. We are highlighting the most important covenants which we consider may affect your future use and enjoyment of the property.

[(i)   User – Clause [ ]
Dwelling-house for the occupation of one family at a time.]

[(ii) Alterations – Clause [ ]
You are not allowed to make alterations to the premises without the consent of the Landlord. If you wish to extend or make external/internal alterations you must first obtain Planning Permission and Building Regulations Approval from the local authority and then get a separate consent from the Landlord. An application for consent can be made to the Landlord or his Managing Agents and a fee may be payable for giving consent. Failure to obtain the Landlord's consent is a breach of the terms of the Lease which can lead to forfeiture and can cause problems when you sell the property.]

[(iii) Pets – Clause [ ]
There is a stipulation in the Lease on the type of pets that can be kept on the premises. You should therefore make a note to see whether or not this will affect you. If you have a pet which is not allowed on the premises under the terms of the Lease, you would be advised not to proceed with your purchase.]

[(iv) Fences Clause [ ]
The fences are party walls and fence (i.e. jointly owned by you and your neighbours) except where they are marked on the plan attached to the Lease and identified with a letter 'T' on the inside or outside. Where the 'T' markings are on the inside, this indicates that the fence will belong to this property. Where it is on the outside, it indicates that the fence belongs to the adjoining properties.
Where the fences/walls separating this property from the adjoining property are party, they are now governed by the provisions of the Party Wall Act 1996. Attached is a brief summary of that Act and how it will affect your future use and enjoyment of the property, and the possible future use of a party wall or fence.]

[(v)   Other Covenants:
These are numerous and are contained in Clause [ ] or in the [ ] Schedule to the Lease which you should read. If there are any which you do not understand or require further explanation or which may affect the proposed use and occupancy of the property, you should raise these with us prior to exchange of contracts.]

7. The Landlord is responsible for insuring the building of which the premises form part. You will be responsible for paying a proportion of that insurance premium.

The Landlord is also responsible for keeping the roofs and outside walls of the premises (except the glass in the windows, but including boundary walls, guttering and downpipes) in good repair and condition.

16.15   LETTERS ADVISING ON METHOD OF JOINT PURCHASE

I confirm your instructions that you are buying the property jointly in the names of [insert names]. We have advised you [when you visited us/by telephone] as to the two different methods of co-ownership and you said that you wished to own the property as [joint tenants/tenants in common].

As a reminder of our conversation, I set out below a summary of the main points of difference between these two types of ownership. We will proceed to carry out the transaction in accordance with your choice of ownership as above. If you wish to change your minds or seek further clarification of this issue, please contact me as soon as possible.

Joint tenants

If you hold the property as joint tenants, you will own the whole of the property jointly and must both agree and join in to any future sale of the property. If one of you were to die, the other would become entitled to the whole of the property in his/her own right and it would not pass to your children or family under your will or on intestacy. This method is popular with married couples but may not be suitable if either of you has children from a previous relationship whom you would want to benefit under your will. You may also prefer not to use this method if you are concerned about the impact of Inheritance Tax on your estates after death. We can provide you with estate planning advice if you require this.

Tenancy in common

Although called a 'tenancy', this method of ownership is applicable to either freehold or leasehold land and enables the owners to divide the ownership of the property into distinct portions which can be left by will or will pass on intestacy. For example, if one person contributes 60% of the purchase price of the property and the other 40%, it may be appropriate for the property to be held as tenants in common in the proportions of 60:40. Each party would then benefit proportionately from an increase in the value of the property (or share the same percentage of any decrease in value). The decision to hold by this method is a private matter which does not affect the legal title to the property, but it is advisable to record the wishes of the parties and their proportionate percentage shares in a separate document which is kept with the title deeds and we can prepare this document for you. Legally, you would both still own the property in its entirety and would both therefore need to consent to and join in to any future sale. This method of holding the property can be appropriate in the following types of situation:

- Where the purchase price is contributed unequally by the parties
- Where the owners are not married to each other
- Where the owners may wish children or relatives from a previous relationship to benefit under their wills
- Where there are considerations relating to Inheritance Tax planning.

If you decide to purchase as tenants in common, I suggest that you each obtain separate advice as to the proportions in which you should hold the property and the tax and other consequences of this decision. It would not be appropriate for me to advise both of you on this issue but I can ask my colleagues to see you each separately for this discussion if you would like me to arrange this.

16.16   LETTER TO CLIENT ENCLOSING CONTRACT FOR SIGNATURE

I now enclose the Contract in this matter for your signature. Can you please sign this where indicated with an 'X' and then return it to me in the stamped addressed envelope enclosed. Please do not date the document. Can you also please let me have your suggestions for a completion date.

16.17   LETTER TO CLIENT REQUESTING AN APPOINTMENT TO SIGN THE CONTRACT

The Contract in this matter is ready for signature. Can you please telephone to arrange a mutually convenient appointment to see me so that I can explain the contract and search results to you and you can sign the contract.

16.18   LETTER TO CLIENT REQUESTING THE RETURN OF THE SIGNED CONTRACT

I refer to my letter of the [date] enclosing the Contract. Please can you return the signed contract to me as soon as possible. If you have any queries, please contact me by telephone or make an appointment to come and see me.

16.19   LETTER TO SELLER'S SOLICITOR RETURNING THE CONTRACT APPROVED

We refer to previous correspondence and now return one part of the Contract approved [or approved as amended in red].

16.20   LETTER TO SELLER'S SOLICITOR ADVISING OF READINESS TO EXCHANGE

We refer to previous correspondence and would advise that we now have signed the Contract on our file ready to exchange. May we please hear from you as soon as possible.

16.21   LETTER TO SELLER'S SOLICITOR FOLLOWING EXCHANGE

Further to our telephone conversation of [date] when exchange of Contracts was effected under Law Society Formula [specify], at [specify] for completion on the [completion date] we enclose our Client's signed Contract together with our cheque in the sum of £ [   ] in respect of the deposit.

We also enclose the draft Transfer in duplicate for approval together with our Requisitions on Title and copies for your use.

16.22   LETTER TO SELLER'S SOLICITOR ENCLOSING DRAFT TRANSFER AND REQUISITIONS

We refer to previous correspondence and we enclose the draft Transfer in duplicate for approval together with Requisitions on Title and copies for your use.

16.23   LETTER TO SELLER'S SOLICITOR ENCLOSING ENGROSSED TRANSFER

We enclose the engrossment of the Transfer signed by our Client for signature by yours in readiness for completion.

16.24   LETTER TO CLIENT CONFIRMING EXCHANGE

I am writing to confirm that Contracts for your purchase of the above property have now been exchanged and completion will take place on the [completion date] as arranged.

16.25   LETTER TO CLIENT ENCLOSING TRANSFER (AND MORTGAGE) FOR SIGNATURE

I enclose the Deed of Transfer (and mortgage) in this matter which require(s) your signature. Can you please sign the document(s) where indicated between the pencil crosses. Your signature(s) should be witnessed by an adult person who should sign their name followed by their printed name, address and occupation, again where indicated. Please do not date the document(s). Can you please do this immediately and return the document(s) to me in the stamped addressed envelope enclosed.

16.26 LETTER TO CLIENT REQUESTING AN APPOINTMENT TO SIGN THE TRANSFER

The purchase deed (or as appropriate) in this matter is now ready for signature. Can you please arrange an appointment to come and see me to sign the documents(s).

16.27 LETTER TO CLIENT REQUESTING THE RETURN OF THE SIGNED TRANSFER (AND MORTGAGE)

I refer to my letter of [date] with enclosures. Please can you return the signed documents as soon as possible.

16.28 LETTER TO CLIENT ENCLOSING BILL, STATEMENT OF ACCOUNT AND COMPLETION STATEMENT

I now enclose our Bill of Charges, VAT invoice, Statement of Account and Completion Statement for your information. As you will see from the Completion Statement, after taking all matters into consideration, there is a final balance due from you of £ [   ]. Will you please arrange to let me have your cheque for that sum no later than [date] to allow clearance in time for completion.

16.29 LETTER TO CLIENT REQUESTING SETTLEMENT OF ACCOUNT

I refer to my letter of [date]. Will you please arrange to let me have your cheque in respect of the final balance due as quickly as possible.

16.30 LETTER TO LENDER ENCLOSING THE REPORT ON TITLE

We enclose Report on Title/Certificate of Title in this matter for your attention. Please ensure that we receive the mortgage advance by [date] at the latest.

16.31 LETTER TO SELLER'S SOLICITOR REQUESTING TITLE DEEDS

We refer to the above matter which was completed on [*completion date*]. As yet, we have not received the Title Deeds and shall be pleased to receive these by return.

16.32 LETTER TO SELLER'S SOLICITOR ACKNOWLEDGING RECEIPT OF THE TITLE DEEDS

We thank you for your letter of [*date*] enclosing the Title Deeds and hereby acknowledge safe receipt.

As requested, we return one copy of the schedule of deeds which we have signed.

16.33 LETTER TO CLIENT FOLLOWING COMPLETION

I confirm completing your purchase of the above property on [*completion date*] as arranged. May I take this opportunity of welcoming you to your new home and I trust your move went well.

I am now proceeding with payment of the stamp duty land tax and then with registering your title to this property at the Land Registry. You will shortly be hearing from your lender with regard to your mortgage repayments.

I enclose a receipted note of my firm's charges together with a completion statement for the work involved in your purchase, which I trust you will find satisfactory.

Thank you for your instructions in this matter. If I can be of any assistance in the future, please do not hesitate to contact me.

16.34 LETTER TO LIFE ASSURANCE COMPANY

We enclose Notice of Assignment in duplicate. Please receipt and return the copy Notice to us as soon as possible.

16.35 LETTER TO FREEHOLDER GIVING NOTICE

We enclose Notice in duplicate for registration together with our cheque in the sum of £ [   ] in respect of the fee. Please receipt and return one copy of the Notice to us as soon as possible.

16.36   LETTER TO CLIENT CONFIRMING COMPLETION AND REGISTRATION

I am writing to confirm that we completed your purchase of the above property on the [*completion date*] as arranged.

I am now proceeding with registering your title to this property at the Land Registry. I shall advise will let you know when this has been completed.

16.37   LETTER TO LAND REGISTRY ENCLOSING APPLICATION FOR REGISTRATION

We enclose herewith HMLR Form AP1 together with the documents listed and our cheque for £ [   ] in respect of the fee.

16.38   LETTER TO SELLER'S SOLICITOR REQUESTING SEALED DISCHARGE

We refer to your undertaking of [*date*]. As yet, we have not received the sealed Form DS1 and shall be pleased to receive this by return.

16.39   LETTER TO SELLER'S SOLICITOR ACKNOWLEDGING RECEIPT OF SEALED DISCHARGE

We thank you for your letter of [*date*] together with enclosure, receipt of which is acknowledged. We confirm that your undertaking is discharged.

16.40   LETTER TO CLIENT FOLLOWING COMPLETION OF REGISTRATION

I refer to previous correspondence and confirm that registration of your title to this property has now been completed at the Land Registry. The Title Deeds have been sent to [*name of lender*] who will keep them until the Mortgage is redeemed. A copy of the Title Deeds is enclosed for you to keep.

I would like to take this opportunity of thanking you for your kind instructions and if I can be of any assistance to you in the future, please do not hesitate to contact me.

16.41   LETTER TO LENDER ENCLOSING TITLE DEEDS

Registration of title in the above matter has now been completed at the Land Registry. We therefore enclose the Title Deeds and Documents in accordance with your instructions and shall be obliged if you would acknowledge safe receipt by signing and returning to us one copy of the enclosed schedule.

16.42   LETTER TO CLIENT CONFIRMING RETENTION OF TITLE DEEDS

I refer to previous correspondence and confirm that registration of your title to this property has now been completed at the Land Registry. The Title Deeds have been placed in our strong room for safe keeping in accordance with your instructions and I enclose our Form of Schedule by way of receipt. A copy of the deeds is enclosed for you to keep.

I would like to take this opportunity of thanking you for your kind instructions and if I can be of any assistance to you in the future, please do not hesitate to contact me.

16.43   UNDERTAKING BY SOLICITOR (WITH FORM OF AUTHORITY FROM CLIENT) TO ACCOUNT TO BANK FOR NET PROCEEDS OF SALE OF THE EXISTING PROPERTY, THE BANK HAVING PROVIDED FUNDS IN CONNECTION WITH THE PURCHASE OF THE NEW PROPERTY

Authority from client(s)

[*date*] ....

To ....[*name and address of solicitors*]
I/We hereby irrevocably authorise and request you to give an undertaking in the form set out below and accordingly to pay the net proceeds of sale after deduction of your costs to:

.... Bank plc .... Branch

Signature of client(s)..

Undertaking

[*date*] ....

To .... Bank plc

If you provide facilities to my/our client ....

for the purchase of the freehold/leasehold property (the new property)

.... [*description of property*] pending the sale by my/our client of the freehold/leasehold property (the existing property)

.... [*description of property*]

I/we undertake:

1. That any sums received from you or your customer will be applied solely for the following purposes:
   (a) in discharging the present mortgage(s) on the existing property [delete if not applicable];
   (b) in acquiring a good marketable title to the new property, subject to the mortgage mentioned below [delete if not applicable];
   (c) in paying any necessary deposit, legal fees, costs and disbursements in connection with the purchase.
   The purchase price contemplated is £ [   ] gross.
   I/We are informed that a sum of £ [   ] is being advanced on mortgage by [*name of lender*] [delete if not applicable]. The amount required from my/our client for the transaction including the deposit and together with costs, disbursements and apportionments is not expected to exceed £ [   ].
2. To hold to your order when received by me/us the documents of title of the existing property pending completion of the sale (unless subject to any prior mortgage(s)) and of the new property (unless subject to any prior mortgage(s)).
3. To pay to you the net proceeds of sale of the existing property when received by me/us. The sale price contemplated is £ [   ] and the only deductions which will have to be made at present known to me/us are:
   (i) the deposit (if not held by me/us),
   (ii) the estate agents' commission,
   (iii) the amount required to redeem any mortgages and charges, which so far as known to me/us at present do not exceed £ [   ],
   (iv) the legal fees, costs and disbursements relating to the transaction.
4. To advise you immediately of any subsequent claim by a third party upon the net proceeds of sale of which I/we have knowledge.

[**Note:**

(1) If any deductions will have to be made from the net proceeds of sale other than those shown above, these must be specifically mentioned.
(2) It would be convenient if this form of undertaking were presented in duplicate so that a copy could be retained by the solicitor.]

17

Remortgage

17.1 LETTER TO THE CLIENT REQUESTING CONFIRMATION OF INSTRUCTIONS

I have today received notification from [*name of lender*] of your proposed remortgage of the above property. Can you please telephone me to confirm your instructions. When telephoning can you please let me know the name and address of your current mortgage lender together with the mortgage account number (you will find these details on a statement of account from your lender).

17.2 LETTER TO THE CLIENT TO CONFIRM INSTRUCTIONS

I have today received notification from [*name of lender*] of your proposed remortgage of the above property.

I confirm having written to [*name of existing lender*] requesting your Title Deeds.

[*name of lender*] will require me to carry out a Local Search with [*local authority*] which service will cost £ [   ]. Please let me have a cheque for that sum as soon as possible so that I can send off the Search Application. I cannot complete the remortgage until I have the result of the Search back from the Council.

I confirm that the legal costs will amount to £ [   ] calculated as follows:

Legal Fees	£ [ ]
VAT	£ [ ]
Official Copies	£ [ ]
Local Search Fee	£ [ ]
Bank Charges to transfer funds	£ [ ]
Bankruptcy Search Fee	£ [ ]
Land Registry Search Fee	£ [ ]
Land Registry Fee to register mortgage	£ [ ]
TOTAL	£ [ ]

Yours sincerely,

17.3   CLIENT CARE LETTER

Thank you for your instructions to act on your behalf in your remortgage of the property at [address] which is a leasehold/freehold property. Please telephone me as soon as possible to let me know the name and address of your current mortgage lender and your mortgage account number so that we can obtain the Deeds. You will find the details of your mortgage lender on your statement of account.

I advised that [confirm any advice given with particular reference to any time limits or steps to be taken by the client].

Our approximate charges for the work are as follows:

Costs £ [ ] plus VAT	
In addition, the following are the disbursements payable and payments to others in the matter:	
Local Search Fee	£ [ ]
Bank Charges to transfer funds	£ [ ]
Bankruptcy Search Fee	£ [ ]
Land Registry Search Fee	£ [ ]
Land Registry Fee to register title	£ [ ]

I hope this letter sets out our charges and disbursements clearly but if you have any queries please contact me to discuss them.

I shall be dealing with the work personally except for [specify areas to be delegated], which will be dealt with by [name] who is a trainee solicitor with this firm. I am a solicitor but not a partner. The partner with overall responsibility for this department is [name]. If you are unhappy about our work, then please contact me in the first instance. If you are unwilling to do this or feel that the matter is too serious, then you should contact [name of partner].

We pride ourselves on giving our clients the very highest level of service but if there is anything you are not happy about, the firm would rather you let us know straight away.

If there is any aspect of our service you are unhappy with, I will either meet with you to discuss the difficulties or your complaint or write to you offering an explanation and try to resolve the difficulty. If you do make a complaint, I will write to you with details of our clients' complaint procedure.

I also confirm that if the transaction does not proceed to completion, we reserve the right to charge an abortive charge on your transaction of not more than £ [   ].

Please will you sign and return to us in the enclosed stamped addressed envelope one copy of this letter as confirmation of your acceptance of our terms as set out in this letter.

Yours sincerely,

[Note: see 15.3.12 for paragraphs relating to money laundering which can be added to a client care letter.]

17.4 LETTER TO LENDER REQUESTING TITLE DEEDS

We have been instructed by the above named to act in the remortgage of the above property which we understand is at present in mortgage to you. Please let us have the Title Deeds on the usual undertaking so that this matter may proceed.

Note: this letter should be referenced to include the name of the borrower, the address of the property and the borrower's Roll number.

17.5 LETTER TO LENDER TO ACKNOWLEDGE RECEIPT OF THE TITLE DEEDS

We acknowledge receipt of the Title Deeds and accordingly enclose your form signed as requested.

17.6 LETTER TO CLIENT ENCLOSING MORTGAGE DEED FOR SIGNATURE

I enclose the Mortgage Deed which requires your signature(s). Can you please sign the document where indicated between the pencil crosses. Your signature(s) should be witnessed by an adult person who should first of all sign their name followed by their printed name, address and occupation, again where indicated. Please do not date the document. Can you please do this immediately and return the document to me in the stamped addressed envelope enclosed.

17.7 LETTER TO CLIENT REQUESTING AN APPOINTMENT TO SIGN THE MORTGAGE DEED

Can you please arrange an appointment to come and see me to sign the Mortgage Deed.

17.8 LETTER TO CLIENT ENCLOSING BILL AND COMPLETION STATEMENT

I now enclose our Bill of Charges and Completion Statement for your information. As you will see from the Completion Statement, after taking all matters into consideration, there is a final balance due to you of £ [   ]. Please let us have details of your bank account so that we can transfer the balance to you after completion.

17.9 LETTER TO LENDER REQUESTING A REDEMPTION FIGURE

Completion of the remortgage of the above property has been arranged for [*completion date*]. May we please have a redemption statement as at that date.

17.10 LETTER TO NEW LENDER ENCLOSING REPORT ON TITLE

We enclose report on title/certificate of title in this matter for your attention.

17.11 LETTER TO CLIENT CONFIRMING COMPLETION

I confirm completing the above matter on [*completion date*] as arranged.

I am now proceeding with registering your new mortgage at the Land Registry. I will let you know when this has been completed.

17.12 LETTER TO CLIENT CONFIRMING COMPLETION AND ENCLOSING BILL AND COMPLETION STATEMENT

I am writing to confirm that the above matter was completed on [*completion date*] as arranged.

I now enclose our Bill of Charges and Completion Statement for your information. As you will see from the Completion Statement, after taking all matters into consideration, there is a final balance due to you of £ [   ]. Please acknowledge safe receipt of the enclosed cheque.

I am now proceeding with registering your new mortgage at the Land Registry. I will let you know when this has been completed.

17.13 LETTER TO LENDER REDEEMING MORTGAGE

We enclose Form DS1 for sealing together with our cheque in the sum of £ [   ] being the amount required to redeem the above account.

We look forward to receiving sealed Form DS1 as soon as possible.

17.14 LETTER TO LENDER REQUESTING SEALED DISCHARGE

We refer to our letter of the [*date*] and shall be pleased to receive sealed Form DS1 as soon as possible.

17.15   LETTER TO LIFE ASSURANCE COMPANY ENCLOSING NOTICE OF REASSIGNMENT

We enclose Notice of Reassignment in duplicate. Can you please receipt and return the copy Notice to us as soon as possible.

17.16   LETTER TO FREEHOLDER

We enclose Notice in duplicate for registration together with our cheque in the sum of £ [   ] in respect of the fee. Can you please receipt and return one copy of the Notice to us as soon as possible.

17.17   LETTER TO LAND REGISTRY ENCLOSING APPLICATION FOR REGISTRATION

We enclose herewith HMLR Form AP1 together with the documents listed and our cheque for £ [   ] in respect of the fee.

17.18   LETTER TO LENDER ENCLOSING TITLE DEEDS

Registration of title in the above matter has now been completed at the Land Registry. We therefore enclose the Title Deeds and Documents in accordance with your instructions and shall be obliged if you would acknowledge safe receipt by signing and returning one copy of the enclosed schedule to us.

17.19   LETTER TO CLIENT FOLLOWING REGISTRATION

I am writing to confirm that registration of your new mortgage has now been completed at the Land Registry. The Title Deeds have been sent to [name of lender] who will keep them until such time as the mortgage is redeemed.

I would like to take this opportunity of thanking you for your kind instructions and if I can be of any assistance to you in the future, please do not hesitate to contact me.

APPENDIX A

Law Society's standard procedures

National Conveyancing Protocol (5th edition) for domestic freehold and leasehold property[1]

ACTING FOR THE SELLER

1. The first step

The seller should inform the solicitor as soon as it is intended to place the property on the market so that delay may be reduced after a prospective purchaser is found.

2. Preparing the package: assembling the information

On receipt of instructions, the solicitor should then immediately take the following steps, at the seller's expense:

2.1 Whenever possible instructions should be obtained from the client in person. The Consumer Protection (Distance Selling) Regulations 2000 should not then apply.

2.2 Check the client's identity if the client is not known to you. Comply with money laundering regulations and follow any guidance issued by the Law Society.

2.3 Give the client information as to costs, information relating to the name and status of the person who will be carrying out the work and, if that person is not a partner, the name of the partner who has overall responsibility for the matter. Give any other information necessary to comply with Rule 15 of the Solicitors' Practice Rules 1990 and Solicitors' Costs Information and Client Care Code 1999. If given orally this information should be confirmed in writing.

2.4 Give the seller details of whom to contact in the event of a complaint about the firm's services (Rule 15).

2.5 Consider with client whether to make local authority and other searches so that these can be supplied to the buyer's solicitor as soon as an offer is made. If thought appropriate request a payment on account in relation to disbursements.

2.6 Ascertain the whereabouts of the documents of title and, if not in the solicitor's custody, obtain them and, or if registration or a dealing has taken place after 13 October 2003, apply for an official copy of entries on the register and the title plan.

2.7 Ask the seller to complete the Seller's Property Information Form and on its return remind the seller of the need to notify you of any changes in the information supplied prior to completion.

2.8 Obtain such original guarantees with the accompanying specification, planning decisions, building regulation approvals and certificates of completion as are in the seller's possession and copies of any other planning consents that are with the title documents or details of any highway and sewerage agreements and bonds or any other relevant certificates relating to the property (e.g. structural engineer's certificate or an indemnity policy).

2.9   Give the seller the Fixtures, Fittings and Contents Form, with a copy to retain, to complete and return prior to the submission of the draft contract.

2.10   If the title is unregistered make an index map search.

2.11   If so instructed requisition a local authority search and enquiries and any other searches (e.g. mining or commons registration searches).

2.12   Obtain details of all mortgages and other financial charges of which the seller's solicitor has notice including, where applicable, improvement grants and discounts repayable to a local authority. Redemption figures should be obtained at this stage in respect of all mortgages on the property so that cases of negative equity or penalty redemption interest can be identified at an early stage.

2.13   Ascertain the identity of all people aged 17 or over living in the dwelling and ask about any financial contribution they or anyone else may have made towards its purchase or subsequent improvement. All persons identified in this way should be asked to confirm their consent to the sale proceeding.

2.14   In leasehold cases, ask the seller to complete the Seller's Leasehold Information Form and to produce, if possible:

(1)   A receipt or evidence from the landlord of the last payment of rent.
(2)   The maintenance charge accounts for the last three years, where appropriate, and evidence of payment.
(3)   Details of the buildings insurance policy.

If any of these are lacking, and are necessary for the transaction, the solicitor should obtain them from the landlord. At the same time investigate whether a licence to assign is required and, if so, enquire of the landlord what references or deeds of covenant are necessary and, in the case of some retirement schemes, if a charge is payable to the management company on change of ownership. On receipt of the form back from the seller, remind the seller of the need to notify you of any changes in the information supplied prior to completion.

2.15   In commonhold cases:

(1)   Ask the seller to complete the Seller's Commonhold Information Form, and to produce, if possible

    (i)   Commonhold Association Memorandum and Articles of Association;
    (ii)   Commonhold Community Statement;
    (iii) Details of the building insurance policy.

(2)   Make a search at Companies House against the commonhold association.
(3)   Obtain an official copy of commonhold title for the common parts.
(4)   Obtain the account from the commonhold association for the unit and ask if there are

    (i)   any other claims or assessments against the unit;
    (ii)   details of the annual budget or estimates;
    (iii) any reserve fund; and
    (iv)   any restricted use areas.

2.16   Check replies given by the seller on the Seller's Property Information Form and, if appropriate, the Seller's Leasehold Information Form and Seller's Commonhold Information Form from the information in your possession (see the guidance from the Law Society's Conveyancing and Land Law Committee [2003] *Gazette*, 16 October, 43).

3. Preparing the package: the draft documents

As soon as the title documents or official copies of the registered title are available, and the seller has completed the Seller's Property Information Form and, if appropriate, the Seller's Leasehold Information Form and the Seller's Commonhold Information Form, the solicitor shall:

3.1 If the title is unregistered:

(1) Make a land charges search against the seller and any other appropriate names.
(2) Make an index map search in the Land Registry (if not already obtained – see 2.10) in order to verify that the seller's title is unregistered and ensure that there are no interests registered at the Land Registry adverse to the seller's title.
(3) Prepare an epitome of title. Mark copies or abstracts of all deeds which will not be passed to the buyer's solicitor as examined against the original.
(4) Prepare and mark as examined against the originals copies of all deeds, or their abstracts, prior to the root of title containing covenants, easements, etc., affecting the property.
(5) Check that all plans on copied documents are correctly coloured.

3.2 If the title is registered, obtain official copy entries of the register, the title plan and copy documents incorporated or referred to in the register entries, if not already obtained (see 2.6).

3.3 Prepare the draft contract and complete and sign the second section of the Seller's Property Information Form and, if appropriate, the Seller's Leasehold Information Form and the Seller's Commonhold Information Form.

3.4 Check contract package is complete and ready to be sent out to the buyer's solicitor.

3.5 Deal promptly with any queries raised by the estate agent.

4. Buyer's offer accepted

When made aware that a buyer has been found the solicitor shall:

4.1 Check with the seller agreement on the price and, if appropriate, that there has been no change in the information already supplied (Seller's Property Information Form, Seller's Leasehold Information Form, Seller's Commonhold Information Form and Fixtures, Fittings and Contents Form). Also check the seller's position on any related purchase. If any part of the purchase price is being apportioned to chattels, which will be in a separate state of severance at completion, advise the seller that apportionment must be a just and reasonable figure, and if in any doubt professional advice from a valuer should be obtained. If appropriate, supply the seller with a copy of the leaflet issued by the Inland Revenue, 'Fixtures and Chattels – Stamp Duty Land Tax'.

4.2 Inform the buyer's solicitor that the Protocol will be used.

4.3 Ascertain the buyer's position on any related sale and in the light of that reply, ask the seller for a proposed completion date.

4.4 Send to the buyer's solicitor as soon as possible the contract package to include:

(1) Draft contract.
(2) Official copy entries of the registered title (including official copies of all documents mentioned), the title plan or the epitome of title (including details of any prior matters referred to but not disclosed by the documents themselves) and the index map search.
(3) The Seller's Property Information Form with copies of all relevant planning decisions, guarantees, etc.

(4) The completed Fixtures, Fittings and Contents Form. Where this is provided it will form part of the contract and should be attached to it.

(5) In leasehold cases

   (i)   the Seller's Leasehold Information Form, with all information about maintenance charges and insurance and, if appropriate, the procedure (including references required) for obtaining the landlord's consent to the sale;

   (ii) a copy of the lease.

(6) In commonhold cases

   (i)   Seller's Commonhold Information Form, with all information obtained under 2.15;

   (ii) a copy of the registered title for the commonhold common parts and a copy of the registered title for the seller's unit.

(7) If available, the local authority search and enquiries and any other searches made by the seller's solicitor.

If any of these documents are not available the remaining items should be forwarded to the buyer's solicitor as soon as they are available.

4.5   Inform the estate agent or property seller when the draft contract has been submitted to the buyer's solicitor.

4.6   Ask the buyer's solicitor if a 10 per cent deposit will be paid and, if not, what arrangements are proposed.

4.7   If and to the extent that the seller consents to the disclosure, supply information about the position on the seller's own purchase and of any other transactions in the chain above, and thereafter, of any change in circumstances.

4.8   Notify the seller of all information received in response to the above.

4.9   Inform the estate agent of any unexpected delays or difficulties likely to delay exchange of contracts.

ACTING FOR THE BUYER

5. The first step

On notification of the buyer's purchase the solicitor should then immediately take the following steps, at the buyer's expense:

5.1   Wherever possible instructions should be obtained from the client in person. The Consumer Protection (Distance Selling) Regulations 2000 should not then apply.

5.2   Check the client's identity if you do not know the client, comply with the Money Laundering Regulations [2003] and follow any guidance issued by the Law Society.

5.3   Give the client information as to costs, information relating to the name and status of the person who will be carrying out the work and, if that person is not a partner, the name of the partner who has overall responsibility for the matter. Give any other information necessary to comply with Rule 15 of the Solicitors' Practice Rules 1990 and Solicitors' Costs Information and Client Care Code 1999. If given orally this information should be confirmed in writing.

5.4   Give the client details of whom to contact in the event of a complaint about the firm's services (Rule 15).

5.5   Request a payment on account in relation to disbursements.

5.6   Confirm to the seller's solicitor that the Protocol will be used.

5.7   Ascertain the buyer's position on any related sale, mortgage arrangements and whether a 10 per cent deposit will be provided.

5.8   If and to the extent that the buyer consents to the disclosure, inform the seller's solicitor about the position on the buyer's own sale, if any, and of any connected transactions, the general nature of the mortgage application, the amount of deposit available and if the seller's target date for completion can be met, and thereafter, of any change in circumstances.

On receipt of the draft contract and other documents:

5.9   Notify the buyer that these documents have been received, check the price and send the client a copy of the Fixtures, Fittings and Contents Form and, if appropriate, a copy of the title plan for checking. If the purchase price is being apportioned between the property and chattels, advise the buyer what constitutes chattels for Stamp Duty Land Tax purposes, that values for the chattels must be just and reasonable, and if in any doubt, professional advice from a valuer should be obtained. If appropriate, supply the buyer with a copy of the leaflet issued by the Inland Revenue 'Fixtures and Chattels – Stamp Duty Land Tax'.

5.10   Subject to 5.20 below, make a local authority search with the usual Part 1 enquiries and any additional enquiries relevant to the property.

5.11   Make a commons registration search, if appropriate.

5.12   Make mining enquiries and drainage enquiries if appropriate and consider any other relevant searches, e.g. environmental searches.

5.13   Check the buyer's position on any related sale and check that the buyer has a satisfactory mortgage offer and all conditions of the mortgage are or can be satisfied.

5.14   Check the buyer understands the nature and effect of the mortgage offer and duty to disclose any relevant matters to the lender.

5.15   Advise the buyer of the need for a survey on the property.

5.16   Check the draft contract to ensure title is satisfactory and add any special conditions necessary to achieve this (e.g. for removal of or consents needed under any restrictions or notices revealed on the title).

5.17   Confirm approval of the draft contract and return it approved as soon as possible, having inserted the buyer's full names and address, subject to any outstanding matters.

5.18   At the same time ask only those specific additional enquiries which are required to clarify some point arising out of the documents submitted or which are relevant to the particular nature or location of the property or which the buyer has expressly requested. Any enquiry, including those about the state and condition of the building, which is capable of being ascertained by the buyer's own enquiries or survey or personal inspection should not be raised. Additional duplicated standard forms should not be submitted; if they are, the seller's solicitor is under no obligation to deal with them nor need answer any enquiry seeking opinions rather than facts.

5.19   If title has been deduced, check the seller's title to the property and raise any requisitions on the title deduced. (See Standard Conditions of Sale (fourth edition) 4.2.1.) Matters relating to the completion arrangements should not be raised at this stage.

5.20   If a local authority search has been supplied by the seller's solicitors with the draft contract, consider the need to make a further local authority search with the usual Part 1 enquiries or raise any of the optional Part 2 enquiries not included in the seller's search or any other additional enquiries relevant to the property. (The local authority search should not be more than three months old at exchange of contracts nor six months old at completion.)

5.21   Ensure that buildings insurance arrangements are in place.

5.22   Check the position over any life policies referred to in the lender's offer of mortgage.

5.23   Check with the buyer if property is being purchased in sole name or jointly with another person. If a joint purchase check whether as joint tenants or tenants in common and advise on the difference in writing.

BOTH PARTIES' SOLICITOR

6.   Prior to exchange of contracts

If acting for the buyer

When all satisfactory replies received to enquiries, requisitions on title and searches:

6.1   Prepare and send to the buyer a contract report and invite the buyer to make an appointment to call to raise any queries on the contract report and to sign the contract ideally in the presence of a solicitor.

6.2   When the buyer signs the contract check:

(1) Completion date.
(2) That the buyer understands and can comply with all the conditions on the mortgage offer if appropriate.
(3) That all the necessary funds will be available to complete the purchase.

If acting for the seller

6.3   Deal with any requisitions on title raised by the buyer's solicitor.

6.4   Advise the seller on the effect of the contract and ask the seller to sign it, ideally in the presence of the solicitor.

6.5   Check the position on any related purchase so that there can be a simultaneous exchange of contracts on both the sale and purchase.

6.6   Check completion date.

7.   Relationship with the buyer's lender

On receipt of instructions from the buyer's lender:

7.1   Check the mortgage offer complies with Practice Rule 6(3)(c) and (e) and is certified to that effect.

7.2   Check any special conditions in the mortgage offer to see if there are additional instructions or conditions not normally required by Practice Rule 6(3)(c).

7.3   Go through any special conditions in the mortgage offer with the buyer.

7.4   Notify the lender if Practice Rule 6(3)(b) or 1.13 or 1.14 of the CML Lenders' Handbook ('Lenders' Handbook') are applicable.

7.5   Consider whether there are any conflicts of interest which prevent you accepting instructions to act for the lender.

7.6   If you do not know the borrower and anyone else required to sign the mortgage, charge or other document, check evidence of identity (Practice Rule 6(3)(c)(i)).

7.7   Consider whether there are any circumstances covered by the Law Society's:

(1) Green Card on property fraud
(2) Blue Card on money laundering
(3) Pink Card on undertakings
(4) Money Laundering Guidance.

7.8   If you do not know the seller's solicitor/licensed conveyancer check that they appear in a legal directory or are on the record of their professional body (see Practice Rule 6(3)(c) (i) and the Lenders' Handbook).

7.9   Carry out any other checks required by the lender provided they comply with Practice Rule 6(3)(c).

7.10   Check the lender's requirements as to whether it requires the original mortgage deed to be lodged with it following registration.

7.11   At all times comply with the requirements of Practice Rule 6(3) and the Lenders' Handbook and ensure if a conflict of interest arises you cease to act for the lender.

8. Exchange of contracts

On exchange, the buyer's solicitor shall send or deliver to the seller's solicitor:

8.1   The signed contract with all names, dates and financial information completed.

8.2   The deposit provided in the manner prescribed in the contract. Under the Law Society's Formula C the deposit may have to be sent to another solicitor nominated by the seller's solicitor.

8.3   If contracts are exchanged by telephone the procedures laid down by the Law Society's Formulae A, B or C must be used and both solicitors must ensure (unless otherwise agreed) that the undertakings to send documents and to pay the deposit on that day are strictly observed.

8.4   The seller's solicitor shall, once the buyer's signed contract and deposit are held unconditionally, having ensured that the details of each contract are fully completed and identical, send the seller's signed contract on the day of exchange to the buyer's solicitor in compliance with the undertaking given on exchange.

8.5   Notify the client that contracts have been exchanged.

8.6   Notify the seller's estate agent or property seller of exchange of contracts and the completion date.

9. Between exchange and the day of completion

As soon as possible after exchange and in any case within the time limits contained in the Standard Conditions of Sale:

9.1   The buyer's solicitor shall send to the seller's solicitor, in duplicate:

(1) Completion Information Form and include any requisitions on title which are necessary and could not be raised prior to exchange of contracts, or ask seller's solicitor to confirm that there is no variation in any replies given prior to exchange.
(2) Draft conveyance/transfer or assignment incorporating appropriate provisions for joint purchase.
(3) Other documents, e.g. draft receipt for purchase price of fixtures, fittings and contents.

9.2   As soon as possible after receipt of these documents the seller's solicitor shall send to the buyer's solicitor:

(1) Replies to Completion Information and Requisitions on Title Form.
(2) Draft conveyance/transfer or assignment approved.
(3) If appropriate, completion statement supported by photocopy receipts or evidence of payment of apportionments claimed.
(4) Copy of licence to assign from the landlord if appropriate.

9.3   The buyer's solicitor shall then:

(1) Engross the approved draft conveyance/transfer or assignment.
(2) Explain the effect of that document to the buyer and obtain the buyer's signature to it (if necessary).
(3) Send it to the seller's solicitor in time to enable the seller to sign it before completion without suffering inconvenience.
(4) If appropriate, prepare any separate declaration of trust, advise the buyer on its effect and obtain the buyer's signature to it.
(5) Advise the buyer on the contents and effect of the mortgage deed and obtain the buyer's signature to that deed. If possible, and in all cases where the lender so requires, a solicitor should witness the buyer's signature to the mortgage deed.
(6) Send the certificate of title (complying with Rule 6(3)(d)) to the lender.
(7) Take any steps necessary to ensure that the amount payable on completion will be available in time for completion including sending to the buyer a completion statement to include legal costs, Land Registry fees and other disbursements and, if appropriate, Stamp Duty Land Tax.
(8) Make the Land Registry and land charges searches and, if appropriate, a company search.
(9) Ensure that you have by this stage obtained sufficient information from each buyer to complete the relevant land transaction return, including national insurance numbers, and prepare the return. After checking with the buyer that the information on the form is accurate, advise the buyer that an Inland Revenue enquiry is possible within the following nine months which might result in costs and penalties. Ask the buyer to sign the form in black ink and return it immediately as penalties will be charged by the Inland Revenue unless the form is lodged within 30 days of completion.
(10) Explain and discuss with the buyer the need to disclose overriding interests in the property and complete Form D1.

9.4   The seller's solicitor shall:

(1) Request redemption figures for all financial charges on the property revealed by the deeds/official copy entries/land charges search against the seller.
(2) On receipt of the engrossment of the transfer or assignment, after checking the engrossment to ensure accuracy, obtain the seller's signature to it after ascertaining that the seller understands the nature and contents of the document. If the document is not to be signed in the solicitor's presence the letter sending the document for signature should contain an explanation of the nature and effect of the document and clear instructions relating to the execution of it.
(3) On receipt of the estate agent's or property seller's commission account obtain the seller's instructions to pay the account on the seller's behalf out of the sale proceeds.
(4) Consider if the consent of any restrictioner (e.g. a managing agent or management company) who will have a continuing interest is needed and if so, take steps to ensure that such consent will be available on completion.

10. Relationship with the seller's estate agent or property seller

Where the seller has instructed estate agents or property seller, the seller's solicitor shall take the following steps:

10.1   Inform them when the draft contracts are submitted (see 4.5).

10.2   Deal promptly with any queries raised by them.

10.3   Inform them of any unexpected delays or difficulties likely to delay exchange of contracts (see 4.9).

10.4   Inform them when exchange has taken place and the date of completion (see 8.6).

10.5   On receipt of their commission account send a copy to the seller and obtain instructions as to arrangements for payment (see 9.4(3)).

10.6   Inform them of completion and, if appropriate, authorise release of any keys held by them (see 11.3(1)).

10.7   If so instructed pay the commission (see 9.4(3) and 11.6(2)).

11. Completion: the day of payment and removals

11.1   If completion is to be by post, the Law Society's Code for Completion shall be used, unless otherwise agreed.

11.2   As soon as practicable and not later than the morning of completion, the buyer's solicitor shall advise the seller's solicitor of the manner and transmission of the purchase money and of steps taken to despatch it.

11.3   On being satisfied as to the receipt of the balance of the purchase money, the seller's solicitor shall:

(1) Notify the estate agent or property seller that completion has taken place and authorise release of the keys.
(2) Notify the buyer's solicitor that completion has taken place and the keys have been released.
(3) Date and complete the transfer.
(4) Despatch the deeds including the transfer or the assignment and the licence to assign to the buyer's solicitor with any appropriate undertakings.

11.4   The seller's solicitor shall check that the seller is aware of the need to notify the local and water authorities of the change in ownership.

11.5   After completion, where appropriate, the buyer's solicitor shall give notice of assignment to the lessor.

11.6   Immediately after completion, the seller's solicitor shall:

(1) Send to the lender the amount required to release the property sold.
(2) Pay the estate agent's or property seller's commission if so authorised.
(3) Account to the seller for the balance of the sale proceeds.

11.7   Immediately after completion, the buyer's solicitor shall:

(1) Date and complete the mortgage document and, if appropriate, give notice of any second or subsequent charge to the first chargee.
(2) Confirm completion of the purchase and the mortgage to the buyer.
(3) Lodge Form SDLT with the Inland Revenue and pay any Stamp Duty Land Tax that is due. On receipt of the certificate of notification from the Inland Revenue, hold it to lodge with the Land Registry application.
(4) Consider the need to register a restriction and, if appropriate, complete Form RX1.
(5) Deal with the registration of the transfer document and mortgage with the Land Registry within the priority period of the search including lodging with the application form (AP1 or FR1) Form D1 and, if appropriate, Form RX1.
(6) If appropriate, send a notice of assignment of a life policy to the insurance company.

(7) On receipt of notification from the Land Registry that registration has been completed and a title information document has been supplied, check its contents carefully and supply a copy of that document to the buyer.
(8) Send the original mortgage deed and/or the title information document to the lender, if appropriate, and deal with any other documents in accordance with its instructions.
(9) Take the buyer's instructions as to any documents not being held by the lender, and if the documents are to be sent to the buyer or anyone else to hold on the buyer's behalf, inform the buyer of the need to keep the documents safely so that they will be available on a sale of the property.
(10) If the sale was a sale of part of the land in the registered title, then on completion of the registration of the transfer of part, the seller's solicitor shall check that the title certificate and amended registered plan are accurate and send a copy to the seller.

Code for completion by post[1]

PREAMBLE

The code provides a procedure for postal completion which practising solicitors may adopt by reference. It may also be used by licensed conveyancers.

Before agreeing to adopt this code, a solicitor must be satisfied that doing so will not be contrary to the interests of the client (including any mortgagee client).

When adopted, the code applies without variation, unless agreed in writing in advance.

PROCEDURE

General

1. To adopt this code, all the solicitors must expressly agree, preferably in writing, to use it to complete a specific transaction.

2. On completion, the seller's solicitor acts as the buyer's solicitor's agent without any fee or disbursements.

Before completion

3. The seller's solicitor will specify in writing to the buyer's solicitor before completion the mortgages or charges secured on the property which, on or before completion, will be redeemed or discharged to the extent that they relate to the property.

4. The seller's solicitor undertakes:

    (i)   to have the seller's authority to receive the purchase money on completion; and
    (ii) on completion to have the authority of the proprietor of each mortgage or charge specified under paragraph 3 to receive the sum intended to repay it,
          BUT
          if the seller's solicitor does not have all the necessary authorities then:
    (iii) to advise the buyer's solicitor no later than 4pm on the working day before the completion date that they do not have all the authorities or immediately if any is withdrawn later; and
    (iv) not to complete until he or she has the buyer's solicitor's instructions.

5. Before the completion date, the buyer's solicitor will send the seller's solicitor instructions as to any of the following which apply:

    (i)   documents to be examined and marked;
    (ii) memoranda to be endorsed;
    (iii) undertakings to be given;
    (iv) deeds, documents (including any relevant undertakings) and authorities relating to rents, deposits, keys, etc. to be sent to the buyer's solicitor following completion; and

(v)   other relevant matters.

In default of instructions, the seller's solicitor is under no duty to examine, mark or endorse any document.

6.   The buyer's solicitor will remit to the seller's solicitor the sum required to complete, as notified in writing on the seller's solicitor's completion statement or otherwise, or in default of notification as shown by the contract. If the funds are remitted by transfer between banks, the seller's solicitor will instruct the receiving bank to telephone to report immediately the funds have been received. Pending completion, the seller's solicitor will hold the funds to the buyer's solicitor's order.

7.   If by the agreed date and time for completion the seller's solicitor has not received the authorities specified in paragraph 4, instructions under paragraph 5 and the sum specified in paragraph 6, the seller's solicitor will forthwith notify the buyer's solicitor and request further instructions.

Completion

8.   The seller's solicitor will complete forthwith on receiving the sum specified in paragraph 6, or at a later time agreed with the buyer's solicitor.

9.   When completing, the seller's solicitor undertakes:

(i)   to comply with the instructions given under paragraph 5; and

(ii)   to redeem or obtain discharges for every mortgage or charge so far as it relates to the property specified under paragraph 3 which has not already been redeemed or discharged.

After completion

10.   The seller's solicitor undertakes:

(i)   immediately completion has taken place to hold to the buyer's solicitor's order every item referred to in (iv) of paragraph 5 and not to exercise a lien over any such item;

(ii)   as soon as possible after completion, and in any event on the same day,

(a)   to confirm to the buyer's solicitor by telephone or fax that completion has taken place; and

(b)   to send written confirmation and, at the risk of the buyer's solicitor, the items listed in (iv) of paragraph 5 to the buyer's solicitor by first class post or document exchange.

Supplementary

11.   The rights and obligations of the parties, under the contract or otherwise, are not affected by this code.

12.   (i)   References to the seller's solicitor and the buyer's solicitor apply as appropriate to solicitors acting for other parties who adopt the code.

(ii)   When a licensed conveyancer adopts this code, references to a solicitor include a licensed conveyancer.

13.   A dispute or difference arising between solicitors who adopt this code (whether or not subject to any variation) relating directly to its application is to be referred to a single arbitrator agreed between the solicitors. If they do not agree on the appointment within one month, the President of the Law Society may appoint the arbitrator at the request of one of the solicitors.

NOTES TO THE CODE

1. This code will apply to transactions where the code is adopted after 1st July 1998.

2. The object of this code is to provide solicitors with a convenient means for completion on an agency basis when a representative of the buyer's solicitor is not attending at the office of the seller's solicitor.

3. As with the Law Society's formulae for exchange of contracts by telephone and fax, the code embodies professional undertakings and is only recommended for adoption between solicitors and licensed conveyancers.

4. Paragraph 2 of the code provides that the seller's solicitors will act as agents for the buyer's solicitors without fee or disbursements. The convenience of not having to make a specific appointment on the date of completion for the buyer's solicitors to attend to complete personally will offset the agency work that the seller's solicitor has to do and any postage payable in completing under the code. Most solicitors will from time to time act for both sellers and buyers. If a seller's solicitor does consider that charges and/or disbursements are necessary in a particular case this would represent a variation in the code and should be agreed in writing before the completion date.

5. In view of the decision in *Edward Wong Finance Company Limited v. Johnson, Stokes and Master* [1984] AC 1296, clause 4(ii) of the code requires the seller's solicitors to undertake on completion to have authority of the proprietor of every mortgage or charge to be redeemed to receive the sum needed to repay such charge.

6. Paragraph 11 of the code provides that nothing in the code shall override any rights and obligations of the parties under the contract or otherwise.

7. The buyer's solicitor is to inform the seller's solicitor of the mortgages or charges which will be redeemed or discharged (see paragraph 3 above) and is to specify those for which an undertaking will be required on completion (paragraph 5(iii)). The information may be given in reply to requisitions on title. Such a reply may also amount to an undertaking.

8. Care must be taken if there is a sale and sub-sale. The sub-seller's solicitor may not hold the title deeds nor be in a position to receive the funds required to discharge the seller's mortgage on the property. Enquiries should be made to ascertain if the monies or some part of the monies payable on completion should, with either the authority of the sub-seller or the sub-seller's solicitor, be sent direct to the seller's solicitor and not to the sub-seller's solicitor.

9. Care must also be taken if there is a simultaneous resale and completion and enquiries should be made by the ultimate buyer's solicitor of the intermediate seller's solicitor as to the price being paid on that purchase. Having appointed the intermediate seller's solicitor as agent the buyer's solicitor is fixed with the knowledge of an agent even without having personal knowledge (see the Society's 'green card' warning on property fraud at Annex 25G, p.501).

10. If the seller's solicitor has to withdraw from using the code, the buyer's solicitor should be notified of this not later than 4pm on the working day prior to the completion date. If the seller's solicitor's authority to receive the monies is withdrawn later the buyer's solicitor must be notified immediately.

These notes refer only to some of the points in the code that practitioners may wish to consider before agreeing to adopt it. Any variation in the code must be agreed in writing before the completion date.

Formulae for exchanging contracts by telephone, fax or telex[1]

INTRODUCTION

It is essential that an agreed memorandum of the details and of any variations of the formula used should be made at the time and retained in the file. This would be very important if any question on the exchange were raised subsequently. Agreed variations should also be confirmed in writing. The serious risks of exchanging contracts without a deposit, unless the full implications are explained to and accepted by the seller client, are demonstrated in *Morris* v. *Duke-Cohan & Co.* (1975) 119 SJ 826.

As those persons involved in the exchange will bind their firms to the undertakings in the formula used, solicitors should carefully consider who is to be authorised to exchange contracts by telephone or telex and should ensure that the use of the procedure is restricted to them. Since professional undertakings form the basis of the formulae, they are only recommended for use between firms of solicitors and licensed conveyancers.

LAW SOCIETY TELEPHONE/TELEX EXCHANGE – FORMULA A (1986)

(for use where one solicitor holds both signed parts of the contract):
A completion date of [*date*] is agreed. The solicitor holding both parts of the contract confirms that he or she holds the part signed by his or her client(s), which is identical to the part he or she is also holding signed by the other solicitor's client(s) and will forthwith insert the agreed completion date in each part.

Solicitors mutually agree that exchange shall take place from that moment and the solicitor holding both parts confirms that, as of that moment, he or she holds the part signed by his or her client(s) to the order of the other. He or she undertakes that day by first class post, or where the other solicitor is a member of a document exchange (as to which the inclusion of a reference thereto in the solicitor's letterhead shall be conclusive evidence) by delivery to that or any other affiliated exchange, or by hand delivery direct to that solicitor's office, to send his or her signed part of the contract to the other solicitor, together, where he or she is the purchaser's solicitor, with a banker's draft or a solicitor's client account cheque for the deposit amounting to £[...].

Note:

1. A memorandum should be prepared, after use of the formula, recording:

   (a) date and time of exchange;
   (b) the formula used and exact wording of agreed variations;
   (c) the completion date;
   (d) the (balance) deposit to be paid;
   (e) the identities of those involved in any conversation.

1 © Law Society 1986 (Revised 1989 and 1996)

LAW SOCIETY TELEPHONE/TELEX EXCHANGE – FORMULA B (1986)

(for use where each solicitor holds his or her own client's signed part of the contract):
A completion date of [*date*] is agreed. Each solicitor confirms to the other that he or she holds a part contract in the agreed form signed by the client(s) and will forthwith insert the agreed completion date.

Each solicitor undertakes to the other thenceforth to hold the signed part of the contract to the other's order, so that contracts are exchanged at that moment. Each solicitor further undertakes that day by first class post, or, where the other solicitor is a member of a document exchange (as to which the inclusion of a reference thereto in the solicitor's letterhead shall be conclusive evidence) by delivery to that or any other affiliated exchange, or by hand delivery direct to that solicitor's office, to send his or her signed part of the contract to the other together, in the case of a purchaser's solicitor, with a banker's draft or a solicitor's client account cheque for the deposit amounting to £[...].

Notes:

1. A memorandum should be prepared, after use of the formula, recording:

    (a) date and time of exchange;
    (b) the formula used and exact wording of agreed variations;
    (c) the completion date;
    (d) the (balance) deposit to be paid;
    (e) the identities of those involved in any conversation.

2. Those who are going to effect the exchange must first confirm the details in order to ensure that both parts are identical. This means in particular, that if either part of the contract has been amended since it was originally prepared, the solicitor who holds a part contract with the amendments must disclose them, so that it can be confirmed that the other part is similarly amended.

9 July 1986, revised January 1996

LAW SOCIETY TELEPHONE/FAX/TELEX EXCHANGE – FORMULA C (1989)

Part I

The following is agreed:
　　Final time for exchange: [...] pm
　　Completion date:
　　Deposit to be paid to:
Each solicitor confirms that he or she holds a part of the contract in the agreed form signed by his or her client, or, if there is more than one client, by all of them. Each solicitor undertakes to the other that:

(a) he or she will continue to hold that part of the contract until the final time for exchange on the date the formula is used, and

(b) if the vendor's solicitor so notifies the purchaser's solicitor by fax, telephone or telex (whichever was previously agreed) by that time, they will both comply with part II of the formula.

The purchaser's solicitor further undertakes that either he or she or some other named person in his or her office will be available up to the final time for exchange to activate part II of the formula on receipt of the telephone call, fax or telex from the vendor's solicitors.

Part II

Each solicitor undertakes to the other henceforth to hold the part of the contract in his or her possession to the other's order, so that contracts are exchanged at that moment, and to despatch it to the other on that day. The purchaser's solicitor further undertakes to the vendor's solicitor to despatch on that day, or to arrange for the despatch on that day of, a banker's draft or a solicitor's client account cheque for the full deposit specified in the agreed form of contract (divided as the vendor's solicitor may have specified) to the vendor's solicitor and/or to some other solicitor whom the vendor's solicitor nominates, to be held on formula C terms.

'To despatch' means to send by first class post, or, where the other solicitor is a member of a document exchange (as to which the inclusion of a reference thereto in the solicitor's letterhead is to be conclusive evidence) by delivery to that or any other affiliated exchange, or by hand delivery direct to the recipient solicitor's office. 'Formula C terms' means that the deposit is held as stakeholder, or as agent for the vendor with authority to part with it only for the purpose of passing it to another solicitor as deposit in a related property purchase transaction on these terms.

Notes:

1. Two memoranda will be required when using formula C. One needs to record the use of part I, and a second needs to record the request of the vendor's solicitor to the purchaser's solicitor to activate part II.

2. The first memorandum should record:

    (a)   the date and time when it was agreed to use formula C;
    (b)   the exact wording of any agreed variations;
    (c)   the final time, later that day, for exchange;
    (d)   the completion date;
    (e)   the name of the solicitor to whom the deposit was to be paid, or details of amounts and names if it was to be split; and
    (f)   the identities of those involved in any conversation.

3. Formula C assumes the payment of a full contractual deposit (normally 10%).

4. The contract term relating to the deposit must allow it to be passed on, with payment direct from payer to ultimate recipient, in the way in which the formula contemplates. The deposit must ultimately be held by a solicitor as stakeholder. Whilst some variation in the formula can be agreed this is a term of the formula which must not be varied, unless all the solicitors involved in the chain have agreed.

5. If a buyer proposes to use a deposit guarantee policy, formula C will need substantial adaptation.

6. It is essential prior to agreeing part I of formula C that those effecting the exchange ensure that both parts of the contract are identical.

7. Using formula C involves a solicitor in giving a number of professional undertakings. These must be performed precisely. Any failure will be a serious breach of professional discipline. One of the undertakings may be to arrange that someone over whom the solicitor has no control will do something (i.e. to arrange for someone else to despatch the cheque or banker's draft in payment of the deposit). An undertaking is still binding even if it is to do something outside the solicitor's control.

8. Solicitors do not as a matter of law have an automatic authority to exchange contracts on a formula C basis, and should always ensure that they have the client's express authority to use formula C. A suggested form of authority is set out below. It should be adapted to cover any special circumstances:

I/We [...] understand that my/our sale and purchase of [...] are both part of a chain of linked property transactions, in which all parties want the security of contracts which become binding on the same day.

I/We agree that you should make arrangements with the other solicitors or licensed conveyancers involved to achieve this.

I/We understand that this involves each property-buyer offering, early on one day, to exchange contracts whenever, later that day, the seller so requests, and that the buyer's offer is on the basis that it cannot be withdrawn or varied during that day.

I/We agree that when I/we authorise you to exchange contracts, you may agree to exchange contracts on the above basis and give any necessary undertakings to the other parties involved in the chain and that my/our authority to you cannot be revoked throughout the day on which the offer to exchange contracts is made.

15th March 1989, revised January 1996

Contaminated Land Warning Card[1]

WARNING – TO ALL SOLICITORS – CONTAMINATED LAND LIABILITIES

The advice contained on this Card is not intended to be a professional requirement for solicitors. Solicitors should be aware of the requirements of Part IIA of the Environmental Protection Act 1990 but they themselves cannot provide their clients with conclusive answers. They must exercise their professional judgement to determine the applicability of this advice to each matter in which they are involved and, where necessary, they should suggest to the client obtaining specialist advice. In the view of the Law Society the advice contained in this Card conforms to current best practice.

Solicitors should be aware that environmental liabilities may arise and consider what further enquiries and specialist assistance the client should be advised to obtain.

CONTAMINATED LAND

1. The contaminated land regime was brought into effect in England on 1 April 2000. It applies to all land, whether residential, commercial, industrial or agricultural. It can affect owners, occupiers, developers, and lenders. The legislation, which is contained in Part IIA, Environmental Protection Act 1990 and in regulations and statutory guidance issued under it (see Contaminated Land (England) Regulations 2000 SI 2000/227 and DETR Guidance on Contaminated Land April 2000) is retrospective. It covers existing and future contamination.

    The National Assembly is expected shortly to introduce similar regulations regarding contaminated land in Wales.

2. Local authorities must inspect and identify seriously contaminated sites. They can issue remediation notices requiring action to remediate contamination, in the absence of a voluntary agreement to do so. In certain cases ('Special Sites') responsibility for enforcement lies with the Environment Agency.

    A negative reply to the standard local authority enquiries from the local authority may merely mean the site has not been inspected. It does not necessarily mean there is no problem.

    Compliance can be costly, and may result in expenditure which could exceed the value of the property.

    Liability falls primarily on those who 'cause or knowingly permit' contamination (a Class A person). If the authority cannot identify a Class A person, liability falls on a Class B person, the current owner, or occupier of the land. Class B persons include lenders in possession. There are complex exclusion provisions for transferring liability from one party to another. Some exclusions apply only on the transfer of land, or the grant of a lease. The applicability of any relevant exclusion needs to be considered before entering such transactions.

    In every transaction you must consider whether contamination is an issue.

CONVEYANCING TRANSACTIONS

In purchases, mortgages and leases, solicitors should:

1. Advise the client of potential liabilities associated with contaminated land.
Generally clients should be advised of the possibility and consequences of acquiring interests in contaminated land and the steps that can be taken to assess the risks.

2. Make specific enquiries of the seller.
In all commercial cases, and if contamination is considered likely to be a risk in residential cases (e.g. redevelopment of brown field land):

3. Make enquiries of statutory and regulatory bodies.

4. Undertake independent site history investigation, e.g. obtaining site report from a commercial company.

In commercial cases, if there is a likelihood that the site is contaminated:

5. Advise independent full site investigation.

6. Consider use of contractual protections and the use of exclusion tests.
    This may involve specific disclosure of known defects, possibly coupled with price reduction, requirements on seller to remedy before completion, and in complex cases the use of warranties and indemnities.

Unresolved problems, consider

7. Advising withdrawal, and noting advice;

8. Advising insurance (increasingly obtainable for costs of remediation of undetected contamination and any shortfall in value because of undisclosed problems).

SPECIFIC TRANSACTIONS

1. Leases

Consider if usual repair and statutory compliance clauses transfer remediation liability to tenant, and advise.

2. Mortgages

Advise lender, if enquiries reveal potential for or existence of contamination, and seek instructions.
    In enforcement cases, consider appointment of receivers, rather than steps resulting in lender becoming mortgagee in possession, and so treated as a Class B person.

3. Share sales and asset purchases

Consider recommending the obtaining of specialist technical advice on potential liabilities, use of detailed enquiries, warranties and indemnities.

OTHER RELEVANT LEGISLATION

Other legislation and common law liabilities (e.g. nuisance) may also be relevant when advising on environmental matters including:

Water Resources Act 1991

Groundwater Regulations 1998

Pollution Prevention and Control (England and Wales) Regulations 2000

Further information

Law Society's *Environmental Law Handbook*
DETR's Website **www.detr.gov.uk**

Money Laundering Warning Card (April 2009)[1]

The Solicitors Regulation Authority is determined to pursue those it regulates who are involved in money laundering.

Your obligations are set out in the Solicitors' Code of Conduct 2007, particularly rules 1 and 4, the Solicitors' Accounts Rules, the Proceeds of Crime Act 2002, the Terrorism Act 2000, and the Money Laundering Regulations 2007.

You must ensure that you do not facilitate laundering even when money does not pass through your firm's accounts. Failure to observe our warnings can lead to disciplinary action, criminal prosecution, or both.

WARNING SIGNS

Unusual payment requests

- Payments from a third party where you cannot verify the source of the funds
- Receipts of cash and requests for payments by cash
- Money transfers where there is a variation between the account holder/signatory
- Payments to unrelated third parties
- Litigation settlements which are reached too easily

Unusual instructions

- Instructions outside the normal pattern of your business
- Instructions changed without a reasonable explanation
- Transactions that take an unusual turn
- Movement of funds between accounts, institutions or jurisdictions without reason

Use of your client account

- Never accept instructions to act as a banking facility, particularly if you do not undertake any related legal work—be aware of note (ix) to rule 15 of the Solicitors' Accounts Rules 1998.
- Be wary if you are instructed to do legal work, receive substantial funds into your client account, but the instructions are later cancelled and you are asked to send the money to a third party or perhaps to your client.

Suspect territory

- Check official sources about suspect territories and sanctions.
- Be wary of funds moved around without a logical explanation.

---

1   © The Law Society 2009. Published by the Solicitors Regulation Authority.

Loss-making transaction

* Instructions potentially leading to financial loss without logical explanation, particularly where your client seems unconcerned

---

Legislation may require you to make an official disclosure to the Serious Organised Crime Agency (SOCA), PO Box 8000, London, SE11 5EN—call 020 7238 8282, or send an email by registering on the secure site at **www.ukciu.gov.uk/saroline.aspx**. You will not commit the offence of 'tipping off' by reporting a matter to the SRA. To report to us on a confidential basis, contact our Fraud and Confidential Intelligence Bureau on 01926 439673 or 0845 850 0999 or email redalert@sra.org.uk.

For conduct advice, contact our Professional Ethics helpline.

For general queries about good-practice anti-money laundering compliance, contact the Law Society's Practice Advice Service on 0870 606 2522 (9:00-17:00 Monday to Friday) or refer to **www.lawsociety.org.uk/moneylaundering**.

Property Fraud Warning Card (April 2009)[1]

The Solicitors Regulation Authority will not tolerate property fraud.

Your obligations are set out in rules 1, 2, 3, 4 and 18 of the Solicitors' Code of Conduct 2007 and its guidance.

IF IN DOUBT – REFUSE TO ACT

You must ensure that you do not facilitate dubious property transactions. Failure to observe our warnings could lead to disciplinary action or criminal prosecution.

If you doubt the propriety of a transaction you should refuse to act. Ensure you verify and question instructions to satisfy yourself that you are not facilitating a dubious transaction.

WHAT IS PROPERTY FRAUD?

Mortgage fraud occurs when a loan is obtained on the basis of untrue statements to the lender, such as when a lender is led to believe that a property is worth more than its true value and therefore lends more than it would if it knew the true position. Always focus on informing the lender of the true price and other relevant facts, while taking into account confidentiality and legal professional privilege.

Some frauds do not involve a mortgage—only the deception of buyers.

WARNING SIGNS

- Back-to-back transactions where a property is bought and then sold quickly, apparently at a higher price. The lender advances money based on the higher price
- Misrepresentation or changes to the purchase price including sellers or developers providing incentives, allowances or discounts unless these are clearly and fully disclosed to the lender
- A representation to you that a deposit or part of the purchase price is paid direct
- 'Gifted deposit' or 'deposit paid' by the seller amounting to a reduction in the price paid by the buyer but distorting the value disclosed to the lender
- Unusual or suspicious instructions such as transactions controlled or funded by a third party; a client using an alias; sales and purchases between associates; parties using the same legal adviser; a request that net proceeds be sent to a third party
- Properties sold between related offshore or corporate companies that are commonly controlled by the same individuals, particularly where the properties are mortgaged at an inflated value

Be aware that variations of these warning signs exist and fraudsters change their methods. You do not need to act for the lender to become implicated. If you are not satisfied of the propriety of the transaction you should refuse to act.

MONEY LAUNDERING

Bear in mind that you may also have legal obligations to report your suspicions to the Serious Organised Crime Agency (SOCA).

For good-practice advice, refer to **www.lawsociety.org.uk/mortgagefraud**.

To report to us on a confidential basis, contact our Fraud and Confidential Intelligence Bureau on 01926 439673 or 0845 850 0999 or email redalert@sra.org.uk.

For conduct advice, contact our Professional Ethics helpline

Undertakings Warning Card
(April 2009)[1]

The SRA takes breaches of undertakings very seriously.

Your obligations are set out in rules 1, 5.01 and 10.05 of the Solicitors' Code of Conduct 2007 and its guidance.

Many transactions depend on the use of undertakings enabling you to negotiate and conduct your client's business successfully.

WHERE YOU GIVE AN UNDERTAKING

Those placing reliance on it will expect you to fulfil it. Ensure your undertakings are

- Specific
- Measurable
- Agreed
- Realistic
- Timed.

A breach of undertaking can lead to a disciplinary finding and costs direction.

Undertakings you give are also summarily enforceable by the High Court. Be aware that you do not become exposed to a liability within the excess of your firm's insurance.

Where you accept an undertaking

Ensure that in doing so your client's position is protected and you are not exposed to a breach.

IF YOU ARE A REGULATED PERSON OR FIRM

- Be clear about who can give undertakings.
- Ensure all staff understand they need your client's agreement.
- Be clear about how compliance will be monitored.
- Maintain a central record to ensure and monitor compliance.
- Prescribe the manner in which undertakings may be given.
- Prepare standard undertakings, where possible, with clear instructions that any departure be authorised in accordance with supervision and management responsibilities.
- Adopt a system that ensures terms are checked by another fee-earner.
- Confirm oral undertakings (given or received) in writing.
- Copy each undertaking and attach it to the relevant file; label the file itself.
- Ensure all staff understand the undertakings they give when using the Law Society's formulae for exchange of contracts and its code for completion by post.

To report to us on a confidential basis, contact our Fraud and Confidential Intelligence Bureau on 01926 439673 or 0845 850 0999 or email redalert@sra.org.uk.

For advice, contact our Professional Ethics helpline.

1   © The Law Society 2009. Published by the Solicitors Regulation Authority.

Council of Mortgage Lenders' Instructions

CML Lenders' Handbook: Part 1[1]

PART 1 – INSTRUCTIONS AND GUIDANCE

1. GENERAL

Those lenders who instruct using the CML Lenders' Handbook certify that these instructions have been prepared to comply with the requirements of Rule 6 (3) of the Solicitors' Practice Rules 1990 (or when applicable the Solicitors' Code of Conduct 2007).

1.1 The CML Lenders' Handbook is issued by the Council of Mortgage Lenders. Your instructions from an individual lender will indicate if you are being instructed in accordance with the Lenders' Handbook. If you are, the general provisions in part 1 and any specific requirements in part 2 must be followed.

1.2 References to 'we', 'us' and 'our' means the lender from whom you receive instructions.

1.3 The Lenders' Handbook does not affect any responsibilities you have to us under the general law or any practice rule or guidance issued by your professional body from time to time.

1.4 The standard of care which we expect of you is that of a reasonably competent solicitor or licensed conveyancer acting on behalf of a mortgagee.

1.5 The limitations contained in rule 6(3)(c) and (e) of the Solicitors' Practice Rules 1990 (and when applicable the Solicitors' Code of Conduct 2007) apply to the instructions contained in the Lenders' Handbook and any separate instructions. This does not apply to licensed conveyancers following clause 3B.

1.6 You must also comply with any separate instructions you receive for an individual loan.

1.7 If the borrower and the mortgagor are not one and the same person, all references to 'borrower' shall include the mortgagor. Check part 2 to see if we lend in circumstances where the borrower and the mortgagor are not one and the same.

1.8 References to 'borrower' (and, if applicable, 'guarantor' or, expressly or impliedly, the mortgagor) are to each borrower (and guarantor or mortgagor) named in the mortgage instructions/offer (if sent to the conveyancer). This applies to references in the Lenders' Handbook and in the certificate of title.

1.9 References to 'mortgage offer' include any loan agreement, offer of mortgage or any other similar document

1.10 If you are instructed in connection with any additional loan (including a further advance) then you should treat references to 'mortgage' and 'mortgage offer' as applying to such 'additional loan' and 'additional loan offer' respectively.

1.11 In any transaction during the lifetime of the mortgage when we instruct you, you must use our current standard documents in all cases and must not amend or generate them without our written consent. We will send you all the standard documents necessary to enable you to comply with our instructions, but please let us know if you need any other documents and we will send these to you. Check part 2 to see who you should contact. If you consider that any of the documentation is inappropriate to the particular facts of a transaction, you should write to us (see part 2) with full details and any suggested amendments.

1.12   In order to act on our behalf your firm must be a member of our conveyancing panel. You must also comply with any terms and conditions of your panel appointment.

1.13.1   If you or a member of your immediate family (that is to say, a spouse, civil partner, co-habitee, parent, sibling, child, step-parent, step-child, grandparent, grandchild, parent-in-law, or child-in-law) is the borrower and you are the sole practitioner, you must not act for us.

1.13.2   Your firm or company must not act for us if the partner or fee earner dealing with the transaction or a member of his immediate family is the seller, unless we say your firm may act (see part 2) and a separate fee earner of no less standing or a partner within the firm acts for us.

1.14   Your firm or company must not act for us if the partner or fee earner dealing with the transaction or a member of his immediate family is the borrower, unless we say your firm may act (see part 2) and a separate fee earner of no less standing or a partner within the firm acts for us.

1.15   If there is any conflict of interest, you must not act for us and must return our instructions.

1.16   Nothing in these instructions lessens your duties to the borrower.

1.17   In addition to these definitions any reference to any regulation, legislation or legislative provision shall be construed as a reference to that regulation, legislation or legislative provision as amended, re-enacted or extended at the relevant time.

2.   COMMUNICATION

2.1   All communications between you and us should be in writing quoting the mortgage account or roll number, the surname and initials of the borrower and the property address. You should keep copies of all written communication on your file as evidence of notification and authorisation. If you use PC fax or e-mail, you should retain a copy in readable form.

2.2   If you require deeds or information from us in respect of a borrower or a property then you must first of all have the borrower's authority for such a request. If there is more than one borrower, you must have the authority of all the borrowers.

2.3   If you need to report a matter to us, you must do so as soon as you become aware of it so as to avoid any delay. If you do not believe that a matter is adequately provided for in the Handbook, you should identify the relevant Handbook provision and the extent to which the issue is not covered by it. You should provide a concise summary of the legal risks and your recommendation on how we should protect our interest. After reporting a matter you should not complete the mortgage until you have received our further written instructions. We recommend that you report such matters before exchange of contracts because we may have to withdraw or change the mortgage offer.

3.   SAFEGUARDS

A   *This section relates to solicitors and those working in practices regulated by the Solicitors Regulation Authority only*

A3.1.1   You must follow the guidance in the Law Society's Green Card (mortgage fraud) and Pink Card (undertakings).

A3.1.2 You must follow the Law Society's guidance relating to money laundering and comply with the current money laundering regulations and the Proceeds of Crime Act 2002 to the extent that they apply.

A3.2 If you are not familiar with the seller's solicitors or licensed conveyancers, you must verify that they appear in a legal directory or they are currently on record with the Law Society or Council for Licensed Conveyancers as practising at the address shown on their note paper. If the seller does not have legal representation you should check part 2 to see whether or not we need to be notified so that a decision can be made as to whether or not we are prepared to proceed.

A3.3 Unless you personally know the signatory of a document, you must ask the signatory to provide evidence of identity, which you must carefully check. You should check the signatory's identity against one of the documents from list A or two of the documents in list B:

List A
- a valid full passport; or
- a valid H M Forces identity card with the signatory's photograph; or
- a valid UK Photo-card driving licence; or
- any other document listed in the additional list A in part 2.

List B
- a cheque guarantee card, credit card (bearing the Mastercard or Visa logo) American Express or Diners Club card, debit or multi-function card (bearing the Switch or Delta logo) issued in the United Kingdom with an original account statement less than three months old; or
- a firearm and shot gun certificate; or
- a receipted utility bill less than three months old; or
- a council tax bill less than three months old; or
- a council rent book showing the rent paid for the last three months; or
- a mortga ge statement from another lender for the mortgage accounting year just ended; or
- any other document listed in the additional list B in part 2.

A3.4 You should check that any document you use to verify a signatory's identity appears to be authentic and current, signed in the relevant place. You should take a copy of it and keep the copy on your file. You should also check that the signatory's signature on any document being used to verify identity matches the signatory's signature on the document we require the signatory to sign and that the address shown on any document used to verify identity is that of the signatory.

B This section applies to licensed conveyancers practices only

B3.1 You must follow the professional guidance of the Council for Licensed Conveyancers relating to money laundering and comply with the current money laundering regulations and the Proceeds of Crime Act 2002 to the extent that they apply and you must follow all other relevant guidance issued by the Council for Licensed Conveyancers.

B3.2 If you are not familiar with the seller's solicitors or licensed conveyancers, you must verify that they appear in a legal directory or they are currently on record with the Law Society or Council for Licensed Conveyancers as practising at the address shown on their note paper. If the seller does not have legal representation you should check part 2 to see whether or not we need to be notified so that a decision can be made as to whether or not we are prepared to proceed.

B3.3 Unless you personally know the signatory of a document, you must ask the signatory to provide evidence of identity, which you must carefully check. You must satisfy yourself that the person signing the document is the borrower, mortgagor or guarantor (as appropriate). If you have any concerns about the identity of the signatory you should notify us immediately.

B3.4   You should check that any document you use to verify a signatory's identity appears to be authentic and current, signed in the relevant place. You should take a copy of it and keep the copy on your file. You should also check that the signatory's signature on any document being used to verify identity matches the signatory's signature on the document we require the signatory to sign and that the address shown on any document used to verify identity is that of the signatory.

4.   VALUATION OF THE PROPERTY

4.1   *Valuation*

4.1.1   Check part 2 to see whether we send you a copy of the valuation report or if you must get it from the borrower.

4.1.2   You must take reasonable steps to verify that there are no discrepancies between the description of the property as valued and the title and other documents which a reasonably competent conveyancer should obtain, and, if there are, you must tell us immediately. The requirements in this clause and clause 4.1.3 apply to valuation reports and home condition reports. Where there is both a valuation report and a home condition report the requirements apply to both.

4.1.3   You should take reasonable steps to verify that the assumptions stated by the valuer (and where applicable a home inspector) about the title (for example, its tenure, easements, boundaries and restrictions on its use) in the valuation and home condition report are correct. If they are not, please let us know as soon as possible (see part 2) as it will be necessary for us to check with the valuer whether the valuation needs to be revised. We are not expecting you to assume the role of valuer. We are simply trying to ensure that the valuer has valued the property based on correct information.

4.1.4   When a home condition report is not provided we recommend that you should advise the borrower that there may be defects in the property which are not revealed by the inspection carried out by our valuer and there may be omissions or inaccuracies in the report which do not matter to us but which would matter to the borrower. We recommend that, if we send a copy of a valuation report that we have obtained, you should also advise the borrower that the borrower should not rely on the report in deciding whether to proceed with the purchase and that he obtains his own more detailed report on the condition and value of the property, based on a fuller inspection, to enable him to decide whether the property is suitable for his purposes.

4.2   *Re-Inspection*

4.2   Where the mortgage offer states that a final inspection is needed, you must ask for the final inspection at least 10 working days before the advance is required (see part 2). Failure to do so may cause delay in the issue of the advance. Your certificate of title must be sent to us in the usual way (see part 2).

5.   TITLE

5.1   *Surrounding Circumstances*

5.1.1   Please report to us (see part 2) if the owner or registered proprietor has been registered for less than six months or the person selling to the borrower is not the owner or registered proprietor unless the seller is:

5.1.1.1   a personal representative of the registered proprietor; or

5.1.1.2   an institutional mortgagee exercising its power of sale; or

5.1.1.3   a receiver, trustee-in-bankruptcy or liquidator; or

5.1.1.4   developer or builder selling a property acquired under a part-exchange scheme.

5.1.2   If any matter comes to your attention which you should reasonably expect us to consider important in deciding whether or not to lend to the borrower (such as whether the borrower has given misleading information to us or the information which you might reasonably expect to have been given to us is no longer true) and you are unable to disclose that information to us because of a conflict of interest, you must cease to act for us and return our instructions stating that you consider a conflict of interest has arisen.

5.2   Searches and Reports

5.2.1   In carrying out your investigation, you must ensure that all usual and necessary searches and enquiries have been carried out. You must report any adverse entry to us but we do not want to be sent the search itself. We must be named as the applicant in the Land Registry search.

5.2.2   In addition, you must ensure that any other searches which may be appropriate to the particular property, taking into account its locality and other features are carried out.

5.2.3   All searches except where there is a priority period must not be more than six months old at completion.

5.2.4   You must advise us of any contaminated land entries revealed in the local authority search. Check part 2 to see if we want to receive environmental or contaminated land reports (as opposed to contaminated land entries revealed in the local authority search). If we do not, you do not need to make these enquiries on our behalf.

5.2.5   Check part 2 to see if we accept:

5.2.5.1   personal searches; or

5.2.5.2   search insurance.

If we do accept personal searches or search insurance, check part 2 to see our requirements as to such searches.

5.2.6   If no requirements are specified in part 2 and we do not indicate that we do not accept personal searches or search insurance you must ensure:

5.2.6.1   a suitably qualified search agent carries out the personal search and has indemnity insurance that adequately protects us; or

5.2.6.2   the search insurance policy adequately protects us.

5.2.7   You must be satisfied that you will be able to certify that the title is good and marketable.

5.3   Planning and Building Regulations

5.3.1   You must by making appropriate searches and enquiries take all reasonable steps (including any further enquiries to clarify any issues which may arise) to ensure the property has the benefit of any necessary planning consents (including listed building consent) and building regulation approval for its construction and any subsequent change to the property (see part 2) and its current use; and

5.3.2   there is no evidence of any breach of the conditions of that or any other consent or certificate affecting the property; and

5.3.3   that no matter is revealed which would preclude the property from being used as a residential property or that the property may be the subject of enforcement action.

5.3.4   If there is such evidence and all outstanding conditions will not be satisfied by completion, then this must be reported to us (see part 2). Check part 2 to see if copies of planning permissions, building regulations and other consents or certificates should be sent to us.

5.3.5   If the property will be subject to any enforceable restrictions, for example, under an agreement (such as an agreement under section 106 of the Town and Country Planning Act 1990) or in a planning permission, which, at the time of completion, might reasonably be expected materially to affect its value or its future marketability, you should report this to us (see part 2).

5.4   Good and Marketable Title

5.4.1   The title to the property must be good and marketable free of any restrictions, covenants, easements, charges or encumbrances which, at the time of completion, might reasonably be expected to materially adversely affect the value of the property or its future marketability (but excluding any matters covered by indemnity insurance) and which may be accepted by us for mortgage purposes. Our requirements in respect of indemnity insurance are set out in paragraph 9. You must also take reasonable steps to ensure that, on completion, the property will be vested in the borrower.

5.4.2   Good leasehold title will be acceptable if:

5.4.2.1   a marked abstract of the freehold and any intermediate leasehold title for the statutory period of 15 years before the grant of the lease is provided; or
5.4.2.2   you are prepared to certify that the title is good and marketable when sending your certificate of title (because, for example, the landlord's title is generally accepted in the district where the property is situated); or
5.4.2.3   you arrange indemnity insurance. Our requirements in respect of indemnity insurance are set out in paragraph 9.

5.4.3.1   A title based on adverse possession or possessory title will be acceptable if the seller is or on completion the borrower will be registered at the Land Registry as registered proprietor of a possessory title or there is satisfactory evidence by statutory declaration of adverse possession for a period of at least 12 years. In the case of lost title deeds, the statutory declaration must explain the loss satisfactorily;

5.4.3.2   we will also require indemnity insurance where there are buildings on the part in question or where the land is essential for access or services;

5.4.3.3   we may not need indemnity insurance in cases where such title affects land on which no buildings are erected or which is not essential for access or services. In such cases, you must send a plan of the whole of the land to be mortgaged to us identifying the area of land having possessory title. We will refer the matter to our valuer so that an assessment can be made of the proposed security. We will then notify you of any additional requirements or if a revised mortgage offer is to be made.

5.5   Flying Freeholds, Freehold Flats, other Freehold Arrangements and Commonhold

5.5.1   If any part of the property comprises or is affected by a flying freehold or the property is a freehold flat, check part 2 to see if we will accept it as security.

5.5.2   If we are prepared to accept a title falling within 5.5.1:

5.5.2.1   (unless we tell you not to in part 2) you must report to us that the property is a freehold flat or flying freehold; and

5.5.2.2   the property must have all necessary rights of support, protection, and entry for repair as well as a scheme of enforceable covenants that are also such that subsequent buyers are required to enter into covenants in identical form; and

5.5.2.3   you must be able to certify that the title is good and marketable; and

5.5.2.4   in the case of flying freeholds, you must send us a plan of the property clearly showing the part affected by the flying freehold. If our requirements in 5.5.2.2 are not satisfied, indemnity insurance must be in place at completion (see paragraph 9).

Other freehold arrangements

5.5.3   Unless we indicate to the contrary (see part 2), we have no objection to a security which comprises a building converted into not more than four flats where the borrower occupies one of those flats and the borrower or another flat owner also owns the freehold of the building and the other flats are subject to long leases.

5.5.3.1   If the borrower occupying one of the flats also owns the freehold, we will require our security to be:

5.5.3.1.1   the freehold of the whole building subject to the long leases of the other flats; and

5.5.3.1.2   any leasehold interest the borrower will have in the flat the borrower is to occupy.

5.5.3.2   If another flat owner owns the freehold of the building, the borrower must have a leasehold interest in the flat the borrower is to occupy and our security must be the borrower's leasehold interest in such flat.

5.5.3.3   The leases of all the flats should contain appropriate covenants by the tenant of each flat to contribute towards the repair, maintenance and insurance of the building. The leases should also grant and reserve all necessary rights and easements. They should not contain any unduly onerous obligations on the landlord.

5.5.4   Where the security will comprise:

5.5.4.1   one of a block of not more than four leasehold flats and the borrower will also own the freehold jointly with one or more of the other flat owners in the building; or

5.5.4.2   one of two leasehold flats in a building where the borrower also owns the freehold reversion of the other flat and the other leaseholder owns the freehold reversion in the borrower's flat; check part 2 to see if we will accept it as security and if so, what our requirements will be.

Commonhold

5.5.5   If any part of the property comprises of commonhold, check part 2 to see if we will accept it as security.

5.5.6   If we are prepared to accept a title falling within 5.5.5, you must:

5.5.6.1   ensure that the commonhold association has obtained insurance for the common parts which complies with our requirements (see 6.13);

5.5.6.2   obtain a commonhold unit information certificate and ensure that all of the commonhold assessment in respect of the property has been paid up to the date of completion;

5.5.6.3   ensure that the commonhold community statement does not include any material restrictions on occupation or use (see 5.4 and 5.6);

5.5.6.4   ensure that the commonhold community statement provides that in the event of a voluntary termination of the commonhold the termination statement provides that the unit holders will ensure that any mortgage secured on their unit is repaid on termination;

5.5.6.5   make a company search to verify that the commonhold association is in existence and remains registered, and that there is no registered indication that it is to be wound up; and

5.5.6.6   within 14 days of completion, send the notice of transfer of a commonhold unit and notice of the mortgage to the commonhold association.

5.6   Restrictions on Use and Occupation

5.6   You must check whether there are any material restrictions on the occupation of the property as a private residence or as specified by us (for example, because of the occupier's employment, age or income), or any material restrictions on its use. If there are any restrictions, you must report details to us (see part 2). In some cases, we may accept a restriction, particularly if this relates to sheltered housing or to first-time buyers.

5.7   Restrictive Covenants

5.7.1   You must enquire whether the property has been built, altered or is currently used in breach of a restrictive covenant. We rely on you to check that the covenant is not enforceable. If you are unable to provide an unqualified certificate of title as a result of the risk of enforceability you must ensure (subject to paragraph 5.7.2) that indemnity insurance is in place at completion of our mortgage (see paragraph 9).

5.7.2   We will not insist on indemnity insurance:

5.7.2.1   if you are satisfied that there is no risk to our security; and

5.7.2.2   the breach has continued for more than 20 years; and

5.7.2.3   there is nothing to suggest that any action is being taken or is threatened in respect of the breach.

5.8   First Legal Charge

5.8   On completion, we require a fully enforceable first charge by way of legal mortgage over the property executed by all owners of the legal estate. All existing charges must be redeemed on or before completion, unless we agree that an existing charge may be postponed to rank after our mortgage. Our standard deed or form of postponement must be used.

5.9   Other Loans

5.9   You must ask the borrower how the balance of the purchase price is being provided. If you become aware that the borrower is not providing the balance of the purchase price from his own funds and/or is proposing to give a second charge over the property, you must report this to us if the borrower agrees (see part 2), failing which you must return our instructions and explain that you are unable to continue to act for us as there is a conflict of interest.

5.10   Leasehold Property

5.10.1   Our requirements on the unexpired term of a lease offered as security are set out in part 2.

5.10.2   There must be no provision for forfeiture on the insolvency of the tenant or any superior tenant.

5.10.3   The only situations where we will accept a restriction on the mortgage or assignment (whether by a tenant or a mortgagee) of the lease is where the person whose consent needs to be obtained cannot unreasonably withhold giving consent. The necessary consent for the particular transaction must be obtained before completion. If the lease requires consent to an assignment or mortgage to be obtained, you must obtain these on or before completion (this is particularly important if the lease is a shared ownership lease). You must not complete without them.

5.10.4 You must take reasonable steps to check that:

5.10.4.1 there are satisfactory legal rights, particularly for access, services, support, shelter and protection; and

5.10.4.2 there are also adequate covenants and arrangements in respect of the following matters: building insurance, maintenance and repair of the structure, foundations, main walls, roof, common parts, common services and grounds (the 'common services').

5.10.5 You should ensure that responsibility for the insurance, maintenance and repair of the common services is that of:

5.10.5.1 the landlord; or

5.10.5.2 one or more of the tenants in the building of which the property forms part; or

5.10.5.3 the management company - see paragraph 5.11.

5.10.6 Where the responsibility for the insurance, maintenance and repair of the common services is that of one or more of the tenants:

5.10.6.1 The lease must contain adequate provisions for the enforcement of these obligations by the landlord or management company at the request of the tenant.

5.10.6.2 In the absence of a provision in the lease that all leases of other flats in the block are in, or will be granted in, substantially similar form, you should take reasonable steps to check that the leases of the other flats are in similar form. If you are unable to do so, you should effect indemnity insurance (see paragraph 9). This is not essential if the landlord is responsible for the maintenance and repair of the main structure.

5.10.6.3 We do not require enforceability covenants mutual or otherwise for other tenant covenants.

5.10.7 We have no objection to a lease which contains provision for a periodic increase of the ground rent provided that the amount of the increased ground rent is fixed or can be readily established and is reasonable. If you consider any increase in the ground rent may materially affect the value of the property, you must report this to us (see part 2).

5.10.8 You should enquire whether the landlord or managing agent foresees any significant increase in the level of the service charge in the reasonably foreseeable future and, if there is, you must report to us (see part 2).

5.10.9 If the terms of the lease are unsatisfactory, you must obtain a suitable deed of variation to remedy the defect. We may accept indemnity insurance (see paragraph 9). See part 2 for our requirements.

5.10.10 You must obtain on completion a clear receipt or other appropriate written confirmation for the last payment of ground rent and service charge from the landlord or managing agents on behalf of the landlord. Check part 2 to see if it must be sent to us after completion. If confirmation of payment from the landlord cannot be obtained, we are prepared to proceed provided that you are satisfied that the absence of the landlord is common practice in the district where the property is situated, the seller confirms there are no breaches of the terms of the lease, you are satisfied that our security will not be prejudiced by the absence of such a receipt and you provide us with a clear certificate of title.

5.10.11 Notice of the mortgage must be served on the landlord and any management company immediately following completion, whether or not the lease requires it. If you cannot obtain receipt of the notice then, as a last resort, suitable evidence of the service of the notice on the landlord should be provided. Check part 2 to see if a receipted copy of the notice or evidence of service must be sent to us after completion.

5.10.12 We will accept leases which require the property to be sold on the open market if re-building or reinstatement is frustrated provided the insurance proceeds and the proceeds of sale are shared between the landlord and tenant in proportion to their respective interests.

5.10.13 You must report to us (see part 2) if it becomes apparent that the landlord is either absent or insolvent. If we are to lend, we may require indemnity insurance (see paragraph 9). See part 2 for our requirements.

5.10.14 If the leasehold title is registered but the lease has been lost, we are prepared to proceed provided you have checked a Land Registry produced copy of the registered lease. Whilst this will not be an official copy of the lease you may accept it as sufficient evidence of the lease and its terms when approving the title for mortgage purposes provided it is, on its face, a complete copy.

5.11 Management Company

5.11.1 In paragraph 5.11 the meanings shall apply:

- 'management company' means the company formed to carry out the maintenance and repair of the common parts;
- 'common parts' means the structure, main walls, roof, foundations, services, grounds and any other common areas serving the building or estate of which the property forms part.

If a management company is required to maintain or repair the common parts, the management company should have a legal right to enter the property; if the management company's right to so enter does not arise from a leasehold interest, then the tenants of the building should also be the members of the management company.

If this is not the case, there should be a covenant by the landlord to carry out the obligations of the management company should it fail to do so.

5.11.1.1 For leases granted before 1 September 2000:
If the lease does not satisfy the requirements of paragraph 5.11.1 but:
you are nevertheless satisfied that the existing arrangements affecting the management company and the maintenance and repair of the common parts; and you are able to provide a clear certificate of title, then we will rely on your professional judgement.

5.11.2 You should make a company search and verify that the company is in existence and registered at Companies House. You should also obtain the management company's last three years' published accounts (or the accounts from inception if the company has only been formed in the past three years). Any apparent problems with the company should be reported to us (see part 2). If the borrower is required to be a shareholder in the management company, check part 2 to see if you must arrange for the share certificate, a blank stock transfer form executed by the borrower and a copy of the memorandum and articles of association to be sent to us after completion (unless we tell you not to). If the management company is limited by guarantee, the borrower (or at least one of them if two or more) must become a member on or before completion.

5.12   Insolvency Considerations

5.12.1   You must obtain a clear bankruptcy search against each borrower (and each mortgagor or guarantor, if any) providing us with protection at the date of completion of the mortgage. You must fully investigate any entries revealed by your bankruptcy search against the borrower (or mortgagor or guarantor) to ensure that they do not relate to them.

5.12.2   Where an entry is revealed against the name of the borrower (or the mortgagor or guarantor):

> 5.12.2.1   you must certify that the entry does not relate to the borrower (or the mortgagor or guarantor) if you are able to do so from your own knowledge or enquiries; or
> 5.12.2.2   if, after obtaining office copy entries or making other enquiries of the Official Receiver, you are unable to certify that the entry does not relate to the borrower (or the mortgagor or guarantor) you must report this to us (see part 2). We may as a consequence need to withdraw our mortgage offer.

5.12.3   If you are aware that the title to the property is subject to a deed of gift or a transaction at an apparent undervalue completed within five years of the proposed mortgage then you must be satisfied that we will acquire our interest in good faith and will be protected under the provisions of the Insolvency (No 2) Act 1994 against our security being set aside. If you are unable to give an unqualified certificate of title, you must arrange indemnity insurance (see paragraph 9).

5.12.4   You must also obtain clear bankruptcy searches against all parties to any deed of gift or transaction at an apparent undervalue.

5.13   Powers of Attorney

5.13.1.1   If any document is being executed under power of attorney, you must ensure that the power of attorney is, on its face, properly drawn up, that it appears to be properly executed by the donor and that the attorney knows of no reason why such power of attorney will not be subsisting at completion.

5.13.1.2   Where there are joint borrowers the power should comply with section 25 of the Trustee Act 1925, as amended by section 7 of the Trustee Delegation Act 1999, or with section 1 of the Trustee Delegation Act 1999 with the attorney making an appropriate statement under section 2 of the 1999 Act.

5.13.1.3   In the case of joint borrowers, neither borrower may appoint the other as their attorney.

5.13.2   A power of attorney must not be used in connection with a regulated loan under the Consumer Credit Act 1974.

5.13.3   Check part 2 to see if:

> 5.13.3.1   the original or a certified copy of the power of attorney must be sent to us after completion;
> 5.13.3.2   where the power of attorney is a general power of attorney and was completed more than 12 months before the completion of our mortgage, you must send us a statutory declaration confirming that it has not been revoked.

5.14   The Guarantee

5.14   Whilst we recommend that a borrower should try to obtain a full title guarantee from the seller, we do not insist on this. We, however, require the borrower to give us a full title guarantee in the mortgage deed. The mortgage deed must not be amended.

5.15   Affordable Housing: Shared Ownership and Shared Equity

5.15   Housing associations, other social landlords and developers sometimes provide schemes under which the borrower will not have 100% ownership of the property and a third party will also own a share or will be taking a charge over the title. In these cases you must check with us to see if we will lend and what our requirements are unless we have already provided these (see part 2).

6.   THE PROPERTY

6.1   Mortgage Offer and Title Documents

6.1.1   The loan to the borrower will not be made until all relevant conditions of the mortgage offer which need to be satisfied before completion have been complied with and we have received your certificate of title.

6.1.2   You must check your instructions and ensure that there are no discrepancies between them and the title documents and other matters revealed by your investigations.

6.1.3   You should tell us (see part 2) as soon as possible if you have been told that the borrower has decided not to take up the mortgage offer.

6.2   Boundaries

6.2   These must be clearly defined by reference to a suitable plan or description. They must also accord with the information given in the valuation report, if this is provided to you. You should check with the borrower that the plan or the description accords with the borrower's understanding of the extent of the property to be mortgaged to us. You must report to us (see part 2) if there are any discrepancies.

6.3   Purchase Price

6.3.1   The purchase price for the property must be the same as set out in our instructions. If it is not, you must tell us (unless we say differently in part 2).

6.3.2   You must tell us (unless we say differently in part 2) if the contract provides for or you become aware of any arrangement in which there is:

    6.3.2.1   a cashback to the buyer; or
    6.3.2.2   part of the price is being satisfied by a non-cash incentive to the buyer or
    6.3.2.3   any indirect incentive (cash or non cash) or rental guarantee.

Any such arrangement may lead to the mortgage offer being withdrawn or amended.

6.3.3   You must report to us (see part 2) if you will not have control over the payment of all of the purchase money (for example, if it is proposed that the borrower pays money to the seller direct) other than a deposit held by an estate agent or a reservation fee of not more than £1000 paid to a builder or developer

6.4   Vacant Possession

6.4   Unless otherwise stated in your instructions, it is a term of the loan that vacant possession is obtained. The contract must provide for this. If you doubt that vacant possession will be given, you must not part with the advance and should report the position to us (see part 2).

6.5   Properties Let at Completion

6.5.1   Unless it is clear from the mortgage offer that the property is let or is to be let at completion then you must check with us whether we lend on 'buy-to-let' properties and that the mortgage is for that purpose (see part 2).

6.5.2   Where the property, or part of it, is already let, or is to be let at completion, then the letting must comply with the details set out in the mortgage offer or any consent to let we issue. If no such details are mentioned, you must report the position to us (see part 2).

6.5.3   Check part 2 for whether counterparts or certified copies of all tenancy agreements and leases in respect of existing tenancies must be sent to us after completion.

6.5.4   Where the property falls within the definition of a house in multiple occupation under the Housing Act 2004 see part 2 as to whether we will accept this as security and if so what our requirements are.

6.6   New Properties - Building Standards Indemnity Schemes

6.6.1   If the property has been built or converted within the past 10 years, or is to be occupied for the first time, you must ensure that it was built or converted under a scheme acceptable to us (see part 2 for the list of schemes acceptable to us and our requirements).

6.6.2   Where the cover under a scheme referred to in clause 6.6.1 is not yet in place before you send us the certificate of title, you must obtain a copy of a new home warranty provider's cover note from the developer. The cover note must confirm that the property has received a satisfactory final inspection and that the new home warranty will be in place on or before legal completion. This does not apply to self-build schemes. Check part 2 to see what new home warranty documentation should be sent to us after completion.

6.6.3   We do not insist that notice of assignment of the benefit of the new home warranty agreement be given to the builder in the case of a second and subsequent purchase(s) during the period of the insurance cover. Check part 2 to see if any assignments of building standards indemnity schemes which are available should be sent to us after completion.

6.6.4   Where the property does not have the benefit of a scheme under 6.6.1 and has been built or converted within the past 6 years check part 2 to see if we will proceed and, if so, whether you must satisfy yourself that the building work is being monitored (or where the work is completed was monitored) by a professional consultant. If we do accept monitoring you should ensure that the professional consultant has provided the lender's Professional Consultant's Certificate which forms an appendix to this Handbook or such other form as we may provide. The professional consultant should also confirm to you that he has appropriate experience in the design or monitoring of the construction or conversion of residential buildings and has one or more of the following qualifications:

> 6.6.4.1   fellow or member of the Royal Institution of Chartered Surveyors (FRICS or MRICS); or
> 6.6.4.2   fellow or member of the Institution of Structural Engineers (F.I.Struct.E or M.I.Struct.E); or
> 6.6.4.3   fellow or member of the Chartered Institute of Building (FCIOB or MCIOB); or
> 6.6.4.4   fellow or member of the Architecture and Surveying Institute (FASI or MASI); or
> 6.6.4.5   fellow or member of the Association of Building Engineers (FB.Eng or MB.Eng); or
> 6.6.4.6   member of the Chartered Institute of Architectural Technologists (formally British Institute of Architectural Technologists) (MCIAT); or
> 6.6.4.7   architect registered with the Architects Registration Board (ARB). An architect must be registered with the Architects Registration Board, even if also a

member of another institution, for example, the Royal Institute of British Architects (RIBA); or

6.6.4.8   fellow or member of the Institution of Civil Engineers (FICE or MICE).

6.6.5   At the time he issues his certificate of practical completion, the consultant must have professional indemnity insurance in force for each claim for the greater of either:

6.6.5.1   the value of the property once completed; or

6.6.5.2   £250,000 if employed directly by the borrower or, in any other case, £500,000.

If we require a collateral warranty from any professional adviser, this will be stated specifically in the mortgage instructions.

6.6.6   Check part 2 to see if the consultant's certificate must be sent to us after completion.

6.7   Roads and Sewers

6.7.1   If the roads or sewers immediately serving the property are not adopted or maintained at public expense, there must be an agreement and bond in existence or you must report to us (see part 2 for who you should report to).

6.7.2   If there is any such agreement, it should be secured by bond or deposit as required by the appropriate authority to cover the cost of making up the roads and sewers to adoptable standards, maintaining them thereafter and procuring adoption.

6.7.3   If there is an arrangement between the developer and the lender whereby the lender will not require a retention, you must obtain confirmation from the developer that the arrangement is still in force.

6.7.4   Where roads and sewers are not adopted or to be adopted but are maintained by local residents or a management company this is acceptable providing that in your reasonable opinion appropriate arrangements for maintenance repairs and costs are in place.

6.8   Easements

6.8.1   You must take all reasonable steps to check that the property has the benefit of all easements necessary for its full use and enjoyment. All such rights must be enforceable by the borrower and the borrower's successors in title. If they are not check part 2 for our requirements.

6.8.2   If the borrower owns adjoining land over which the borrower requires access to the property or in respect of which services are provided to the property, this land must also be mortgaged to us.

6.9   Release of Retentions

6.9.1   If we make a retention from an advance (for example, for repairs, improvements or road works) we are not obliged to release that retention, or any part of it, if the borrower is in breach of any of his obligations under the mortgage, or if a condition attached to the retention has not been met or if the loan has been repaid in full. You should, therefore not give an unqualified undertaking to pay the retention to a third party.

6.9.2   Check part 2 to see who we will release the retention to.

6.10   Neighbourhood Changes

6.10   The local search or the enquiries of the seller's conveyancer should not reveal that the property is in an area scheduled for redevelopment or in any way affected by road proposals. If it is please report to us (see part 2).

6.11   Rights of Pre-emption and Restriction on Resale

6.11   You must ensure that there are no rights of pre-emption, restrictions on resale, options or similar arrangements in existence at completion which will affect our security. If there are, please report this to us (see part 2).

6.12   Improvements and Repair Grants

6.12   Where the property is subject to an improvement or repair grant which will not be discharged or waived on completion, check part 2 to see whether you must report the matter to us.

6.13   Insurance

6.13   Where we do not arrange the insurance, you must:

6.13.1   report to us (see part 2) if the property is not insured in accordance with our requirements (one of our requirements, see part 2, will relate to whether the property is insured in the joint names of us and the borrower or whether our interest may be noted);

6.13.2   arrange that the insurance cover starts from no later than completion;

6.13.3   check that the amount of buildings insurance cover is at least the amount referred to in the mortgage offer. If the property is part of a larger building and there is a common insurance policy, the total sum insured for the building must be not less than the total number of flats multiplied by the amount set out in the mortgage offer for the property – check part 2 for our requirements on this;

6.13.4   ensure that the buildings insurance cover is index linked;

6.13.5   ensure that the excess does not exceed the amount set out in part 2;

6.13.6   check part 2 to see if we require you to confirm that all the following risks are covered in the insurance policy:

6.13.6.1   fire;
6.13.6.2   lightning;
6.13.6.3   aircraft;
6.13.6.4   explosion;
6.13.6.5   earthquake
6.13.6.6   storm;
6.13.6.7   flood;
6.13.6.8   escape of water or oil;
6.13.6.9   riot;
6.13.6.10   malicious damage;
6.13.6.11   theft or attempted theft;
6.13.6.12   falling trees and branches and aerials;
6.13.6.13   subsidence;
6.13.6.14   heave;
6.13.6.15   landslip;
6.13.6.16   collision;
6.13.6.17   accidental damage to underground services;
6.13.6.18   professional fees, demolition and site clearance costs; and
6.13.6.19   public liability to anyone else.

6.13.7   Check part 2 to see if we require you to obtain before completion the insurer's confirmation that the insurer will notify us if the policy is not renewed or is cancelled or if you do not obtain this, report to us (see part 2).

6.13.8   Check part 2 to see if we require you to send us a copy of the buildings insurance policy and the last premium receipt to us.

7.   OTHER OCCUPIERS

7.1   Rights or interests of persons who are not a party to the mortgage and who are or will be in occupation of the property may affect our rights under the mortgage, for example, as overriding interests.

7.2   If your instructions state the name of a person who is to live at the property, you should ask the borrower before completing the mortgage that the information given by us in our mortgage instructions or mortgage offer about occupants is correct and nobody else is to live at the property.

7.3   Unless we state otherwise (see part 2), you must obtain a signed deed or form of consent from all occupants aged 17 or over of whom you are aware who are not a party to the mortgage before completion of the mortgage.

7.4   We recognise that in some cases the information given to us or you by a borrower may be incorrect or misleading. If you have any reason to doubt the accuracy of any information disclosed, you should report it to us (see part 2) provided the borrower agrees; if the borrower does not agree, you should return our instructions.

8.   SEPARATE REPRESENTATION

8.   Unless we otherwise state (see part 2), you must not advise:

8.1.1   any borrower who does not personally benefit from the loan; or
8.1.2   any guarantor; or
8.1.3   anyone intending to occupy the property who is to execute a consent to the mortgage and you must arrange for them to seek independent legal advice.

8.2   If we do allow you to advise any of these people, you must only do so after recommending in the absence of any other person interested in the transaction that such person obtains independent legal advice. Any advice that you give any of these people must also be given in the absence of any other person interested in the transaction. You should be particularly careful if the matrimonial home or family home is being charged to secure a business debt. Any consent should be signed by the person concerned. A power of attorney is not acceptable.

9.   INDEMNITY INSURANCE

9.   You must effect an indemnity insurance policy whenever the Lenders' Handbook identifies that this is an acceptable or required course to us to ensure that the property has a good and marketable title at completion. This paragraph does not relate to mortgage indemnity insurance. The draft policy should not be sent to us unless we ask for it. Check part 2 to see if the policy must be sent to us after completion. Where indemnity insurance is effected:

9.1   you must approve the terms of the policy on our behalf; and
9.2   the limit of indemnity must meet our requirements (see part 2); and
9.3   the policy must be effected without cost to us; and
9.4   you must disclose to the insurer all relevant information which you have obtained; and

9.5   the policy must not contain conditions which you know would make it void or prejudice our interests; and

9.6   you must provide a copy of the policy to the borrower and explain to the borrower why the policy was effected and that a further policy may be required if there is further lending against the security of the property; and

9.7   you must explain to the borrower that the borrower will need to comply with any conditions of the policy and that the borrower should notify us of any notice or potential claim in respect of the policy; and

9.8   the policy should always be for our benefit and, if possible, for the benefit of the borrower and any subsequent owner or mortgagee. If the borrower will not be covered by the policy, you must advise the borrower of this.

10.   THE LOAN AND CERTIFICATE OF TITLE

10.1   You should not submit your certificate of title unless it is unqualified or we have authorised you in writing to proceed notwithstanding any issues you have raised with us.

10.2   We shall treat the submission by you of the certificate of title as a request for us to release the mortgage advance to you. Check part 2 to see if the mortgage advance will be paid electronically or by cheque and the minimum number of days' notice we require. See part 2 for any standard deductions which may be made from the mortgage advance.

10.3.1   You are only authorised to release the loan when you hold sufficient funds to complete the purchase of the property and pay all stamp duty land tax and registration fees to perfect the security as a first legal mortgage or, if you do not have them, you accept responsibility to pay them yourself.

10.3.2   Before releasing the loan when the borrower is purchasing the property you must either hold a properly completed and executed stamp duty land tax form or you must hold an appropriate authority from the borrower allowing you to file the necessary stamp duty land tax return(s) on completion.

10.3.3   You must ensure that all stamp duty land tax returns are completed and submitted to allow registration of the charge to take place in the priority period afforded by the search.

10.3.4   You must hold the loan on trust for us until completion. If completion is delayed, you must return it to us when and how we tell you (see part 2).

10.4   You should note that although your certificate of title will be addressed to us, we may at some time transfer our interest in the mortgage. In those circumstances, our successors in title to the mortgage and persons deriving title under or through the mortgage will also rely on your certificate.

10.5   If, after you have requested the mortgage advance, completion is delayed you must telephone or fax us immediately after you are aware of the delay and you must inform us of the new date for completion (see part 2).

10.6   See part 2 for details of how long you can hold the mortgage advance before returning it to us. If completion is delayed for longer than that period, you must return the mortgage advance to us. If you do not, we reserve the right to require you to pay interest on the amount of the mortgage advance (see part 2).

10.7   If the mortgage advance is not returned within the period set out in part 2, we will assume that the mortgage has been completed, and we will charge the borrower interest under the mortgage.

11.   THE DOCUMENTATION

11.1   The Mortgage

11.1   The mortgage incorporates our current mortgage conditions and, where applicable, loan conditions. If the mortgage conditions booklet is supplied to you with your instructions you must give it to the borrower before completion of the mortgage.

11.2   You should explain to each borrower (and any other person signing or executing a document) his responsibilities and liabilities under the documents referred to in 11.1 and any documents he is required to sign.

11.3   Signing and Witnessing of Documents

11.3   It is considered good practice that the signature of a document that needs to be witnessed is witnessed by a solicitor, legal executive or licensed conveyancer. All documents required at completion must be dated with the date of completion of the loan.

12.   INSTALMENT MORTGAGES AND MORTGAGE ADVANCES RELEASED IN INSTALMENTS

12.1   Introduction

12.1.1   If the cost of the building is to be paid by instalments as work progresses (for example, under a building contract) the amount of each instalment which we will be able to release will be based on a valuation made by our valuer at the time. Whilst we will not be bound by the terms of any building contract we will meet the reasonable requirements of the borrower and the builder as far as possible.

12.1.2   The borrower is expected to pay for as much work as possible from his own resources before applying to us for the first instalment. However, we may, if required, consider advancing a nominal sum on receipt of the certificate of title to enable the mortgage to be completed so long as the legal estate in the property is vested in the borrower.

12.1.3   The borrower is responsible for our valuer's fees for interim valuations as well as the first and final valuations.

12.2   Applications for Part of the Advance

12.2   As in the case of a normal mortgage account, funds for instalment mortgages may be sent to you. However, instalments (apart from the first which will be sent to you to enable you to complete the mortgage) can be sent directly to the borrower on request. We may make further payments and advances without reference to you.

12.3   Requests for Intermediate Funds

12.3   To allow time for a valuation to be carried out, your request should be sent to us (see part 2) at least 10 days before the funds are required.

12.4   Building Contract as Security

12.4   We will not lend on the security of a building contract unless we tell you to the contrary. As a result the mortgage must not be completed and no part of the advance released until the title to the legal estate in the property has been vested by the borrower.

13. MORTGAGE INDEMNITY INSURANCE OR HIGHER LENDING CHARGE

13.   You are reminded to tell the borrower that we (and not the borrower) are the insured under any mortgage indemnity or similar form of insurance policy and that the insurer will have a subrogated right to claim against the borrower if it pays us under the policy. Different lenders call the various schemes of this type by different names. They may not involve an insurance policy.

14.   AFTER COMPLETION

14.1   Registration

14.1.1.1   You must register our mortgage as a first legal charge at the Land Registry. Before making your Land Registry application for registration, you must place a copy of the results of the Official Search on your file together with certified copies of the transfer, mortgage deed and any discharges or releases from a previous mortgagee.

14.1.1.2   Where the borrower or mortgagor is a company an application to register the charge must be lodged at Companies House within the required time period.

14.1.2   Our mortgage conditions and mortgage deed have been deposited at the Land Registry and it is therefore unnecessary to submit a copy of the mortgage conditions on an application for registration.

14.1.3   Where the loan is to be made in instalments or there is any deferred interest retention or stage release, check part 2 to see whether you must apply to Land Registry on form CH2 for entry of a notice on the register that we are under an obligation to make further advances. If the mortgage deed states that it secures further advances, and that the lender is under an obligation to make them, there is no need to submit a form CH2 provided the mortgage deed also states that application is made to the Registrar for a note to be entered on the register to that effect and the mortgage deed bears a Land Registry MD reference at its foot.

14.1.4   The application for registration must be received by the Land Registry during the priority period afforded by your original Land Registry search made before completion and, in any event, in the case of an application for first registration, within two months of completion. Please check part 2 to see if we require the original mortgage deed to be returned to us.

14.2   Title Deeds

14.2.1   All title deeds, official copies of the register (where these are issued by the Land Registry after registration), searches, enquiries, consents, requisitions and documents relating to the property in your possession must be held to our order and you must not create or exercise any lien over them. Check part 2 for our requirements on what you should do with these documents following registration. If registration at the Land Registry has not been completed within three months from completion you should advise us in writing with a copy of any correspondence with the Land Registry explaining the delay.

14.2.2   You must only send us documents we tell you to (see part 2). You should obtain the borrower's instructions concerning the retention of documents we tell you not to send us.

14.3   Your Mortgage File

14.3.1   For evidential purposes you must keep your file for at least six years from the date of the mortgage before destroying it. Microfiching or data imaging is suitable compliance with this requirement. It is the practice of some fraudsters to demand the conveyancing file on completion in order to destroy evidence that may later be used against them. It is important to retain these documents to protect our interests.

14.3.2   Where you are processing personal data (as defined in the Data Protection Act 1998) on our behalf, you must;

14.3.2.1   take such security measures as are required to enable you to comply with obligations equivalent to those imposed on us by the seventh data protection principle in the 1998 Act; and

14.3.2.2   process such personal data only in accordance with our instructions. In addition, you must allow us to conduct such reasonable audit of your information security measures as we require to ensure your compliance with your obligations in this paragraph.

14.3.3   Subject to any right of lien or any overriding duty of confidentiality, you should treat documents comprising your file as if they are jointly owned by the borrower and us and you should not part with them without the consent of both parties. You should on request supply certified copies of documents on the file or a certified copy of the microfiche to either the borrower or us, and may make a reasonable charge for copying and certification.

15.   LEGAL COSTS

15.   Your charges and disbursements are payable by the borrower and should be collected from the borrower on or before completion. You must not allow non-payment of fees or disbursements to delay the payment of stamp duty land tax, the lodging of any stamp duty land tax return and registration of documents. For solicitors the Law Society recommends that your costs for acting on our behalf in connection with the mortgage should, in the interest of transparency, be separately identified to the borrower.

16.   TRANSACTIONS DURING THE LIFE OF THE MORTGAGE

16.1   Request for Title Documents

16.1   All requests for title documents should be made in writing and sent to us (see part 2). In making such a request you must have the consent of all of the borrowers to apply for the title documents.

16.2   Further Advances

16.2   Our mortgage secures further advances. Consequently, when a further advance is required for alterations or improvements to the property we will not normally instruct a member of our conveyancing panel but if you are instructed the appropriate provisions of this Handbook will apply.

16.3   Transfers of Equity

16.3.1   You must approve the transfer (which should be in the Land Registry's standard form) and, if we require, the deed of covenant on our behalf. Check part 2 to see if we have standard forms of transfer and deed of covenant. When drafting or approving a transfer, you should bear in mind that:

16.3.1.1   although the transfer should state that it is subject to the mortgage (identified by date and parties), it need give no details of the terms of the mortgage;

16.3.1.2   the transfer need not state the amount of the mortgage debt. If it does, the figure should include both principal and interest at the date of completion, which you must check (see part 2 for where to obtain this);

16.3.1.3   there should be no statement that all interest has been paid to date.

16.3.2   You must ensure that every person who will be a borrower after the transfer covenants with us to pay the money secured by the mortgage, except in the case of:

16.3.2.1   an original party to the mortgage (unless the mortgage conditions are being varied); or

16.3.2.2   a person who has previously covenanted to that effect.

16.3.3   Any such covenant will either be in the transfer or in a separate deed of covenant. In a transfer, the wording of the covenant should be as follows, or as close as circumstances permit: 'The new borrower agrees to pay the lender all the money due under the mortgage and will keep to all the terms of the mortgage.' If it is in the transfer, you must place a certified copy of the transfer with the deeds (unless we tell you not to in part 2).

16.3.4   If we have agreed to release a borrower or a guarantor and our standard transfer form (if any) includes no appropriate clause, you must add a simple form of release. The release clause should be as follows, or as close as circumstances permit: 'The lender releases ... from [his/her/their] obligations under the mortgage.' You should check whether a guarantor who is to be released was a party to the mortgage or to a separate guarantee.

16.3.5   You must obtain the consent of every guarantor of whom you are aware to the release of a borrower or, as the case may be, any other guarantor.

16.3.6   You must only submit the transfer to us for execution if it releases a party. All other parties must execute the transfer before it is sent to us. See part 2 for where the transfer should be sent for sealing. Part 2 also gives our approved form of attestation clause.

16.4   Properties to be let after Completion (other than 'Buy-to-Let')

16.4.1   If after completion the borrower informs you of an intention to let the property you should advise the borrower that any letting of the property is prohibited without our prior consent. If the borrower wishes to let the property after completion then an application for consent should be made to us by the borrower (see part 2). Check part 2 to see whether it is necessary to send to us a copy of the proposed tenancy when making the application.

16.4.2   If the application for our consent is approved and we instruct you to act for us, you must approve the form of tenancy agreement on our behalf in accordance with our instructions.

16.4.3   Please also note that:

16.4.3.1   an administration fee may be payable for our consideration of the application whether or not consent is granted; and

16.4.3.2   the proposed rent should cover the borrower's gross mortgage payments at the time; and

16.4.3.3   you should draw the borrower's attention to the fact that, under the terms of the mortgage, we may reserve the right to charge a higher rate of interest to the borrower or change the terms of the mortgage.

16.5   Deeds of Variation etc

16.5.1   If we consent to any proposal for a deed of variation, rectification, easement or option agreement, we will rely on you to approve the documents on our behalf.

16.5.2   Our consent will usually be forthcoming provided that you first of all confirm in writing to us (see part 2) that our security will not be adversely affected in any way by entering into the deed. If you are able to provide this confirmation then we will not normally need to see a draft of the deed. If you cannot provide confirmation and we need to consider the matter in detail then an additional administration fee is likely to be charged.

16.5.3   Whether we are a party to the deed or give a separate deed or form of consent is a matter for your discretion. It should be sent to us (see part 2) for sealing or signing with a brief explanation of the reason for the document and its effect together with your confirmation that it will not adversely affect our security.

16.6   Deeds of Postponement or Substitution

16.6   If we agree to enter into an arrangement with other lenders concerning the order of priority of their mortgages, you will be supplied with our standard form of deed or form of postponement or substitution. We will normally not agree to any amendments to the form. In no cases will we postpone our first charge over the property.

17.   REDEMPTION

17.1   Redemption Statement

17.1.1   When requesting a redemption statement (see part 2) you should quote the expected repayment date and whether you are acting for the borrower or have the borrower's authority to request the redemption statement in addition to the information mentioned in paragraph 2.1. You should request this at least five working days before the expected redemption date. You must quote all the borrower's mortgage account or roll numbers of which you are aware when requesting the repayment figure. You must only request a redemption statement if you are acting for the borrower or have the borrower's written authority to request a redemption statement.

17.1.2   To guard against fraud please ensure that if payment is made by cheque then the redemption cheque is made payable to us and you quote the mortgage account number or roll number and name of the borrower.

17.2   Discharge

17.2   On the day of completion you should send the discharge and your remittance for the repayment to us (see part 2). Check part 2 to see if we discharge via a DS1 form or direct notification to the Land Registry.

APPENDIX C

Fees

Land Registration Fee Order 2009, SI 2009/845[1]

Made 1st April 2009
Laid before Parliament 2nd April 2009
Coming into force 6th July 2009
The Lord Chancellor makes the following Order in exercise of the powers conferred on him by sections 102 and 128(1) of the Land Registration Act 2002.
In accordance with section 102 of that Act, he has received the advice and assistance of the Rule Committee, appointed under section 127 of that Act.
Also in accordance with section 102 of that Act, the Treasury has consented to the making of this Order.

PART 1

General

1. CITATION, COMMENCEMENT AND INTERPRETATION

(1) This Order may be cited as the Land Registration Fee Order 2009 and shall come into force on 6 July 2009.

(2) In this Order–

'account holder' means a person holding a credit account,
'the Act' means the Land Registration Act 2002,
'CLRA' means the Commonhold and Leasehold Reform Act 2002,
'charge' includes a sub-charge,
'common parts' has the same meaning as in the CLRA,
'a commonhold' has the same meaning as in the CLRA,
'commonhold association' has the same meaning as in the CLRA,
'commonhold community statement' has the same meaning as in the CLRA,
'commonhold land' has the same meaning as in the CLRA,
'commonhold unit' has the same meaning as in the CLRA,
'credit account' means an account authorised by the registrar under article 14(1),
'developer' has the same meaning as in the CLRA,
'large scale application' has the same meaning as in article 6(1)(b),
'monetary consideration' means a consideration in money or money's worth (other than a nominal consideration or a consideration consisting solely of a covenant to pay money owing under a mortgage),

'premium' means the amount or value of any monetary consideration given by the lessee as part of the same transaction in which a lease is granted by way of fine, premium or otherwise, but, where a registered leasehold estate of substantially the same land is surrendered on the grant of a new lease, the premium for the new lease shall not include the value of the surrendered lease,

'profit' means a profit a prendre in gross,

'remote terminal' means a remote terminal communicating with the registrar's computer system in accordance with a notice given under Schedule 2 to the rules,

'rent' means the largest amount of annual rent the lease reserves within the first five years of its term that can be quantified at the time an application to register the lease is made,

'the rules' means the Land Registration Rules 2003 and a rule referred to by number means the rule so numbered in the rules,

'Scale 1' means Scale 1 in Schedule 1,

'Scale 2' means Scale 2 in Schedule 2,

'scale fee' means a fee payable in accordance with a scale set out in Schedule 1 or 2 whether or not reduced in accordance with article 2(6),

'scale fee application' means an application which attracts a scale fee, or which would attract such a fee but for the operation of article 6,

'share' in relation to land, means an interest in that land under a trust of land,

'surrender' includes a surrender not made by deed,

'termination application' has the same meaning as in the CLRA,

'unit-holder' has the same meaning as in the CLRA,

'voluntary application' means an application for first registration (other than for the registration of title to a rentcharge, a franchise or a profit) which is not made wholly or in part pursuant to section 4 of the Act (when title must be registered).

(3) Expressions used in this Order have, unless the contrary intention appears, the meaning which they bear in the rules.

PART 2

Scale fees

2. APPLICATIONS FOR FIRST REGISTRATION AND APPLICATIONS FOR REGISTRATION OF A LEASE BY AN ORIGINAL LESSEE

(1) The fee for an application for first registration of an estate in land is payable under Scale1 on the value of the estate in land comprised in the application assessed under article 7, unless the application is–

   (a) for the registration of title to a lease by the original lessee or his personal representative, where paragraph (2) applies,

   (b) a voluntary application, where either paragraph (6) or article 6(3) applies, or

   (c) a large scale application, where article 6 applies.

(2) The fee for an application by the original lessee or his personal representative for the registration of title to a lease, or for the registration of the grant of a lease, is payable under Scale 1–

   (a) on an amount equal to the sum of the premium and the rent, or

   (b) where

(i) there is no premium, and

(ii) either there is no rent or the rent cannot be quantified at the time the application is made,

on the value of the lease assessed under article 7 subject to a minimum fee of £50,

unless either of the circumstances in paragraph (3) applies.

(3) Paragraph (2) shall not apply if the application is –

(a) a voluntary application, where paragraph (6) applies, or
(b) a large scale application, where article 6 applies.

(4) The fee for an application for the first registration of a rentcharge is £50.

(5) The fee for an application for the first registration of a franchise or a profit is payable under Scale 1 on the value of the franchise or the profit assessed under article 7.

(6) The fee for a voluntary application (other than a large scale application, where article 6(3) applies) is the fee which would otherwise be payable under paragraph (1) or (2) reduced by 25 per cent and, where the reduced fee would be a figure which includes pence, the fee must be adjusted to the nearest £10.

(7) In paragraph (2) 'lease' means–

(a) a lease which grants an estate in land whether or not the grant is a registrable disposition, or
(b) a lease of a franchise, profit or manor the grant of which is a registrable disposition.

3. TRANSFERS OF REGISTERED ESTATES FOR MONETARY CONSIDERATION, ETC.

(1) Subject to paragraphs (2), (3) and (4), the fee for an application for the registration of –

(a) a transfer of a registered estate for monetary consideration,
(b) a transfer for the purpose of giving effect to a disposition for monetary consideration of a share in a registered estate, or
(c) a surrender of a registered leasehold estate for monetary consideration, other than a surrender to which paragraph (3) of Schedule 4 applies, is payable under Scale 1 on the amount or value of the consideration.

(2) Paragraph (1) shall not apply if the application is –

(a) a large scale application, where article 6 applies, or
(b) for the registration of a transfer of a registered estate made pursuant to an order of the Court under the Matrimonial Causes Act 1973 or the Civil Partnership Act 2004, where article 4(1)(h) applies.

(3) Where a sale and sub-sale of a registered estate are made by separate deeds of transfer, a separate fee is payable for each deed of transfer.

(4) Where a single deed of transfer gives effect to a sale and a sub-sale of the same registered estate a single fee is assessed upon the greater of the monetary consideration given by the purchaser and the monetary consideration given by the sub-purchaser.

(5) The fee for an application to cancel an entry in the register of notice of an unregistered lease which has determined is payable under Scale 1 on the value of the lease immediately before its determination assessed under article 7.

4. TRANSFERS OF REGISTERED ESTATES OTHERWISE THAN FOR MONETARY CONSIDERATION, ETC.

(1) Unless the application is a large scale application (where article 6 applies), the fee for an application for the registration of –

    (a) a transfer of a registered estate otherwise than for monetary consideration (unless paragraph (2) applies),

    (b) a surrender of a registered leasehold estate otherwise than for monetary consideration,

    (c) a transfer of a registered estate by operation of law on death or bankruptcy, of an individual proprietor,

    (d) an assent of a registered estate (including a vesting assent),

    (e) an appropriation of a registered estate,

    (f) a vesting order or declaration to which section 27(5) of the Act applies,

    (g) an alteration of the register, or

    (h) a transfer of a registered estate made pursuant to an order of the Court under the Matrimonial Causes Act 1973 or the Civil Partnership Act 2004,

is payable under Scale 2 on the value of the registered estate which is the subject of the application, assessed under article 7, but after deducting from it the amount secured on the registered estate by any charge subject to which the registration takes effect.

(2) Where a transfer of a registered estate otherwise than for monetary consideration is for the purpose of giving effect to the disposition of a share in a registered estate, the fee for an application for its registration is payable under Scale 2 on the value of that share.

5. CHARGES OF REGISTERED ESTATES OR REGISTERED CHARGES

(1) The fee for an application for the registration of a charge is payable under Scale 2 on the amount of the charge assessed under article 8 unless it is an application to which paragraph (2), (3) or (4) applies.

(2) No fee is payable for an application to register a charge lodged with or before the completion of either a scale fee application or an application to which paragraph (17) in Part 1 of Schedule 3 applies ('the primary application') that will result in the chargor being registered as proprietor of the registered estate included in the charge unless–

    (a) the charge includes a registered estate which is not included in the primary application, where paragraph (4) applies, or

    (b) the primary application is a voluntary application, in which case this paragraph shall apply only if the application to register the charge accompanies the primary application.

(3) No fee is to be paid for an application to register a charge made by a predecessor in title of the applicant that is lodged with or before completion of an application for first registration of the estate included in the charge.

(4) Where a charge also includes a registered estate which is not included in the primary application ('the additional property') any fee payable under Scale 2 is to be assessed on an amount calculated as follows:

$$\frac{\text{Value of the additional property}}{\text{Value of all the property included in the charge}} \times \text{Amount secured by the charge}$$

(5) The fee for an application for the registration of–

(a) a transfer of a registered charge for monetary consideration, or

(b) a transfer for the purpose of giving effect to a disposition for monetary consideration of a share in a registered charge,

is payable under Scale 2 on the amount or value of the consideration.

(6) The fee for an application for the registration of the transfer of a registered charge otherwise than for monetary consideration is payable under Scale 2 on–

(a) the amount secured by the registered charge at the time of the transfer, or

(b) where the transfer relates to more than one charge, the aggregate of the amounts secured by the registered charges at the time of the transfer.

(7) The fee for an application for the registration of a transfer for the purpose of giving effect to a disposition otherwise than for monetary consideration of a share in a registered charge is payable under Scale 2 on –

(a) the proportionate part of the amount secured by the registered charge at the time of the transfer, or

(b) where the transfer relates to more than one charge, the proportionate part of the aggregate of the amounts secured by the registered charges at the time of the transfer.

(8) This article takes effect subject to article 6 (large scale applications).

6. LARGE SCALE APPLICATIONS, ETC.

(1) In this article –

(a) 'land unit' means –

(i) the land registered under a single title number other than, in the case of an application to register a charge, any estate under any title number which is included in a primary application within the meaning of article 5(2), or

(ii) on a first registration application, a separate area of land not adjoining any other unregistered land affected by the same application.

(b) 'large scale application' means a scale fee application which relates to 20 or more land units, other than an application to register a disposition by the developer affecting the whole or part of the freehold estate in land which has been registered as a freehold estate in commonhold land, or a low value application,

(c) 'low value application' means a scale fee application, other than an application for first registration, where the value of the land or the amount of the charge to which it relates (as the case may be) does not exceed £30,000.

(2) Subject to paragraphs (3) and (4), the fee for a large scale application is the greater of–

(a) the scale fee, and

(b) a fee calculated on the following basis–

(i) where the application relates to not more than 500 land units, £12 for each land unit, or

(ii) where the application relates to more than 500 land units, £6,000 plus £6 for each land unit in excess of 500.

(3) If a large scale application is a voluntary application, the fee payable under paragraph (2) is reduced by 25 per cent and, where the reduced fee would be a figure which includes pence, the fee must be adjusted to the nearest £10.

(4) The maximum fee payable for a large scale application for first registration is £52,000 unless the application is a voluntary application in which case the maximum fee is £39,000.

PART 3

Valuation

7.   VALUATION (FIRST REGISTRATION AND REGISTERED ESTATES)

(1) The value of the estate in land, franchise, profit, manor or share is the maximum amount for which it could be sold in the open market free from any charge–

  (a)   in the case of a surrender, at the date immediately before the surrender, and
  (b)   in any other case, at the date of the application.

(2) As evidence of the amount referred to in paragraph (1), the registrar may require a written statement signed by the applicant or his conveyancer or by any other person who, in the registrar's opinion, is competent to make the statement.

(3) Where an application for first registration is made on–

  (a)   the purchase of a leasehold estate by the reversioner,
  (b)   the purchase of a reversion by the leaseholder, or
  (c)   any other like occasion,

and an unregistered interest is determined, the value of the land is the combined value of the reversionary and determined interests assessed in accordance with paragraphs (1) and (2).

8.   VALUATION (CHARGES)

(1) On an application for registration of a charge, the amount of the charge is–

  (a)   where the charge secures a fixed amount, that amount,
  (b)   where the charge secures further advances and the maximum amount that can be advanced or owed at any one time is limited, that amount,
  (c)   where the charge secures further advances and the total amount that can be advanced or owed at any one time is not limited, the value of the property charged,
  (d)   where the charge is by way of additional or substituted security or by way of guarantee, an amount equal to the lesser of–
    (i)   the amount secured or guaranteed, and
    (ii) the value of the property charged, or
  (e)   where the charge secures an obligation or liability which is contingent upon the happening of a future event ('the obligation'), and is not a charge to which sub-paragraph (d) applies, an amount equal to –
    (i)   the maximum amount or value of the obligation, or
    (ii) if that maximum amount is greater than the value of the property charged, or is not limited by the charge, or cannot be calculated at the time of the application, the value of the property charged.

(2) Where a charge of a kind referred to in paragraph (1)(a) or (1)(b) is secured on unregistered land or other property as well as on a registered estate or registered charge, the fee is payable on an amount calculated as follows –

$$\frac{\text{Value of the registered estate or registered charge}}{\text{Value of all the property charged}} \times \text{Amount of the charge}$$

(3) Where one deed contains two or more charges made by the same chargor to secure the same debt, the deed is to be treated as a single charge, and the fee for registration of the charge is to be paid on the lesser of –

  (a) the amount of the whole debt, and
  (b) an amount equal to the value of the property charged.

(4) Where one deed contains two or more charges to secure the same debt not made by the same chargor, the deed is to be treated as a separate single charge by each of the chargors and a separate fee is to be paid for registration of the charge by each chargor on the lesser of–

  (a) the amount of the whole debt, and
  (b) an amount equal to the value of the property charged by that chargor.

(5) In this article 'value of the property charged' means the value of the registered estate or the amount of the registered charge or charges affected by the application to register the charge, less the amount secured by any prior registered charges.

PART 4

Fixed Fees and Exemptions

9. FIXED FEES

(1) Subject to paragraph (2) and to article 10, the fees for the applications and services specified in Schedule 3 shall be those set out in that Schedule.

(2) Where an application is one specified in paragraphs (1), (2) or (10) in Part 1 of Schedule 3 affecting the whole or part of the freehold estate in land which has been registered as a freehold estate in commonhold land registered in the name of the developer under more than one title number, the fee is to be assessed as if the application affects only one title.

10. EXEMPTIONS

No fee is payable for any of the applications and services specified in Schedule 4.

PART 5

General and Administrative Provisions

11. COST OF SURVEYS, ADVERTISEMENTS AND SPECIAL ENQUIRIES

The applicant is to meet the costs of any survey, advertisement or other special enquiry that the registrar requires to be made or published in dealing with an application.

12. APPLICATIONS NOT OTHERWISE REFERRED TO

The fee payable for an application in respect of which no other fee is payable under this Order shall be £50.

13. METHOD OF PAYMENT

(1) Except where the registrar otherwise permits, every fee shall be paid by means of a cheque or postal order crossed and made payable to Land Registry.

(2) Where there is an agreement with the applicant, a fee may be paid by direct debit to such bank account of the land registry as the registrar may from time to time direct.

(3) Where the amount of the fee payable on an application is immediately quantifiable, the fee shall be payable on delivery of the application.

(4) Where the amount of the fee payable on an application is not immediately quantifiable, the applicant shall pay the sum of £50 towards the fee when the application is made and shall lodge at the same time an undertaking to pay on demand the balance of the fee due, if any.

(5) Where an outline application is made, the fee payable shall be the fee payable under paragraph (9) of Part 1 of Schedule 3 in addition to the fee otherwise payable under this Order.

14. CREDIT ACCOUNTS

(1) Any person may, if authorised by the registrar, use a credit account in accordance with this article for the payment of fees for applications and services of such kind as the registrar shall from time to time direct.

(2) To enable the registrar to consider whether or not a person applying to use a credit account may be so authorised, that person shall supply the registrar with such information and evidence as the registrar may require to satisfy him of that person's fitness to hold a credit account and the ability of that person to pay any amounts which may become due from time to time under a credit account.

(3) To enable the registrar to consider from time to time whether or not an account holder may continue to be authorised to use a credit account, the account holder shall supply the registrar, when requested to do so, with such information and evidence as the registrar may require to satisfy him of the account holder's continuing fitness to hold a credit account and the continuing ability of the account holder to pay any amounts which may become due from time to time under the account holder's credit account.

(4) Where an account holder makes an application where credit facilities are available to him, he may make a request, in such manner as the registrar directs, for the appropriate fee to be debited to the account holder's credit account, but the registrar shall not be required to accept such a request where the amount due on the account exceeds the credit limit applicable to the credit account, or would exceed it if the request were to be accepted.

(5) Where an account holder makes an application where credit facilities are available to him, and the application is accompanied neither by a fee nor a request for the fee to be debited to his account, the registrar may debit the fee to his account.

(6) The registrar shall send a statement of account to each account holder at the end of each calendar month or such other interval as the registrar shall direct.

(7) The account holder must pay any sums due on his credit account before the date and in the manner specified by the registrar.

(8) The registrar may at any time terminate or suspend any or all authorisations given under paragraph (1).

(9) In this article 'credit limit' in relation to a credit account authorised for use under paragraph (1) means the maximum amount (if any) which is to be due on the account at any time, as notified by the registrar to the account holder from time to time, by means of such communication as the registrar considers appropriate.

15. REVOCATION

The Land Registration Fee Order 2006 is revoked.

SCHEDULE 1

SCALE 1

NOTE 1: Where the amount or value is a figure which includes pence, it must be rounded down to the nearest £1.

NOTE 2: The third column, which sets out the reduced fee payable where article 2(6) (voluntary registration: reduced fees) applies, is not part of the scale.

Amount or value	Fee	Reduced fee where article 2(6) (voluntary registration: reduced fees) applies
£	£	£
0–50,000	50	40
50,001–80,000	80	60
80,001–100,000	130	100
100,001–200,000	200	150
200,001–500,000	280	210
500,001–1,000,000	550	410
1,000,001 and over	920	690

SCHEDULE 2

SCALE 2

NOTE: Where the amount or value is a figure which includes pence, it must be rounded down to the nearest £1.

Amount or value	Fee
£	£
0–100,000	50
100,001–200,000	70
200,001–500,000	90
500,001–1,000,000	130
1,000,001 and over	260

SCHEDULE 3

Articles 9 & 13

PART 1

FIXED FEE APPLICATIONS

Fee

(1) To register:

(a) a standard form of restriction contained in Schedule 4 to the rules, or

(b) a notice (other than a notice to which section 117(2)(b) of the Act applies), or

(c) a new or additional beneficiary of a unilateral notice

- total fee for up to three registered titles affected   £50

- additional fee for each subsequent registered title affected   £25

Provided that no such fee is payable if, in relation to each registered title affected, the application is accompanied by a scale fee application or another application which attracts a fee under this paragraph.

(2) To register a restriction in a form not contained in Schedule 4 to the rules – for each registered title   £100

(3) To register a caution against first registration (other than a caution to which section 117(2)(a) of the Act applies)   £50

(4) To alter the cautions register – for each individual caution register   £50

(5) To close or partly close a registered leasehold or a registered rentcharge title other than on surrender – for each registered title closed or partly closed   £50

Provided that no such fee is payable if the application is accompanied by a scale fee application.

(6) To upgrade from one class of registered title to another   £50

Provided that no such fee is payable if the application for upgrading is accompanied by a scale fee application.

(7) To cancel an entry in the register of notice of an unregistered rentcharge which has determined – for each registered title affected   £50

Provided that no such fee is payable if the application is accompanied by a scale fee application.

(8) To enter or remove a record of a defect in title pursuant to section 64(1) of the Act   £50

Provided that no such fee is payable if the application is accompanied by a scale fee application.

(9) An outline application made under rule 54:

(a) where delivered from a remote terminal   £3

(b) where delivered by any other permitted means   £6

Such fee is payable in addition to any other fee which is payable in respect of the application.

(10)   For an order in respect of a restriction under section 41(2) of the Act –   £50
for each registered title affected

(11)   To register a person in adverse possession of a registered estate – for   £150
each registered title affected

(12)   For registration as a person entitled to be notified of an application for   £50
adverse possession – for each registered title affected

(13)   For the determination of the exact line of a boundary under rule 118 –   £100
for each application

(14)   To register a freehold estate in land as a freehold estate in commonhold
land which is not accompanied by a statement under section 9(1)(b) of
the CLRA:

        (a) up to 20 commonhold units   £50

        (b) for every 20 commonhold units, or up to 20 commonhold units,   £15
thereafter

(15)   To add land to a commonhold:

        (a) adding land to the common parts title   £50

        (b) adding land to a commonhold unit   £50

        (c) adding commonhold units

        – up to 20 commonhold units   £50

        – for every 20 commonhold units, or up to 20 commonhold units,   £15
thereafter

(16)   To apply for a freehold estate in land to cease to be registered as a   £50
freehold estate in commonhold land during the transitional period, as
defined in the CLRA

(17)   To register a freehold estate in land as a freehold estate in commonhold
land, which is accompanied by a statement under section 9(1)(b) of
the CLRA

        – for each commonhold unit converted   £50

(18)   To register an amended commonhold community statement which
changes the extent of the common parts or any commonhold unit:

        (a) for the common parts   £50

        (b) for up to three commonhold units   £50

        (c) for each subsequent commonhold unit   £25

Provided that no such fee shall be payable if, in relation to each
registered title affected, the application is accompanied by a scale fee
application or another application that attracts a fee under this Part.

(19)   To register an amended commonhold community statement, which   £50
does not change the extent of a registered title within the commonhold

Provided that no such fee shall be payable if, in relation to each
registered title affected, the application is accompanied by a scale fee
application or another application that attracts a fee under this Part.

(20)   To register an alteration to the Memorandum or Articles of Association   £50
of a commonhold association

(21)   To make a termination application

        – for each registered title affected   £50

(22)   To note the surrender of a development right under section 58 of the   £50
        CLRA

PART 2

SERVICES – INSPECTION AND COPYING

NOTE: In this Part 'lease' means a lease or a copy of a lease.

(1)   Inspection, from a remote terminal:

        (a) for each individual register   £4

        (b) for each title plan   £4

        (c) for any or all of the documents (other than leases) referred to in an £6
        individual register – for each registered title

        (d) for each lease kept by the registrar which is referred to in an   £12
        individual register or which relates to an application to him

        (e) for the individual register and title plan of a commonhold common
        parts title –

                for each registered title   £4

        (f) for each individual caution register   £4

        (g) for each caution plan   £4

        (h) for any other document kept by the registrar which relates to an   £6
        application to him - for each document

(2)   Inspection (otherwise than under paragraph (1)):

        (a) for each individual register   £8

        (b) for each title plan   £8

        (c) for any or all of the documents (other than leases) referred to in an £12
        individual register – for each registered title

        (d) for each lease kept by the registrar which is referred to in an   £24
        individual register or which relates to an application to him

        (e) for the individual register and title plan of a commonhold common   £8
        parts title – for each registered title

        (f) for each individual caution register   £8

        (g) for each caution plan   £8

        (h) for any other document kept by the registrar which relates to an   £12
        application to him – for each document

(3)   Official copy in respect of a registered title:

        (a) for each individual register

        (i) where an official copy in electronic form is requested from a remote   £4
        terminal

        (ii) where an official copy in paper form is requested by any permitted   £8
        means

        (b) for each title plan

        (i) where an official copy in electronic form is requested from a remote   £4
        terminal

(ii) where an official copy in paper form is requested by any permitted   £8
means

(c) for each commonhold common parts individual register and title
plan

(i) where an official copy in electronic form is requested from a remote   £4
terminal

(ii) where an official copy in paper form is requested by any permitted   £8
means

(4)   Official copy in respect of the cautions register

(a) for each individual caution register

(i) where an official copy in electronic form is requested from a remote   £4
terminal

(ii) where an official copy in paper form is requested by any permitted   £8
means

(b) for each caution plan

(i) where an official copy in electronic form is requested from a remote   £4
terminal

(ii) where an official copy in paper form is requested by any permitted   £8
means

(5)   Official copy of any or all of the documents (other than a lease)
referred to in an individual register – for each registered title

(a) where an official copy in electronic form is requested from a   £6
remote terminal

(b) where an official copy in paper form is requested by any permitted   £12
means

(6)   Official copy of a lease kept by the registrar which is referred to in an
individual register or which relates to an application to him – for each
lease

(a) where an official copy in electronic form is requested from a   £12
remote terminal and a copy of the lease is held in electronic form by
the registrar

(b) where an official copy in electronic form is requested from a   £24
remote terminal and a copy of the lease is not held in electronic form
by the registrar

(c) where an official copy in paper form is requested by any permitted   £24
means

(7)   Official copy of any other document kept by the registrar which relates
to an application to him – for each document

(a) where an official copy in electronic form is requested from a   £6
remote terminal and a copy of the document is held in electronic form
by the registrar

(b) where an official copy in electronic form is requested from a remote terminal and a copy of the document is not held in electronic form by the registrar   £12

(c) where an official copy in paper form is requested by any permitted means   £12

(8)   Copy of an historical edition of a registered title (or of part of the edition where rule 144(4) applies) – for each title   £10

PART 3

SERVICES - SEARCHES

(1)   An official search of an individual register or of a pending first registration application made to the registrar from a remote terminal – for each title   £4

(2)   An official search of an individual register by a mortgagee for the purpose of section 56(3) of the Family Law Act 1996 made to the registrar from a remote terminal   £4

(3)   An official search of an individual register or of a pending first registration application other than as described in paragraphs (1) and (2) – for each title   £8

(4)   The issue of a certificate of inspection of a title plan   £8

(5)   An official search of the index map

(a) where no or not more than five registered titles are disclosed   £5

(b) where more than five registered titles are disclosed

(i) for the first five titles   £5

(ii) for every ten titles, or up to ten titles, thereafter   £3

(6)   Search of the index of proprietors' names – for each name   £12

(7)   An official search of the index of relating franchises and manors – for each administrative area

(a) where the application is made from a remote terminal   £4

(b) where the application is made by any other permitted means   £8

PART 4

SERVICES – OTHER INFORMATION

(1)   Application for return of a document under rule 204   £10

(2)   Application that the registrar designate a document an exempt information document   £26

SCHEDULE 4

Article 10

EXEMPTIONS

No fee is payable for:

(1) reflecting a change in the name, address or description of a registered proprietor or other person referred to in the register, or in the cautions register, or changing the description of a property,

(2) giving effect in the register to a change of proprietor where the registered estate or the registered charge, as the case may be, has become vested without further assurance (other than on the death or bankruptcy of a proprietor) in some person by the operation of any statute (other than the Act), statutory instrument or scheme taking effect under any statute or statutory instrument,

(3) registering the surrender of a registered leasehold estate where the surrender is consideration or part consideration for the grant of a new lease to the registered proprietor of substantially the same premises as were comprised in the surrendered lease and where a scale fee is paid for the registration of the new lease,

(4) registering a discharge of a registered charge,

(5) registering a home rights notice, or renewal of such a notice, or renewal of a home rights caution under the Family Law Act 1996,

(6) entering in the register the death of a joint proprietor,

(7) cancelling the registration of a notice, (other than a notice in respect of an unregistered lease or unregistered rentcharge), caution against first registration, caution against dealings, including a withdrawal of a deposit or intended deposit, inhibition, restriction, or note,

(8) the removal of the designation of a document as an exempt information document,

(9) approving an estate layout plan or any draft document with or without a plan,

(10) an order by the registrar (other than an order under section 41(2) of the Act),

(11) deregistering a manor,

(12) an entry in the register of a note of the dissolution of a corporation,

(13) registering a restriction in Form A in Schedule 4 to the rules,

(14) an application for day list information on any one occasion from a remote terminal,

(15) an application to lodge a caution against first registration or to make a register entry where in either case the application relates to rights in respect of the repair of a church chancel.

Land Charges Fees Rules 1990, SI 1990/327, Schedule 1[1]

	Service		Amount of Fee
1.	Registration, renewal, rectification or cancellation of an entry in any register	per name	£1
2.	Certificate of cancellation	per name	£1
3.	Entry of priority notice	per name	£1
4.	Inspection of an entry in the register	per entry	£1
5.	Office copy of an entry in the register (including any plan) whether the application is made in writing or by telephone or teleprinter or facsimile transmission or to the registrar's computer system by means of the applicant's remote terminal	per copy	£1
6.	Official search in the index (including issue of printed certificate of result):–		
	written application	per name	£1
	telephone application	per name	£2
	teleprinter application	per name	£2
	facsimile transmission application	per name	£2
	application made to the registrar's computer system by means of the applicant's remote terminal	per name	£2
7.	Official search in the index (including visual display of result of search and issue of printed certificate of such result)	per name	£2

[1] © Crown Copyright 1990. Schedule is as amended by the Land Charges (Amendment) Rules 1994, SI 1994/286.

Stamp Duty (Exempt Instruments) Regulations 1987, SI 1987/516, reg.2(1) and Schedule

2. (1) An instrument which –

   (a) is executed on or after 1st May 1987,
   (b) is of a kind specified in the Schedule hereto for the purposes of this regulation, and
   (c) is certified by a certificate which fulfils the conditions of regulation 3 to be an instrument of that kind,

   shall be exempt from duty under the provisions specified in paragraph (2) of this regulation.

SCHEDULE

Regulation 4

An instrument which effects any one or more of the following transactions only is an instrument specified for the purposes of regulation 2 –

A. The vesting of property subject to a trust in the trustees of the trust on the appointment of a new trustee, or in the continuing trustees on the retirement of a trustee.

B. The conveyance or transfer of property the subject of a specific devise or legacy to the beneficiary named in the will (or his nominee).

C. The conveyance or transfer of property which forms part of an intestate's estate to the person entitled on intestacy (or his nominee).

D. The appropriation of property within section 84(4) of the Finance Act 1985 (death: appropriation in satisfaction of a general legacy of money) or section 84(5) or (7) of that Act (death: appropriation in satisfaction of any interest of surviving spouse or civil partner and in Scotland also of any interest of issue).

E. The conveyance or transfer of property which forms part of the residuary estate of a testator to a beneficiary (or his nominee) entitled solely by virtue of his entitlement under the will.

F. The conveyance or transfer of property out of a settlement in or towards satisfaction of a beneficiary's interest, not being an interest acquired for money or money's worth, being a conveyance or transfer constituting a distribution of property in accordance with the provisions of the settlement.

G. The conveyance or transfer of property on and in consideration only of marriage to a party to the marriage (or his nominee) or to trustees to be held on the terms of a settlement made in consideration only of the marriage.

GG. The conveyance or transfer of property on and in consideration only of the formation of a civil partnership to a party to the civil partnership (or his nominee) or to trustees to be held on the terms of a settlement made in consideration only of the civil partnership.

H. The conveyance or transfer of property within section 83(1) or (1A) of the Finance Act 1985 (transfers in connection with divorce or dissolution of civil partnership etc.).

I. The conveyance or transfer by the liquidator of property which formed part of the assets of the company in liquidation to a shareholder of that company (or his nominee) in or towards satisfaction of the shareholder's rights on a winding-up.

J. The grant in fee simple of an easement in or over land for no consideration in money or money's worth.

K. The grant of a servitude for no consideration in money or money's worth.

L. The conveyance or transfer of property operating as a voluntary disposition inter vivos for no consideration in money or money's worth nor any consideration referred to in section 57 of the Stamp Act 1891 (conveyance in consideration of a debt etc.).

M. The conveyance or transfer of property by an instrument within section 84(1) of the Finance Act 1985 (death: varying disposition).

N. The declaration of any use or trust of or concerning a life policy, or property representing, or benefits arising under, a life policy.